AF865330

The True Significance of Sacred Tradition and Its Great Worth

By St. Raphael M. Hawaweeny

Northern Illinois University Press, DeKalb 60115

25 24 23 22 21 20 19 18 17 16 1 2 3 4 5
978-0-87580-745-4 (cloth)
978-1-60909-205-4 (e-book)

Cover design by Shaun Allshouse
Book design by Yuni Dorr

Pen and ink drawing of the Patriarchal Seal by Deacon Matthew Garrett, iconographer. Author's collection.

Library of Congress Cataloging-in-Publication Data
Names: Hawāwīnī, Rafā'īl, author. | Viscuso, Patrick, 1956– translator.
Title: The true significance of sacred tradition and its great worth : a translation of a nineteenth-century Orthodox theological work written in response to Roman Catholic and Protestant missionaries in the East / St. Raphael M. Hawaweeny ; [translator] Patrick Demetrios Viscuso.
Other titles: Alēthēs tēs hieras Paradoseōs ennoia kai to mega autēs axiōma. English
Description: DeKalb : NIU Press, 2016. | In English; translated from Greek. | Includes bibliographical references.
Identifiers: LCCN 2016011471 (print) | LCCN 2016038606 (ebook) | ISBN 9780875807454 (cloth) | ISBN 9781609092054 (ebook)
Subjects: LCSH: Orthodox Eastern Church—Doctrines. | Orthodox Eastern Church—Relations—Catholic Church. | Catholic Church—Relations—Orthodox Eastern Church.
Classification: LCC BX323 .H378 2016 (print) | LCC BX323 (ebook) | DDC 230/.19—dc23
LC record available at https://lccn.loc.gov/2016011471
ISBN 978-1-5017-9163-5 (pbk.)

The True Significance of Sacred Tradition and Its Great Worth

by St. Raphael M. Hawaweeny

A Nineteenth-Century Orthodox Response to Roman Catholic and Protestant Missionaries in the East

EDITED AND TRANSLATED BY
Patrick Demetrios Viscuso

Foreword by
His All-Holiness Ecumenical Patriarch Bartholomew

NIU Press / DeKalb, IL

To my wife, Susan,

and

my son, Sebastian

Contents

Foreword

It is with paternal joy that we welcome and offer our blessing for the publication of this thesis written by one of our beloved alma mater's esteemed students, Raphael Hawaweeny, and submitted toward the fulfillment of academic requirements at the historic and holy Theological School of Halki.

Much of the cause for our personal delight in receiving and reading this book derives from the wonderful and moving insights that it provides in returning our memory and heart to a time when this unique Theological School still vibrantly functioned, when the value of learning classical and foreign languages was held in high regard and when students of theology engaged with sources both inside and outside of their traditions in order to present our world with scholarly studies that are not disconnected from, but firmly contribute to contemporary society.

Throughout this work, moreover, we are reminded of areas in which exceptional progress has been made. Whereas in the past, for instance, we saw a multitude of controversies among Orthodox Christians fueled by ethnophyletism, in the present we have before us the recent unanimous decision taken by all Orthodox Primates throughout the world to convene the long-anticipated Holy and Great Council in June 2016. Also, just as it was common in previous centuries to see the proselytizing ambitions of Christian groups target the Orthodox communities living under harsh circumstances, today the standard for almost any Christian community is to embrace, respect and understand one another through authentic, fruitful and constructive dialogue.

Therefore, we warmly appreciate and extend our wholehearted gratitude to our beloved Rev. Dr. Patrick Viscuso for bringing ever so vividly to mind the beauty and achievements of past generations, as well as the many valuable lessons learned along the way. It is our fervent prayer and hope that the authentic words of this prominent Christian figure, Raphael Hawaweeny, may encourage all of us to serve our fellow human beings with humility and generosity for the benefit not just of our own communities but of the entire oikoumene, the world within which we all share and live together.

✠ BARTHOLOMEW
Archbishop of Constantinople-New Rome
and Ecumenical Patriarch

February 2016

Preface

> "It is, of course, naïve to expect total reconciliation. Some grievances are so deep that the people who suffered them will never be satisfied. But the point is not satisfaction—the point is that the present is superior to the past, and it has to be cultivated as such."[1]
>
> —*Colum McCann*

The work of St. Raphael Hawaweeny highlights the sharp contrasts between the present and the recent past. The adversarial relations between Eastern and Western Christianity that characterized the world of St. Raphael have changed radically, but only recently.

The "dialogue of love" initiated by the pope and ecumenical patriarch in 1964 was nothing short of miraculous. Those who had shared the most in common—the priesthood, the Eucharist, sacramental life, ascetical discipline, devotion to the Mother of God, and so much more—were in bitter disagreement. This changed dramatically when the mutual excommunications of 1054 AD were lifted in 1965. A series of ecclesial acts—actions and words set within the context of church life—were intentionally designed to reverse the alienation and to express mutual love. Numerous speeches, letters, declarations, common prayers, visits, and other events from 1964 to 1979 provided the foundation for formal theological dialogue.

The 1979 declaration by Ecumenical Patriarch Dimitrios I and Pope John Paul II, which opened the official theological dialogue between the Roman Catholic and Orthodox Churches, represented another turning point, particularly in the expression of the declaration's stated aims: "an advance towards the reestablishment of full communion between the Catholic and Orthodox sister Churches" and "a contribution to the multiple dialogues that are pursuing their courses in the Christian world as it seeks its unity."[2]

The modern development of the theological expression of "sister church," which can be traced to 1962—when Ecumenical Patriarch Athenagoras referred to the Roman Catholic Church as such—represents a shift in paradigm regarding the future life of the church of East and West.[3]

This vision was captured in Pope Paul VI's apostolic brief *Anno Ineunte* ("At the Beginning of the Year of Faith") of July 25, 1967, in which the pope stated that the Roman Catholic and Orthodox Churches "in virtue of apostolic succession are united more closely by the priesthood and the Eucharist. . . . In each local Church this mystery of divine love is enacted. . . . And now, after a long period of division and mutual misunderstanding, the Lord is enabling us to discover ourselves as 'sister Churches' once more, in spite of the obstacles which were once raised between us."[4]

As Pope Paul VI states, there had been a long period of mutual misunderstanding. Nonetheless, the official dialogue between the Roman Catholic and Orthodox Churches has produced common documents on foundational theological themes. The Roman Catholic Church has begun from the foundation of "an unqualified recognition of the validity of Orthodox sacraments," expressed eloquently in the documents of the Second Vatican Council.[5] The North American Orthodox-Catholic Theological Consultation, founded in 1965, has produced numerous groundbreaking agreed statements, including the finalization of a document entitled "The *Filioque*: A Church-Dividing Issue?" (2003), in which the consultation reviewed the history of this extremely divisive question and recommended that all the churches return to the original form of the Nicene-Constantinopolitan Creed, without the *Filioque*.

Nevertheless, despite the progress made through the dialogues of love and truth, one should not underestimate the strength of Orthodox thought and feeling regarding past Roman Catholic proselytization. The Jesuit priest Fr. Robert Francis Taft, former vice-rector of the Pontifical Oriental Institute, also acknowledges the "historically ludicrous, self-centered, self-congratulatory perception of reality" by which "the Roman Catholic Church saw itself as the original one and only true Church of Christ from which all other Christians had separated for one reason or another in the course of history, and Catholics held, simplistically, that the solution to divided Christendom consisted in all other Christians returning to Rome's maternal bosom."[6]

One might well understand the reasons lying behind the statement of His Beatitude Archbishop Hieronymos of Athens to Cardinal Jan Willebrands on the occasion of the latter's visit to the Greek Holy Synod in May 1971, a mere seven years after the initiation of the "dialogue of love":

> The faithful of our Church have, over the centuries, grown accustomed to discerning in actions of your Church intentions, which were anything else but fraternal, and as a rule now find it difficult to convince themselves that the fervent attempts towards Christian unity being exerted by the Holy See are free from past tendencies. Hence the necessary time must be given to our faithful to realize from the events themselves that hands which are now being extended are in truth brotherly.[7]

In this light, one can also understand the disruptions in the theological dialogue that occurred from 2000 to 2005 as both churches grappled with the problem of the reemergence of Greek Catholic groups in Eastern Europe after the fall of communism.

As a concluding reflection, if one were to ask me what is the major challenge that remains to the restoration of communion between the sees of the Christian East and West, I would say that on one level it is the issue and definition of universal primacy and the place of the *prōtos*, or first among the many, in the hierarchical ordering of the church. However, on a deeper level, I would say that the restoration of communion is not only vertical, it is also horizontal. Without the recognition of ourselves in each other, without my acceptance as a priest of other priests, of laity of other laity, of monks and nuns of their brothers and sisters in both East and West, no restoration of communion will be possible, since it will not live in true ecclesial reality.

None of my work would have been possible without the support of His Eminence Professor Dr. Elpidophoros Lambriniadis, metropolitan of Bursa, abbot of the Halki Holy Trinity Patriarchal and Stauropegial Monastery, who provided a copy of the handwritten text of St. Raphael's theological thesis. I am deeply grateful for his generosity, which exemplifies the sacred Tradition of the School of Theology, its graduates, and our beloved Ecumenical Patriarchate.

I express my gratitude to my colleagues, especially Dr. David Olster, Dr. John Birkenmeier, Dr. Robert Haddad, Dr. Anton Vrame, the Very Rev. Dr. Demetrios Constantelos, Dr. Roy Robson, the Rev. Msgr. Paul McPartlan, Dr. Tom Papademetriou, Dr. Dimitris Kastristis, the Very Rev. Antoun Aaraj, and Mr. John Margetis for their support in creating this volume. I would like to thank Khouria Gabriela Fulton and the faculty of the Antiochian House of Studies for their encouragement and support of my efforts. Furthermore, I wish to acknowledge the generosity of Dr. Margaret Mullet, former director of Byzantine Studies, and Dr. Deborah Brown, librarian (Dumbarton Oaks Research Library and Collection); the Very Rev. Dr. Joachim Cotsonis, director of the Archbishop Iakovos Library and Learning Resource Center (Holy Cross Greek Orthodox School of Theology); and Ms. Julia Ritter, curator and librarian (Antiochian Heritage Museum and Library), for extending the resources of their respective institutions. I thank Amy Faranto, Nathan Holmes, Lori Propheter, Yuni Dorr, Pat Yenerich, and Cara Carlson of Northern Illinois Press for all of their hard work in producing this volume. I wish to also express my special thanks to the Very Rev. Dr. Joseph Allen, whose loyal friendship is a constant assistance.

Most of all, I thank my wife, Susan, and son, Sebastian, who continue to make sacrifices that enable my scholarship.

Finally, my gratitude is especially heartfelt for the spiritual guidance of His Eminence Metropolitan Joseph, the primate of the Antiochian Orthodox Christian Archdiocese of North America, and His Grace Bishop Thomas, the hierarchical overseer of the Antiochian House of Studies and bishop of Charleston, Oakland, and the Mid-Atlantic of the Antiochian Archdiocese. I remain thankful to His Eminence Metropolitan Philip, of blessed memory, founder of the Antiochian House of Studies. I express my gratitude for having been granted the privilege and honor of teaching canon law at the Antiochian House of Studies, where many hours of research were performed.

Εἰς πολλὰ ἔτη Δέσποτα.

NOTES

1. "Ireland's Troubled Peace," *New York Times*, May 15, 2014.

2. E. J. Storman, ed. and trans., *Towards the Healing of Schism: The Sees and Rome and Constantinople; Public Statements and Correspondence between the Holy See and the Ecumenical Patriarchate, 1958–1984* (Mahwah, NJ: Paulist Press, 1987), 13.

3. Ronald G. Roberson, "The Joint International Commission for Theological Dialogue between the Catholic Church and the Orthodox Church," in *Celebrating a Century of Ecumenism: Exploring the Achievements of International Dialogue*, ed. John A. Radano (Grand Rapids, MI: Eerdmans, 2012), 250. In the Roman Catholic Church, the correct use of the expression *sister churches* is set forth in Congregation for the Doctrine of the Faith, "Note on the Expression 'Sister Churches,'" June 30, 2000, http://www.vatican.va/roman_curia/congregations/cfaith/documents/rc_con_cfaith_doc_20000630_chiese-sorelle_en.html. For the history and theological discussion surrounding "sister church," see Will T. Cohen, "The Concept of 'Sister Churches' in Orthodox-Catholic Relations since Vatican II" (PhD diss., The Catholic University of America, 2010).

4. Storman, *Towards the Healing of Schism*, 162.

5. Roberson, "Joint International Commission," in *Celebrating a Century of Ecumenism,* 249; *Unitatis Redintegratio*, 15.

6. Christopher B. Warner, "Building Bridges Between Orthodox and Catholic Christians," *Catholic World Report*, May 1, 2013, http://www.catholicworldreport.com/Item/2223/Building_Bridges_between_Orthodox_and_Catholic_Christians.aspx. Shortly after the publication of Warner's article, Roman Catholic writers criticized Taft's comments: see Michael J. Miller, "'Sister Churches': A Clarification," *Catholic World Report*, May 2, 2013, http://www.catholicworldreport.com/Blog/2227/sister_churches_a_clarification.aspx.

7. Aidan Nichols, *Rome and the Eastern Churches*, 2nd ed. (San Francisco: Ignatius Press, 2010), 285.

The True Significance of Sacred Tradition and Its Great Worth

By St. Raphael M. Hawaweeny

PART 1

Introduction

THIS BRIEF ESSAY WILL PRESENT systematically a general historical context for the theological thesis of St. Raphael Hawaweeny (1860–1915), which was written as part of the requirements for graduation from the Theological School of the Great Church of Christ, an institution of the Ecumenical Patriarchate located on the island of Halki in the Sea of Marmara, near present-day Istanbul. St. Raphael was the first Orthodox bishop consecrated in the Western Hemisphere, and as a missionary he crossed the continent while establishing parishes and serving widespread communities. In 2000 the Orthodox Church in America and the Antiochian Orthodox Christian Archdiocese of North America recognized him as a saint.[1]

This examination will explore questions regarding the history of the Ottoman Empire, the organization of the *millet* system, the relationship of Orthodoxy to nationalism, and the course of study at the Theological School of the Ecumenical Patriarchate. In addition, the content of the theological thesis will be outlined and summarized. On the basis of this background, the reader will have a foundation for understanding the translation of this nineteenth-century Orthodox theological work.[2]

THE OTTOMAN EMPIRE, THE *MILLET* SYSTEM, AND THE ORTHODOX CHURCH

The Ottoman Empire was the Islamic successor state to the Roman Empire of the East, otherwise known as Byzantium.[3] The Ottomans originated in late-thirteenth-century northwest Anatolia (present-day Turkey) and through conquests, beginning with the Byzantine city of Prousa, subsequently encompassed most of the Middle East, the Balkans, and parts of Central Europe. Their capital was eventually located in Istanbul (or Kostantiniyye, namely Constantinople), the former Byzantine capital taken by Mehmed II "the Conqueror" in 1453. The name *Ottoman* derives from Osman Bey (d. ca. 1324), to whom is attributed the foundation of the dynasty of sultans that ruled the empire until 1923.

The Ottoman Empire used a governing structure that has come to be known as the *millet* system, under which its subjects were organized on the basis of religious affiliation.[4] According to the modern scholar Halil İnalcik, "individuals were not considered citizens in the modern sense of the word: rather they were perceived as members of a community, which was the only type of entity officially recognized within the larger political framework . . . based on the Sultan's recognition . . . of the existence and limited authority of such communities."[5]

During a significant portion of Ottoman history, most of the Orthodox population of the empire was viewed as belonging to the *millet-i Rum*, or Roman nation, administered by the Ecumenical Patriarchate of Constantinople, which was known as the Great Church of Christ.[6] The ecumenical patriarch not only functioned as a religious leader, but came to be considered an official (ἐθνάρχης) who was made responsible for the loyalty of his flock as subjects (*re ʻâyâ*) of the Islamic state. In addition to his spiritual functions, the patriarch had limited authority within the *millet*, which included cognizance especially of personal legal matters such as those related to marriage, divorce, and inheritance. Islamic courts exercised cognizance over criminal matters. The strength of the patriarch's position and influence over the Ottoman central administration "depended on the situation at a given time."[7] The patriarch eventually maintained a complex administrative bureaucracy and system of religious courts that were supported by taxes, which the church collected from the *millet-i Rum*.

With the Ottoman conquest of Antioch, Jerusalem, and Alexandria in the sixteenth century, the authority of Constantinople was extended over the Orthodox patriarchates of these cities, which formerly had enjoyed a high degree of independence after being separated from the Byzantine Empire by the Arab conquests of the seventh century.[8] At Antioch the authority of Constantinople was manifested initially by the removal and replacement of patriarchs and by periodic interventions, usually at the request of rival local parties that often competed for the patriarchal throne. Constantinople was able to assert this authority on the basis of its privileged status and its close position vis-à-vis the Ottoman central government, which was known as the Sublime Porte.[9]

By the eighteenth century the church was administered under a system of leadership known as *gerondismos* (γεροντισμός, "the rule of elders"), a name derived from the word *gerondes* (γέροντες, "elders"), which in turn referred to the senior metropolitans of neighboring sees to Istanbul; these metropolitans dominated the Holy Synod by governing with the patriarch and controlling elections to the patriarchal throne.[10] This system was modified in the mid-nineteenth century.

As a result of reforms within the empire, changes took place in the Ecumenical Patriarchate's governance structure.[11] Beginning in 1862 the patriarch, with the assistance of two bodies, administered the *millet-i Rum*. These two bodies were the Permanent National Mixed Council, which included eight laypersons whom the Constantinopolitan Orthodox community elected as well as four senior bishops; and the Holy Synod, which consisted of twelve senior metropolitans. The Permanent National Mixed Council had cognizance over various *millet* institutions, finances, and legal matters related to wills and donations. Other reforms included attempts to reduce the authority of *millet* courts, make changes in taxation, promote religious toleration, establish a limited constitutional monarchy, and advance the equality of all Ottoman subjects.

ROMAN CATHOLIC AND PROTESTANT PROSELYTIZATION OF THE ORTHODOX

From the sixteenth century onward, the Roman Catholic Church launched major proselytization efforts directed toward Orthodox Christians living under Ottoman rule. These efforts were conducted with the financial and political support of the Great Western powers, particularly the French, and involved Jesuits; Franciscans; Dominicans; and other Roman Catholic societies, orders, and congregations. From Rome's point of view, eventual "centralization of these missionary activities under a congregation reporting directly to the pope" was needed, and to this end, by a papal bull of January 14, 1622, the Sacred Congregation for the Propagation of the Faith (usually called *Propaganda* to simplify its title, *Sacra Congregatio de Propaganda Fide*) was created.[12]

According to the modern historian Charles Frazee, "By constitution and structure, it became one of the most efficient organs of the modern Roman Catholic Church."[13] Its jurisdiction extended to all missionary territories that lacked resident Roman Catholic bishops. At the same time, educational establishments were established in Rome, such as the Greek Pontifical College of St. Athanasius, where Roman Catholic missionaries sent Orthodox students for conversion and training, so that they might in turn be used as native clergy for further proselytization work.[14] Beginning in 1626 *Propaganda* began publishing in Rome polemical works in Latin, Greek, and Arabic, taking the advantage over the Orthodox, who had "little opportunity to reply in print" because of severe restrictions on publishing in the Ottoman Empire.[15]

Roman Catholic historians note the sixteenth and seventeenth centuries as the golden age for such "missions," which resulted in the establishment of Catholic groups that retained Eastern rites and customs, and eventually had their own hierarchy; in places some of these Catholic rites even had a patriarchate.[16] Roman Catholic documents from the period called for reunion between the Roman Church and the Orthodox Church, but union was often expressed as a "return to the See of Rome," with only one partner—the Orthodox—needing to move.

One cannot overestimate the lasting bitterness and suspicion that was engendered by such missionary efforts. Often welcomed at first by local Orthodox hierarchy and clergy who were struggling under Ottoman rule, especially in the eighteenth century, Latin missionaries were "deeply impressed by the extent to which the Christian East agreed with Roman Catholicism as well as by the warm friendship" shown to them and "found it difficult to treat the Orthodox simply as aliens, as schismatics or heretics whom they must shun."[17] Jesuits in particular strove to render help to Christian populations living under the difficult conditions of Islamic rule, which even led them to share in worship and sacraments (particularly preaching and confession). Nevertheless, while striving to win the "confidence and affection of the Orthodox," at the same time, the missionaries pursued a deliberate policy "to infiltrate among them" and "to work upon them from within."[18]

The Roman Catholic missionaries purposely adopted a “Trojan horse” policy, that of “not creating a Roman Catholic community distinct from and in rivalry to the Orthodox, but fostering a Catholic nucleus inside the canonical boundaries of the Orthodox communion” through the signing of secret formal professions of faith evaluated and often composed by *Propaganda*.[19] Converts were told to continue outwardly as members of their previous church and to receive communion there as before.[20] Consequently, throughout the seventeenth century, “there was built up a powerful crypto-Roman party within the outward boundaries of the Orthodox Church.”[21] As the modern scholar Kallistos Ware observes, “This nucleus, so Roman Catholic clergy hoped, would slowly grow until it was in a position to take over the leadership of the Eastern patriarchates and to proclaim organic unity as a *fait accompli*.”[22]

An example of these secret submissions reads as follows (from Parthenios II, a metropolitan of the Island of Chios, who eventually became patriarch of Constantinople in 1644), in addressing the pope:

> To your Beatitude I render all due obedience and submission, acknowledging you to be the true successor of the leader of the Apostles, and the chief shepherd of the Catholic Church throughout the whole world. With all piety and obedience I bow before your holy feet and kiss them, asking your blessing, for with full power you guide and tend the whole of Christ’s chosen flock. So I confess and so I believe; and I am zealous that my subjects also should be such as I am myself. Finding them eager, I guide them in the ways of piety; for there are not a few who think just as I do.[23]

Such a policy was extremely successful in Antioch in 1724, resulting in the division of the ancient Antiochian patriarchate into Roman Catholic and Orthodox hierarchies. In analyzing the effectiveness of the Roman Catholic missionaries, the historian Robert Haddad observes:

> The success of the Latin missionaries was symptomatic of Ottoman distress, for they were organically part of the expansion that would force the world into the European orbit before the twentieth century. Constantinople’s grip over the whole of Antioch, like Istanbul’s over Syria, slackened further after 1680 as a substantial minority of Melkites[24] turned Uniate, entering that European orbit to be nurtured and protected,

diplomatically and materially, by the men of the First Rome and the French monarch.[25]

In response to the Roman Catholic successes and to stem the "Uniate tide," Constantinople intervened at Antioch in 1724 with the support of the Ottoman government and took control of the patriarchate by electing its own candidates to fill the patriarchal throne until 1898.[26] Nevertheless, according to Robert Haddad, these efforts did not counter the Uniate effort, mainly because of provincial Syrian rulers:

> Direct Greek control over Antioch merely inhibited the Uniate advance. Local Syrian authorities tended to favour the Uniates as parties perched, like themselves, at the edge of Ottoman legitimacy. Complemented by pope and Catholic king, they continued to mediate relations between Constantinople and Antioch and between Istanbul and Syria, thus ensuring the survival and moderate expansion of the Uniates despite Ottoman refusal to accord them *de jure* recognition until 1839.[27]

In light of these proselytization efforts, the Ecumenical Patriarchate's consequent policy (established in 1750) of receiving converts from Roman Catholicism into the Orthodox communion through baptism must also be understood as an Orthodox attempt to draw a clear and strong boundary between the two churches to prevent other such engineered divisions. Eventually, in the nineteenth century this policy was moderated to reception through chrismation, another means established in church history for reception of heretics and schismatics.[28]

Adversarial relations also existed with Protestant missionaries working in the Ottoman Empire, who were active in attempting to make converts from the Orthodox throughout the Middle East, although with less success than Roman Catholicism, which did not require a fundamental change in the liturgical life of proselytes.[29] In the last part of the nineteenth century, the number of American missionaries accounted for half of all Protestant missionaries worldwide. The United States was the leading missionary nation and dominated Protestant efforts in the Ottoman Empire.[30]

Throughout the nineteenth century, the following major organizations were responsible for most of the American missionaries in the Middle East: the American Board of Commissioners for Foreign

Missions (ABCFM), the Board of Foreign Missions of the Presbyterian Church (BFMPC), the Southern Methodist mission board, and the mission boards of the Northern Baptists and Methodists. Calvinist Congregationalists and Presbyterians constituted the majority of American Protestant missionaries. The missionaries generally had two goals: Christianizing and civilizing.[31]

Rufus Anderson, the foreign secretary for the ABCFM from 1826 to 1866, summarized the American Protestant strategy toward the Eastern churches as follows:

> We may not hope for the conversion of the Mohammedans, unless true Christianity be exemplified before them by the Oriental Churches. To them the native Christians represent the Christian religion, and they see that these are no better than themselves. They think them worse; and therefore the Moslem believes the Koran to be more excellent than the Bible.
>
> It is vain to say, that the native Christians have so far departed from the truth that they do not feel the power of the Gospel, and that therefore the immorality of their lives is not to be attributed to its influence. The Mohammedan has seen no other effect of it, and he cannot be persuaded to read the Bible to correct the evidence of his observation, and perhaps also of his own painful experience.
>
> Hence a wise plan for the conversion of the Mohammedans of Western Asia necessarily involved first, a mission to the Oriental Churches. It was needful that the lights of the Gospel should once more burn on those candlesticks, that everywhere there should be living examples of the religion of Jesus Christ, that Christianity should no longer be associated in the Moslem mind with all that is sordid and base.[32]

At the end of the nineteenth century, the Reverend Henry H. Jessup synopsized the views of Presbyterian missionaries regarding the Eastern churches:

> In the year 1819 the first American missionaries came to Western Asia, bringing the Gospel of Christ to the Mohammedans, but in their explorations they came in contact with these various Oriental Christian sects. They found them to be ignorant, illiterate, superstitious, idolatrous . . . It is a painful and sickening spectacle to enter a Greek church and see the crowds of worshippers burning incense, lighting tapers, and bowing before the filthy,

> painted boards and then devoutly kissing them and crossing themselves . . . The Greek Church stands condemned from its own authorized symbols as polytheistic, idolatrous, and unscriptural.[33]

Fundamental to the Protestant missionaries' approach was the notion that education had to precede the reform of the Eastern churches.[34] Colleges and universities throughout the Middle East owe their foundation to missionary efforts to civilize in order to evangelize, that is, "to create the conditions for preaching the Gospel" in order "to facilitate the acceptance of the higher religion—Christianity."[35] Such institutions include "the American University in Cairo, the American University in Beirut, Bosphorus University, Tarsus American College, the International College in Beirut, and Anatolia College (now in Greece)."[36]

The conditions that would facilitate the acceptance of the higher religion were linked to Anglo-Saxon Protestantism. In 1876 the general secretary of the ABCFM stated:

> It is now the English language, saturated with Christian ideas, gathering up into itself the best thought of all the ages, that is the great agent of Christian civilization throughout the world; at this moment affecting the destinies and molding the character of half the human race. French influence, so dominant in the literary world, has passed away. The encyclopedists have left but the shadow of a name. The Nazarene has triumphed.[37]

The missionaries often saw themselves as the guardians of the "less developed races" such as the Arabs, Armenians, and other "Orientals."[38] As a result of their efforts,

> despite initial setbacks, missionaries had established a considerable, permanent, presence in the region by the 1900s. It was concentrated in three areas and principally directed by two organizations. In Anatolia, the ABCFM had 166 missionaries with 137 churches and just fewer than 14,000 communicants at its peak before World War I. In Iran, the BFMPC had 36 missionaries, 35 churches, and over 3,000 communicants; in Syria it had 31 missionaries, 34 churches, and just fewer than 3,000 communicants. The United Presbyterian Board was also active in Egypt and the Dutch Reformed Board had a tiny Arabian Mission in the Persian Gulf that

included Samuel Zwemer, one of the most renowned American missionaries to the Middle East.[39]

ORTHODOXY AND SECULAR NATIONALISM IN THE NINETEENTH CENTURY

Generally, before the nineteenth century, religious institutions, such as patriarchates, monasteries, and holy places, were the focal points for the collective life of Orthodox under Ottoman rule. As the modern scholar Paschalis Kitromilides stated:

> These elements—a common unitary religious community and common Orthodox convictions—composed the identity of the Orthodox commonwealth, for which the Greek language supplied the instrument of communication, and classical culture and Christian political thought the sources of cohesion and legitimacy.[40]

In these prenational societies under the Ottomans, "linguistic difference was not a source of conflict since people were multi-lingual and in the absence of state boundaries, they could cross potential ethnolinguistic distinctions much more easily."[41] The Greek language was used for common communication among the higher clergy without any national overtones and was viewed as the language of the church and part of its patristic inheritance.

Among the Orthodox population, time was organized according to the church calendar, with its feast days and commemorations of saints that marked the seasons and harvests, and space was structured through "places of worship, great shrines of the faith and humble chapels isolated in the countryside, graves of the saints, places of martyrdom, environments sanctified by miracles. Pride of place was reserved for shrines sheltering miraculous icons or holy relics."[42] An individual's life was organized around the sacraments of the Orthodox Church. In general, the sharing of a common religious inheritance and "framework of values and emotional and aesthetic affinities" enabled Orthodox "to transcend linguistic barriers and cultural borders and softened the physical and psychological differences created by geographical distance."[43]

The rise of Greek, Arab, Serbian, Bulgarian, Albanian, Rumanian, and Russian nationalism shattered the collective Orthodox identity of the *millet-i Rum*. During the nineteenth century the secular concept of "nation" that originated in Western Europe infected the Orthodox world of the Balkans and the Middle East. Nation-states and national identities were created on the basis of secular values that often distorted the symbols of the common Orthodox heritage by substituting material principles for spiritual ones. After the revolts of various "nations" against Ottoman rule, the Greek language was no longer regarded as a nonnational means of communication, but rather was identified with Greek ethnicity.[44]

Throughout the nineteenth century the Ecumenical Patriarchate continued to reject these new secular, parochial, and ethnic tendencies by appealing to the universal values of Orthodoxy. As stated by Paschalis Kitromilides, "the deep antinomy between the new political morality associated with the secular state and the tradition of the Great Church can be comprehended if the ecumenical and transcendental values which composed the teaching of Christianity, and in particular the Orthodox worldview, are juxtaposed to the secular, non-ecumenical and violent values of nationalism, which were the substrate of the constitution of the secular state."[45]

In 1844 Patriarch Germanos IV of Constantinople (1842–45) established "The Theological School of the Great Church of Christ" in the stauropegial Monastery of the Holy Trinity in Halki, one of the Prince Islands located near Constantinople, for the purpose of "the education and moral formation proper to clergymen of the Most High."[46] During the period 1844–99, the School had seven grades, or classes.[47] The old structures of the monastery and the School survived until a devastating earthquake in 1894. The School was then completely rebuilt in a new location on the island and reopened in 1896.

The Ecumenical Patriarchate's foundation of a theological school was an attempt to address theological education universally for the entire *millet-i Rum*, not for any specific "nation" in the sense of ethnicity. Consequently, from its establishment the Ecumenical Patriarchate envisioned the School as open to the entire Orthodox Church and took steps to accomplish this aim. According to Apostolos Mexēs, a modern historian who also served as a professor of the School,

Students supported by the hierarchs constituted the first pupils of the Theological School . . . who formerly studied in the schools of the capital and of foreign lands, a considerable number being deacons and hieromonks advanced in age. On the one hand, in order that the number of students of the School might be increased, and on the other, that all of the Orthodox Churches of the East might be as much as possible represented in it, the ecumenical patriarch sent encyclicals to all the hierarchs of the Ecumenical Throne; the patriarchs of Antioch, Alexandria, and Jerusalem; and the archbishop of Cyprus, through which he announced the Theological School's establishment under good auspices and expressed the desire of the church that supported students would be sent who are appropriately prepared. This was an excellent measure that demonstrated the increased prestige of the Ecumenical Throne and contributed to the achievement of the desired unity of the local Orthodox Churches.

All the eparchies and the remaining Orthodox Churches hastened eagerly to respond to the invitation of the Ecumenical Patriarchate. Consequently, within a short time, in addition to Bulgarians and Serbians coming from eparchies of the region of the Ecumenical Patriarchate, the students of the School included ones who also came from the other Orthodox patriarchates and autocephalous churches. The number of foreign languages increased so significantly in level that the teachers having difficulties were placed in an embarrassing position. And in these circumstances, the sagacity of the headmaster Kōnstantinos Typaldos[48] was appreciated when he discovered a solution that so wisely settled matters. The wise headmaster prescribed special studies during the first year for those who did not know the Greek language. In the course of time, starting from the views that a purpose of the Theological School was the education of the sacred clergy and its students were intended as confessors, teachers, priests, and shepherds of the Orthodox of the region of the Ecumenical Throne, of which a numerous part speaks foreign languages, it was proposed and approved by the Synod that—in addition to classes in theology, the humanities, and Hebrew—Slavonic, Arabic, and Armenian would be taught in the Theological School.[49]

Of these languages Slavonic was promoted inasmuch as in numerous eparchies the Sacred Liturgy was also celebrated either entirely in Slavonic or even mixed with Greek, and thus it was necessary for the clergy who were to instruct the Slavic-speaking masses to be conversant in their tongue.[50]

The pan-Orthodox character of the school reflected the role of the Ecumenical Patriarchate as the leader of a collective Orthodox community that transcended national barriers.

In this context, at the outset of the School's foundation, the teaching of the Greek language was viewed as a way to help prepare its students as sacred clergy ("confessors, teachers, priests, and shepherds of the Orthodox") rather than a way to reflect and impose Greek ethnicity. Other languages were equally considered within the context of improving the clergy's communications with the faithful, rather than being based on considerations of secular nationhood.

ST. RAPHAEL HAWAWEENY AND THE THEOLOGICAL SCHOOL IN HALKI

St. Raphael Hawaweeny was the third son of Mikha'il al-Hawaweeny and his wife Mariam (née Najjar) and was born near the feastday of the Archangels, November 8, 1860, in Beirut. His family, originally Damascene, had fled the 1860 Druze massacres of the Christian population, which took place during July of the same year. The family returned to Damascus in 1861 and enrolled St. Raphael in a parochial school under the Patriarchate of Antioch. Eventually he was accepted as a minor seminarian under Patriarch Hierotheos of Antioch (1850–85) and completed his gymnasium studies, which included Arabic, Greek, Turkish, mathematics, history, geography, church catechism, and Byzantine chant. These studies corresponded to the academic prerequisites necessary for his acceptance into the Theological School of the Great Church of Christ.[51]

According to the 1874 *Regulations* of the School in force during St. Raphael's matriculation, the requirements for entrance included the following:

> In order to be admitted into the School, the students ought: 1.) to be children of the Orthodox Church; 2.) to be neither younger than eighteen years of age nor older than twenty-two, outside of those who have already completed gymnasium studies, who are accepted even up to twenty-five years of age; 3.) not to be subject either to organic or to any chronic illness; 4.) to hold a certificate that has been certified by the Hierarch concerning their

> honest character and good conduct; and 5.) to know the following subjects: grammar, etymology, and principles of the syntax of the Greek language, with their application in writing, practical arithmetic, political geography, sacred history, and sacred catechism.[52]

Although he fulfilled the academic requirements, St. Raphael was nearly denied admission by the School's physician due to physical weakness, consistent with the third condition of not being "subject either to organic or to any chronic illness." The School also required its approximately sixty students to be supported by patrons, most often hierarchs.

St. Raphael is reported to have enjoyed the initial patronage of a local merchant who was encouraged by Ecumenical Patriarch Iōacheim III (1878–84, 1901–12). When this support was withdrawn in 1884 owing to Iōacheim's resignation over a disagreement with the Ottoman government regarding reform of *millet* privileges, Archimandrite Chrysanthos Saliba (later metropolitan of Akkar) became St. Raphael's new patron.

According to the 1874 *Regulations*, patrons were responsible for reimbursing the School for all expenses if a student might be expelled for any cause.[53] Prior to beginning their studies, students were also required to make a formal promise to their patron "that, upon reaching the age prescribed by the sacred canons, they will become clergy."[54] In turn, patrons were required to indemnify the School for each year of study in the event that the student might "wish not to be a clergyman after reaching the age according to the canons."[55] In addition, the following provision was also made:

> The funds that the patron ought to pay if the student might not be a clergyman after reaching the legal age remain as a deposit in the treasury of the School, and are returned to the patron whenever the student might become a clergyman.[56]

Just prior to his matriculation in 1879, St. Raphael was tonsured a monk. In December 1885, prior to his graduation in 1886, St. Raphael was ordained as a hierodeacon in the School's chapel by Prokopios, metropolitan of Melnik (1875–91).

The School's monastic foundation was reflected in its student life, which included the wearing of the *skoufos* (σκοῦφος), a short cylinder-shaped cap mostly worn by monks and monastic clergy, and a black tunic reaching the feet;[57] silence during meals, which were all taken in common and accompanied by the reading of an "ecclesiastical book";[58] the description of student accommodations as cells, with severe restrictions on mutual visitations;[59] strict controls on all outside visitors, who were forbidden any overnight accommodation;[60] regulation of all articles brought into the School by porters and caretakers;[61] supervision of even walks outside of the School;[62] and restrictions on travel during recesses from classes, with written permission required from the School's headmaster (σχολάρχης) to visit Constantinople and from the student's patron for any other trips.[63]

The authority of the headmaster may be compared to that of an abbot. He was required to be a clergyman and to remain at the School except on rare occasions. The headmaster's authority was pervasive over all personnel, professors, and students. His permission was required for all actions governing any aspect of the School's life. During St. Raphael's matriculation the headmaster was the archimandrite Germanos Grēgoras (1877–98), who had previously directed the School of the Holy Cross under the Patriarchate of Jerusalem (1858–62).

The 1874 *Regulations* listed a staff of ten professors and described them as "obedient to the headmaster" and ideally clergy.[64] The professors were also required to reside at the School and to dine in common with the students.[65] Their travel was also subject to restrictions and necessitated the concurrence of the headmaster.[66]

The 1874 *Regulations* described the seven-year course of study in the following summary:

> The classes taught in the School are those of sacred theology with required humanities. The classes of sacred theology are presently the following: church history, sacred commentary and exegesis of Holy Scripture, dogmatic and moral theology, patrology and Hebrew archeology, pastoral theology, homiletics, catechesis, teleturgical and church law, and theological exercises. The humanities classes are sacred history, sacred catechesis, anthropology, psychology, logic, ethics and history of philosophy, Greek and Latin language and philology, rhetoric and composition, geometry, mathematics, arithmetic, algebra, mathematical geography, political

history, chronology, Slavonic and Bulgarian language, Turkish and French, and theoretical and practical church music.[67]

Greek language study occurred in the following progression:

First Year: St. John Chrysostom, Xenophon, Arrian, Plutarch; syntax and composition
Second Year: St. Basil the Great, St. Gregory the Theologian, Plato, Lysias, Demosthenes; syntax and composition
Third Year: Herodotus, Thucydides; philology
Fourth Year: Homer, Euripides, Theocritus, the poems of St. Gregory the Theologian; philology
Fifth Year: Sophocles, Aeschylus, Pindar; philology

A similar progression was made with Latin:

Second Year: Cornelius Nepos, Eutropius; grammar
Third Year: Caesar, Livy, St. Ambrose; syntax
Fourth Year: Sallust, Ovid, Cicero, Tertullian; philology
Fifth Year: Virgil, Horace, St. Augustine; philology

The study of both languages involved a similar grounding in classics and patristic texts, and in this way reflected their purpose at the School for apprehending church Tradition rather than inculcating ethnicity.

In addition, students were required to take two years of classes in Slavonic, one year of Bulgarian, three years of Turkish, and two years of French, which reflected the pan-Orthodox character of studies.

Three types of examinations were conducted: those throughout the year; annual examinations for the entire school body; and a special set of examinations, oral and written, for the diploma. In addition, there were homiletic exercises in the sixth and seventh years.

Prior to the examinations for the diploma, a theological thesis was required, which was described in the 1874 *Regulations*:

> At least one month before the annual examinations, each of the undergraduates (τελειοδιδάκτων) ought to present to the headmaster a thesis on a

> theological subject that he chose with the approval of the headmaster, written in refined Greek language (καθαρεύουσαν Ἑλληνικὴν γλῶσσαν), and having at least the length of a folio (ἑνὸς τυπογραφικοῦ φύλλου).[68]

The graduation ceremonies were also described by the 1874 *Regulations*:

> The presentation of the diplomas takes place solemnly on the first Sunday after the conclusion of the examinations for a diploma, as follows. After a sacred celebration takes place, the headmaster makes a suitable public address, and then the secretary reads the approval given by the examination committee. One of the members of the trustee board reads aloud each of the diplomas. The headmaster, when he invites up each graduate and bestows the diploma, declares him a teacher of **Orthodox Christian theology**.[69]

ST. RAPHAEL'S THEOLOGICAL THESIS

Composed during his seventh year of studies, St. Raphael's thesis is entitled "The True Significance of Sacred Tradition and Its Great Worth" and is preceded by a page stating that its subject concerns "sacred Tradition and its undeniable authority." The thesis was handwritten in thirty-nine pages and is dated May 1, 1886.

As required by the 1874 *Regulations* of the School, the work is written in "refined Greek language" (καθαρεύουσαν Ἑλληνικὴν γλῶσσαν). The term *kathareuousa* (καθαρεύουσα) often refers to a form of Modern Greek that was consciously purified of foreign elements (from καθαρεύειν, "to be pure") and was regarded as a literary language for scholarship and official documents. *Kathareuousa* was also considered an expression of Greek nationalism in its emphasis on a return to a language untainted by foreign influences. Many advocates of *kathereouosa* in the eighteenth and nineteenth centuries associated themselves and the Greek language with Ancient Greece rather than with the patristic and Byzantine periods.[70]

However, the grammar and vocabulary used in the thesis are clearly similar to those in the writings of patristic authorities and reflect the course of Greek and Latin studies at the Theological School, which incorporated texts from classical authors and the Fathers for syntax and philology. Rather than a contrived modern language, the thesis is written in a form of Greek that would be apprehensible to Byzantine and late patristic authors. In this way, the language used clearly represents the continuation of a church Tradition or patristic inheritance rather than an artificial return to classical models in order to express a purified Greek identity.

This identification with the church's patristic inheritance is further underscored by the fact that the thesis contains numerous texts from eighteen patristic authors, six of whom are Latin; when the Latin authors are cited, the quotations are accompanied by Greek translation. The Latin Fathers are St. Ambrose, St. Augustine, St. Cyprian, St. Jerome, Tertullian, and St. Vincent of Lérins. The Greek Fathers are St. Basil the Great, St. Clement of Alexandria, St. Cyril of Alexandria, St. Dionysius the Areopagite, Eusebius of Caesarea, St. Gregory the Theologian, St. Irenaeus of Lyons (whose work is cited from Latin texts where the Greek no longer survives), St. John Chrysostom, St. Justin Martyr, Origen, and Sozomen. A text is also reproduced from the memoirs of the Byzantine author Sylvester Syropoulos (fifteenth century) concerning the Council of Florence (1438–39). The thesis quotes only once from a classical work, Homer's *Odyssey* (9.51), and this is done only in order to emphasize the disunity brought about by the Protestant Reformation.[71]

The work cites seventeen modern writings from fifteen separate authors. The pan-Orthodox nature of the thesis is illustrated by the inclusion of three Slavic authors in Greek translation: Antonii Amfiteatrov (1815–79), archbishop of Kazan (1867–69); Philaret Drozdov (1782–1867), metropolitan of Moscow (1821–67); and Makarii Bulgakov (1816–82), metropolitan of Moscow (1879–82), who wrote standard texts used in Orthodox seminaries in the Church of Russia.[72] The remaining citations of Orthodox works include two by Eugenios Voulgarēs (1716–1806), a major Orthodox theologian of the eighteenth century, whose career included teaching at Mount Athos, Constantinople, and the Church of Russia. Voulgarēs died as a hierarch of the Russian Orthodox Church and was a strong opponent of the *Unia* and Roman Catholic missionaries among the Orthodox.[73]

It is interesting to note that five of the remaining authors are Roman Catholics who wrote before the First Vatican Council. The presence of these works reflects the inclusion of Western European scholarship and languages in the curriculum of the School as well as the holdings of its library. The writers are Claude Fleury (1640–1723), a church historian; Heinrich Klee (1800–40), a systematic theologian; Johann Adam Möhler (1796–1838), a theologian whose work continues to influence ecumenical thought, particularly regarding relations with Protestants; as well as Nicolas-Sylvestre Bergier (1718–90) and Abbé Pierrot (d. ca. 1864), joint authors of an ecclesiastical encyclopedia.[74]

The thesis is structured in the following manner: introductory material summarizing its content, two main sections devoted to a refutation of Roman Catholic and Protestant views of sacred Tradition, and a concluding part that consists entirely of a long quotation from the second article of the *Confession* of Dositheos II, patriarch of Jerusalem (1669–1707), which was adopted by the Council of Jerusalem (1672) to refute Protestant theological positions.

The introductory part of the thesis outlines Orthodox theological positions on the relationship between written and oral expressions of divine revelation:

> Of these two ways of transmitting divine truths, the one by word, that is, living voice, constitutes sacred Tradition, [and] the other by letter, that is, writing, constitutes holy Scripture, in both of which all Christian truth, that is, divine revelation is contained. But just as the written word is nothing other than the more brief and at the same time more constant representation of the spoken word, so also holy Scripture can be viewed as the brief and at the same time constant expression of sacred Tradition. Hence sacred Tradition and holy Scripture are thus very closely tied to one another, so that each by necessity requires the other, and the absence of one in these important points is detrimental to the other.

Once he has described the relationship between sacred Tradition and holy Scripture, St. Raphael states that the overemphasis of either distorts ecclesiastical life:

> In this way, when holy Scripture is disregarded, sacred Tradition runs the danger of distortion because the human can be mixed up easily with the divine, the profane with the holy, and truth with falsehood. On the other hand, when sacred Tradition is removed, holy Scripture is subject to many misinterpretations because when holy Scripture is left to each one's free

> understanding and interpretation, a certain strange diversity within the one and same Christian teaching can hence result.

After establishing the notion of such distortions, Roman Catholics and Protestants are introduced as examples of modern "heresies" teaching falsehoods:

> But in order that we pass over such heretics that appeared in more ancient times, whose remains or even names that scarcely survive today set forth before us shining evidence of their false teachings, come, let us now examine the more modern and at the same time more important of the two aforesaid one-sided heresies: I speak of the papists and the Protestants.

Such a characterization of Roman Catholicism and Protestantism as "heresies" most likely reflects not only theological considerations, but also the adversarial relationship between the Orthodox Churches and Western Christianity that resulted from aggressive missionary efforts directed against Eastern Christians during this period. The choice of this approach to the subject of sacred Tradition—as well as its required approval by the headmaster—almost certainly suggests the influence of the prior attempts of Roman Catholics to engineer secret conversions at the School itself.[75]

St. Raphael next outlines the main arguments against both Roman Catholicism and Protestantism as heretical bodies:

> Whereas the Orthodox Christian who freely searches the Scriptures subjects his individual precarious interpretation to the certain judgment of the universal Church, "taking captive," according to the divine Paul, "every thought to the obedience of Christ" (2 Cor. 10:5), the papist who is prevented from the free search of the Scriptures blindly follows papist traditions in many fables, so resting his conscience upon the so-called infallible judgments of the Roman pontifex as the supreme interpreter of holy Scripture, and the Protestant who, basing himself only on his individual conscience, interprets the Scriptures in a completely arbitrary way. Thus papism, which centers in this manner all ecclesiastical life in one sole person, the pope, established in Rome a religious, so to speak, oracle, in whom the apostolic Traditions, distorted in many ways and confused with human nonsense, are presented as incontestable writ of divine origin! The Protestant, who

> also rejected sacred Tradition along with this papist prattle, was deprived of any firm basis in the interpretation of holy Scripture and so, one-sidedly following Scripture, dismembered the one Church into so many parts,
>
> "As many as the leaves and flowers multiply in spring"![76]
>
> Because papism, thus impelled by an uncivilized spirit and centralization, mixes the human with the divine for the attainment of this very aim and so distorts and falsifies sacred Traditions, Protestantism, spurred on by a tendency to struggle against these arrogant claims of papism, stumbled into the opposite excess of indiscipline and decentralization, completely rejecting sacred Traditions as human writ.

The reference to an "oracle" established in Rome is most likely a reference to the doctrine of papal infallibility, which was defined at the First Vatican Council (1869–70) within ten years of the saint's matriculation to Halki.

The introduction then concludes with an explanation of the thesis title and summary of its academic task:

> On account of this, come, let us discuss certain brief points concerning sacred Tradition, demonstrating on the one hand its true significance against the papists who distort it, and on the other hand its great worth against the Protestants who reject it.

The first section, which deals with the refutation of Roman Catholicism, is divided into four parts, each devoted to a separate topic dealing with sacred Tradition: content, sources, characteristic marks, and the storehouse where it is protected.

The content of sacred Tradition is defined as "the unwritten word that is handed over by the Savior through the Apostles to the Church and recorded in large measure by the holy Fathers." Tradition is distinguished as divine in its content and as human in being delivered over by men. The process of its delivery is further subdivided into apostolic, ecclesiastical, and purely human. The apostolic and ecclesiastical transmissions are identified with the divine content. Purely human traditions are generally all things that distort true belief, among which is considered "the primacy of the pope and generally all innovations of the papal Church."

Eight sources of sacred Tradition are identified: ancient symbols or creeds, the Apostolic Canons (although it is acknowledged that they are not authored by the Apostles, but rather their successors), ancient liturgies, ancient martyrologies, canonical legislation, patristic writings, customs (practices with regard to time, space, and rites), and the witness of ancient heresies, "which truly distorted certain proofs of orthodox teaching, on account of which they were also condemned by the church, but when separated they preserved many things safe and unadulterated."

The characteristic marks of sacred Tradition are internal and external. The internal marks are its agreement with itself, other traditions, and holy Scripture. The external marks are its catholicity, antiquity, and agreement, namely, "the three designated by Vincent, bishop of Lérins . . . the things *quod ubique* (what everywhere), *quod semper* (what always), *quod ab omnibus* (what by all) *creditum est* (was believed)."

After the fall of the formerly Orthodox Church of Rome into innovation, the only remaining storehouse and protection of sacred Tradition is the Eastern Orthodox Church. The fall of the Roman Church is attributed to arrogance, vanity, and ambition, which in turn corrupt and lead to innovations:

> In this manner, proportionately to her ambitious proclivities, advancing from error to error in spiritual and worldly affairs, it has left nothing unshaken, nothing without innovation, nothing without perversion—neither doctrines, nor mysteries, nor customs—but it spoiled and distorted everything written and unwritten! In truth, time lacks even to simply enumerate the shameless innovations of the papist Church, which both church and civil history report with horror, but lest I appear to say unsubstantiated things, let it be permitted for me that I make a brief comparison of the present-day so-called papist Church with our Orthodox Church, or rather with itself, when at one time, being in agreement in everything with our own Church, it was called an orthodox Church of Rome, because nothing more disinterested and impartial than history can demonstrate for us which of the two discussed Churches is the faithful and true guardian of sacred Traditions.

The following chart illustrates the comparison made between Orthodoxy, characterized as the formerly orthodox Church of Rome before its innovations, and Roman Catholicism, namely, the "papist Church":

ORTHODOX CHURCH OF ROME	PAPIST CHURCH
Pope as "first among equals" and subject to the decisions of ecumenical councils	Pope as an infallible supreme hierarch (*summus pontifex*) above the ecumenical councils
Holy Spirit proceeds from Father	Holy Spirit proceeds from Father and Son (*Filioque*)
Baptism by triple immersion	Baptism by sprinkling and infusion
Celebration of chrismation immediately after baptism	Confirmation at the age of twelve
Eucharist: leavened bread, epiclesis, and communion of both species for the entire Church	Eucharist: unleavened bread, words of institution, and exclusion of the laity from communion of the precious blood of Christ
Repentance	Subdivision of the mystery into: contrition, confession, and satisfaction; absolutions based on excess merits and release from purifying fire
Celibacy obligatory only for bishops	Celibacy obligatory for all clergy
Dissolution of marriage based on spousal infidelity	Indissoluble marriage
Unction celebrated by any priest for the sick	Unction only celebrated by the bishop for the dying as a last anointing (*extrema unctio*)
No fasting or kneeling on the Sabbath	Permitted fasting and kneeling on Sabbath
No breaking of the fast on Wednesdays and Fridays	Permitted breaking of the fast on Wednesdays and Fridays
No consumption of blood or clotted blood	Permitted consumption of blood and clotted blood
No playing of any musical instrument in church	Permitted playing of musical instruments in church
No veneration of statues or unwritten images	Permitted veneration of statues and unwritten images
No ordination of more than one priest during one and the same Liturgy	Permitted ordination of more than one priest during one and the same Liturgy
No offering each day of more than one sacrifice on the same altar	Permitted offering each day of more than one sacrifice on the same altar
No shaving of the hair and the beard	Permitted shaving of the hair and beard

On the basis of this comparison, the conclusion is reached that the storehouse of sacred Tradition is the "orthodox Eastern Church, which neither added or subtracted nor altered a jot or tittle from the divine deposit handed over to it from apostolic times until the present day."

The second section is introduced by a description of Protestantism as originating from a revolt against papism that went to the opposite extreme of "spiritual anarchy and religious mob rule." The Protestant revolt was to discard all sacred Tradition and consider holy Scripture "as the sole source of Christian faith," which "when each of them interprets [Scripture] arbitrarily, without sacred Tradition, he is basing his religious conviction upon his individual conscience."

The revolt's main consequence was the destruction of the "unity of faith," which surpasses papism into the "abyss of spiritual destruction." The main point is then made that holy Scripture is not the sole and sufficient source for the Christian religion and requires for its completion and explanation sacred Tradition, which has the same authority. The remainder of this section is divided into three parts, each devoted to a demonstration of the latter's "great worth," according to evidence of holy Scripture, the witness of the church including the holy Fathers, and sacred Tradition's indispensability.

In the first part, treatment of holy Scripture is divided into the Old Testament and Christian eras and is based on the view that the oral transmission of divine revelation precedes and provides the context for understanding its written expression.

Moses urged the Israelites not simply to read the law of God as recorded at the end of his life, but to "remember the days of old, understand generation from generation: ask your father, and he shall proclaim to you; your elders, and they shall tell you."[77] Throughout the duration of the Judaic Kingdom, there are "two means of transmission of divine revelation . . . parallel to one another, one of tradition and the other of Scripture." The Protestant argument that writings should not be added to interpret Scripture, an argument based on Deuteronomy 4:2, "You shall not add to the word which I command you," is opposed by two points: that the passage refers to adding what is detrimental, not written; and if otherwise true, the words of the Prophets could not have been added to Scripture.

During the Christian era the original transmission of the Christian faith occurs first by living voice and then similarly through written and oral means. The Lord Jesus Christ "preached the gospel of salvation only by word of mouth" and "wrote nothing either concerning His life or concerning His teachings." Only through His living voice, the Lord attended to the foundation of His church and commissioned the Apostles, who in turn orally preached the divine word "but then some of them and their disciples, thus only a certain number, motivated by various reasons, wrote some brief memorials of their particular teaching by word of mouth."

However, the Apostles' writings illustrate that they did not record everything that was taught by a living voice. Among the examples provided are texts of St. Paul—"About the remaining things, when I come, I will give direction"[78]—and of the Apostle John—"Having many things to write to you by ink and pen, but I hope to immediately see you and will speak to you face to face."[79]

In fact, the majority of the Apostles "wrote nothing at all" and "successfully preached the word of God everywhere . . . established Churches, many of which until the beginning of the third century and after . . . knew nothing outside of sacred Tradition." Few translations and even copies of written Scriptures existed among early Christians. Nevertheless, "true faith and salvation existed for so many millions."

The Apostles acknowledge that the oral tradition provides the source for their own writings and the context for their understanding. When St. Paul writes, "Therefore, brethren, stand fast and hold firm to the traditions that you were taught whether by word or our letter,"[80] the Apostle is ordering the observance of traditions already in hand and that these as well as those in writings are equally valued. The Protestant argument against Tradition, which is based on passages such as Galatians 1:8–9, which forbids the preaching of "a gospel besides that which you received," is said to be founded on a misunderstanding that the reception of divine revelation is confined to written transmission. Consequently, Protestants fail to comprehend that the point in such passages is not the addition of written words, but of false teachings.

In the second part, concerning the witness of "the one, holy, catholic, and apostolic Church," the great worth of sacred Tradition is demonstrated based on the church's nature. The Lord establishes an eternal church that exists wherever two or three are "gathered in my name"[81] through the promised abiding presence of the Holy Spirit.[82] The ecumenical and local councils are the voice of this church. These councils constantly affirm that divine truth is expressed through Tradition and, most importantly, use the latter rather than Scripture to refute heretics, who distort the written word.

In addition to the universal church, the Fathers also witness to the great authority of sacred Tradition. The following chart lists the Fathers and texts that are cited:

FATHER	TEXT
St. Ignatius the God-bearer	"... exhorted the parishes in each city in which he stayed ... he encouraged them to hold fast to the Tradition of the Apostles, which he regarded necessary to be given fixed form for certainty, when witnessing [to the Tradition] in writing at that time." (Eusebius, *Church History* 3.36)
St. Polycarp	"In the time of Anicetus, when he stayed in Rome, he turned many from the aforementioned heretics to the Church of God, while preaching that this one and only truth was received from the Apostles, which was handed over by the Church." (Irenaeus, *Against Heresies* 3.3)
St. Papias	"Not from books did I receive so much to benefit me, as from a voice living and enduring." (Eusebius, *Church History* 3.39)
St. Dionysius the Areopagite	"Therefore we accept as clearly necessary for man's salvation the divine law, prophetic ordinances, and the evangelic commands in the Apostolic Constitutions and sacred unwritten traditions of the Church, the transgressors of which are called heretics." (*Concerning Ecclesiastical Hierarchy* 1)
Hegesippus	"Therefore he collected the unerring tradition of apostolic preaching in five books with the most simple style of writing." (Eusebius, *Church History* 4.8)
St. Irenaeus	"Anyone who wishes to see the truth is able to see in every Church the apostolic Tradition that is known to the entire world." (*Against Heresies* 3.3)
Tertullian	"We have the Apostles of the Lord as our authorities, who not even themselves chose to introduce anything on their own authority, but faithfully handed on to the nations the rule received from Christ." (*On the Prescription of Heretics* 6)
St. Clement of Alexandria	"But those who preserve the true Tradition of blessed teaching directly from the holy Apostles John, James, and Paul, being handed on from father to son (but a few similar to fathers), came by God's will to us also to deposit those ancestral and apostolic seeds." (*Stromata* 1.1.11–12)
Origen	"Therefore, because the apostolic tradition must be preserved, which is handed over in the order of succession from the Apostles and exists in our Churches to the present day, only this truth must be accepted that differs in no respect from ecclesiastical and apostolic Tradition." (*On First Principles*, preface, 2)

St. Cyprian	"It is easy for pious and simple souls both to avoid falsehood and to find the truth, for at the same time that we turn to the source of divine Tradition, falsehood is destroyed." (*Epistle 63*)
St. Basil the Great	"Of the dogmas and preaching that are preserved in the Church, some we possess from written teaching, others we have received from the Tradition of the Apostles that was preserved for us in secret; both of which have the same force in relation to right belief. And no one will speak against these, no one who has even at least a little experience of the institutions of the Church. For if we were to attempt to reject unwritten customs, as not having great value, we might be negligent in these principal customs, injuring the Gospel [and] instead turning the preaching into a mere word. For example, to take the first and most general custom, who taught in writing those who have trusted in the name of our Lord Jesus Christ to seal themselves by the sign of the Cross? What writing taught us to turn toward the East during prayer? Which of the saints has left us in writing the words of the invocation at the displaying of the bread of the Eucharist and the cup of blessing? For we are certainly not content with what the Apostle or the Gospel has recorded, but we both proclaim and say other words that have great importance to the mystery, which we receive from unwritten teaching. By which writings do we bless the water of baptism, the oil of the chrism, and above all the very one being baptized? Is it not by silent and mystical tradition? What then? What written word taught the very anointment of the oil? From where is man baptized three times? But from what Scripture are many customs of baptism, such as the renunciation of Satan and his angels? Do they not come from this unpublished and secret teaching, which our fathers guarded in a silence not meddled with and examined out of curiosity?" (*Concerning the Holy Spirit* 27)
St. Gregory the Theologian	"[Julian], seeing that our reasoning is strong, both in doctrines and in testimonies from above . . . but still greater and more well known in the types of the Church that have been handed down and preserved at present, that not even this might remain without guile, what does he plot, and what does he do?" (*First Invective against Julian* 110)
St. Gregory the Theologian	"Preserving the good deposit, which we received from the Fathers while worshiping Father, Son, and Holy Spirit, knowing the Father in the Son, the Son in the Spirit, in whom we have been baptized, in whom we have believed, to whom we have sworn allegiance." (*Oration* 6.22)
St. John Chrysostom	"Hence it is clear that they [the Apostles] did not hand over everything by letter, but many things also equally by word of mouth, and both the former and latter are trustworthy. Therefore we also believe that the Tradition of the Church is trustworthy. It is a tradition; seek nothing further." (*Homily 4 on 2 Thes.*)

Any Protestant use of patristic writings to disprove such affirmation of sacred Tradition's worth is portrayed as misunderstandings of the texts, which concern the rejection of false traditions, but not sacred Tradition. In this connection, a text of St. Irenaeus is cited: "Read carefully the Gospel given to us by the Apostles and the Prophets, and you will find in them . . . all the aforementioned teaching of our Lord."[83] The point is made that St. Irenaeus was not rejecting sacred Tradition in favor of holy Scripture, but addressing Marcionites, who, on the basis of false tradition, did not accept the inspiration of the Old and New Testaments by one and the same God.

Two Protestant positions are then outlined. The first is that the tradition of the first three or four centuries is the true apostolic Tradition and that afterward the Fathers "deviated from correct Christian teaching, either accepting many dubious works as genuine or falling into other errors and fallacies" under the influence of "Platonic philosophy."

The counterargument is made that if this were true, then the promises of the Lord—to be always with the church and guide it with the Holy Spirit—would be false. For if the Apostles appointed such successors, then they would be no better, and therefore the apostolic Tradition would also be suspect. In many cases the Apostles themselves taught their successors from childhood. If these successors had taught things publicly contrary to the Apostles, the church would have rejected them as it did others without any hesitation, including many brilliant men (for example, Paul of Samosata, Sabellius, Arius, Nestorius, Eutyches, and Dioscorus). Moreover, the Fathers were defending the church using sacred Tradition because their opponents misused Scripture to distort and misinterpret. In the face of "fearsome opposition," the Fathers would not have distorted "one single doctrine of Christian faith."

The second Protestant position is based on the view that the primitive Church represented true Christianity. During the early centuries "when no corruption had yet entered the Church . . . the Christian faith was still limited to a few doctrines," and only later when "the pure apostolic Tradition was altered . . . the doctrines were multiplied." Protestants who believe this are said to confuse the creation of new doctrines with the explanation and formulation of the content of divine revelation in response to theological questions that arose on occasion. The church's formulation of truths, more clearly in response to soul-destroying false teachings, should not be confused with the introduction of new doctrines.

The following conclusion is reached:

> Let us only ask our opponents this: how was it possible for the "apostolic Tradition known to the entire world" (Irenaeus) to be changed and corrupted generally in every local Church, many of which the Apostles established and sealed by their blood? Was not even one Church among these able to remain faithful to the apostolic teaching? But then one must admit either of the two as true by necessity: either that the true Church of Christ failed for many centuries, as the Protestant reformers maintain, though this very thing is completely absurd and contrary to the divine promises of the Savior (Mt. 28:20; Jn. 16:13); or that the Church of Christ never failed, and then the Protestants who assert that they returned to the authentic apostolic teaching are telling lies.

In the third part of the section dealing with Protestantism, the great worth of sacred Tradition is demonstrated by its indispensible use for "the correct solution of various questions that relate to the authenticity and inspiration of the sacred books of Scripture, second for the true interpretation and comprehension of holy Scripture, and third for knowledge of certain truths not contained in the Scripture but necessary to faith and Christian life."

In order to determine "the authenticity and inspiration of the sacred books of Scripture," human reason alone is disqualified as a means since it results in accepting simply what is in agreement with one's subjective point of view. The internal evidence of Scripture cannot be used since there are no texts concerning the canon and authenticity of the books that constitute it, and what passages may exist are not certain because of the inexactitude of manuscripts, translations, and other factors. Finally, since many Protestants admit that the witness of the Fathers is the only sure principle for judging the authenticity of the scriptural canon, they should also accept the trustworthiness of the unwritten Tradition that patristic authority represents.

To support the necessity of sacred Tradition for "true interpretation and comprehension of Scripture," the examples of the Lord in interpreting Scripture for the disciples and the Apostles in explaining the books of the Old Testament to the faithful are brought forward. Many things in Scripture are beyond the comprehension of the human mind or are simply allusions that Tradition correctly explains. Three positions attributed to Protestants are then set forth and refuted.

The first position is that human reason alone can be used for understanding Scripture. The opposing argument is made: that human reason cannot be used as a sole guide because it is finite and many truths are supernatural and incomprehensible. The result of using only reason can be the rejection of any doctrine inaccessible to reasons, exemplified by the Socinians and Quakers.

The second is that Scripture alone can be used to interpret Scripture. The counterargument is based on the assertion that such interpretation would be subjective and nothing makes one opinion more correct than another.

The final is that internal enlightenment alone is the guide for correct interpretation of Scripture. Because it is subjective and prone to false inspiration, such enlightenment may not only lead to false interpretation, but may be given priority over Scripture itself. The example of the Swedenborgians is cited.

In supporting the "absolute necessity" of sacred Tradition "for knowledge of certain truths, which are not contained in holy Scripture but are essential to the faith and the Christian life," the main focus is on refuting the Protestant position that "anything not mentioned in Scripture is a human regulation." The assertion is made that sacred Tradition is the authentic expression of the Truth taught by the Apostles and Fathers. The counterargument is then set forth: that Protestants follow human tradition when accepting the teachings of their sects' founders, such as Luther and Calvin. Divine teaching is based on a divine mission. Consequently, in contrast to the Apostles, who teach the world based on the commission of Christ Himself, the so-called "reformers" of the church are motivated only by conceit and "claiming to be wise, became foolish."[84] The argument concludes with an address to Protestantism in general: "How, while on the one hand do you reject the sacred Traditions for the reason that they do not exist in Scripture, on the other hand you accept and observe others although [they are] not contained in Scripture, such as the observance of Sunday, the feast of Pascha, infant baptism, and other such matters?"

The entire thesis concludes with a long quotation from the second article of the *Confession* of Dositheos II, patriarch of Jerusalem (1669–1707), a work that was adopted by the Council of Jerusalem (1672) to refute

Protestant theological positions. Patriarch Dositheos II called the council on the occasion of the Church of the Nativity's reconsecration. As its main subject, the council addressed the *Confession* attributed to Kyrillos I Loukaris, patriarch of Constantinople.[85] The latter *Confession* was published for the first time at Constantinople in 1629, was republished in Western Europe, and was Calvinist in theological orientation. The council attempted to prove that the latter was a fabrication and concentrated its legislation on a refutation of Loukaris's Protestant theology.[86]

In St. Raphael's thesis the *Confession* of Dositheos is treated as an authoritative expression of the Orthodox faith: "the most true and at the same time most clear witness of our holy Church concerning the true meaning of sacred Tradition and its great and undeniable worth." The specific portion quoted deals with the relationship of sacred Tradition to Scripture and affirms that the "witness of the Catholic Church" is to be treated "no less than that which divine Scripture holds." The thesis ends with the *Confession*'s affirmation that in contrast to human reason, it is impossible for the "Catholic Church . . . to sin or completely deceive or be deceived, but it is like the divine Scripture, having undiminished and eternal authority."

CONCLUSIONS

The theological thesis of St. Raphael Hawaweeny reflects the collective life of Orthodox under Ottoman rule, where the Greek language was used for common communication among the higher clergy without any national overtones and was viewed as the language of the church and part of its patristic inheritance. In this sense, the thesis reflects an Orthodox worldview that transcends linguistic barriers and cultural borders.

Academically, the work is a product of a rigorous curriculum that emphasized disciplined and structured study of the primary sources in original languages. The thesis includes a wide scope of sources and incorporates Western European scholarship in German and French. Combined with the orientation of the School toward a monastic environment and its promotion of early celibate ordination, the high degree of academic rigor in the thesis also reflects the School's purpose of providing leadership for the *millet-i Rum* as a whole.

The strength of language used and the presentation of Roman Catholic and Protestant positions and their refutation appear to reflect an active dialogue with Western Christianity. Given the aggressive activity of Western Europeans and Americans in the Ottoman Empire as well as the adversarial relations existing during this period, the thesis gives the appearance of a resource designed for preparation in replying to the arguments advanced by missionaries, whether Roman Catholic or Protestant. It is ironic that this preparation would be most applicable when the author became an Orthodox missionary bishop in a predominantly Western Christian environment.[87]

NOTES

1. For excellent overviews of St. Raphael's life, see Basil Essey, "Saint Raphael Hawaweeny, Bishop of Brooklyn: 'The Good Shepherd of the Lost Sheep in America,'" in *The Orthodox Christian World*, ed. Augustine Casiday (London: Routledge, 2012), 338–44; Basil Essey et al., *Our Father among the Saints Raphael, Bishop of Brooklyn, "Good Shepherd of the Lost Sheep in America"* (Englewood, NJ: Antakya Press, 2000); and Antony Gabriel, *The Ancient Church on New Shores, Antioch in North America* (self-published, 2012).

2. This brief study is not intended to be an exhaustive treatment of Ottoman history or to address the numerous points in dispute within current scholarship concerning matters such as tax farming, the existence or changing nature of *millets*, the *millet* as indicative of rift between Muslim and non-Muslim, the role of *archons*, the rise of the *Phanariots*, the bases for Ottoman relations with non-Muslim subjects in Islamic law, the scope of *berâts* as authorizing documents, the status of the ecumenical patriarch as an Ottoman official, and the character of the ecclesiastical authority of hierarchs. For examples of such scholarship, see Elif Bayraktar Tellan, "The Patriarch and the Sultan: The Struggle for Authority and the Quest for Order in the Eighteenth-Century Ottoman Empire" (PhD diss., İhsan Doğramacı Bilkent University, 2011); and Tom Papademetriou, *Render unto the Sultan: Power, Authority, and the Greek Orthodox Church in the Early Ottoman Centuries* (Oxford: Oxford University Press, 2015).

3. Byzantium is often dated from the foundation of its capital in Constantinople during the fourth century until the Ottoman conquest of Constantinople in 1453. There is disagreement on this point, with some scholars opting for later dating of the Byzantine era. For an overview of Ottoman origins, see Caroline Finkel, *Osman's Dream: The Story of the Ottoman Empire 1300–1923* (London: Murray, 2006), 1–47.

4. The general discussion above of *millets*, the administration of the Great Church, and this administration's reform represents a traditional view, but there is an ongoing debate over whether the term *millet* became descriptive of organizing non-Muslims only in the late Ottoman period. See the survey of recent scholarly literature concerning *millets* by Papademetriou, *Render unto the Sultan*, 19–62. By 1914 there were seventeen *millets*.

5. Halil İnalcik, "The Status of the Greek Orthodox Patriarch under the Ottomans," *Turcica: Revue des études turques* 21–23 (1991): 420.

6. Prior to the Ottoman conquest of the Byzantine Empire, the governance of the church was centralized in the churches of Rome, Constantinople, Alexandria, Antioch, and Jerusalem, with its foundations fixed through four authoritative gatherings of bishops known as ecumenical councils (Nicea in 325, Constantinople in 381, Ephesos in 431, and Chalcedon in 451) that ranked these churches' order of primacy. The patriarch of Constantinople, who held the title of ecumenical patriarch, administered the church of the Eastern Byzantine capital with a synod of metropolitan bishops who represented sees from throughout Asia Minor. The pope of Alexandria and the patriarchs of Antioch and Jerusalem with their respective synods had authority over the rest of the Middle East, which was under Islamic rule after the Arab invasions of the mid-seventh century. The church's division into an Orthodox East and Latin West is traditionally dated to the mutual excommunications of 1054 promulgated by representatives from the Sees of Rome and Constantinople. Until that time, the pope of Rome was regarded as holding the first place in the order of primacy. After the schism the patriarch of Constantinople assumed this role for the Orthodox East. By the end of the nineteenth century, with the expansion of the Orthodox Church, other self-governing, or autocephalous, churches emerged and were ranked below the ancient patriarchates in the order of primacy. These included the Orthodox Church of Russia as well as others in the Balkans and Eastern Europe.

7. İnalcik, "Status of the Greek Orthodox Patriarch," 418.

8. In the fourteenth century the Patriarchate of Antioch was transferred to Damascus after the depopulation of the city due to repeated invasion.

9. For an excellent discussion of the relationship between the patriarchates and Constantinople, see Robert Haddad, "Constantinople over Antioch, 1516–1724: Patriarchal Politics in the Ottoman Era," *Journal of Ecclesiastical History* 41 (1990): 217–38.

10. The title "metropolitan" originally referred to the chief bishop of a province or eparchy, whose episcopal seat is in the metropolis, or capital, of the eparchy. He chaired a synod of bishops drawn from the area of the eparchy. By the eighteenth century metropolitans of the patriarchate were equivalent to resident bishops and no longer had a provincial synod or other bishops in their territories. Some came to reside in Istanbul away from their official sees and became dominant in the Holy Synod.

11. These changes took place during the *Tanzimât* ("reorganization") period, which is dated from 1839 to 1876 and was marked by a series of reform measures taken by sultans and Ottoman officials. See the studies by: Roderic H. Davison, *Reform in the Ottoman Empire, 1856-1876* (Princeton, NJ: Princeton University Press, 1963); M. Hanioğlu, *A Brief History of the Late Ottoman Empire* (Princeton, NJ: Princeton University Press, 2008); and C. V. Findley, *Bureaucratic Reform in the Ottoman Empire* (Princeton, NJ: Princeton University Press, 1980).

12. Charles Frazee, *Catholics and Sultans: The Church and the Ottoman Empire, 1453–1923* (London: Cambridge University Press, 1983), 88; Frazee's work extensively covers the Roman Catholic efforts. Two of the most insightful studies on Syria during the period in question are by Robert Haddad: *Syrian Christians in Muslim Society* (Princeton, NJ: Princeton University Press, 1970); and "Conversion of Eastern Orthodox Christians to the Unia in the Seventeenth and Eighteenth Centuries," in *Conversion and Continuity: Indigenous Communities in Islamic Lands, Eighth to Eighteenth Centuries*, ed. Michael

Gervers and Ramzi Bikhazi, Papers in Mediaeval Studies 9 (Toronto: Pontifical Institute of Medieval Studies, 1990), 449–59.

13. Frazee, *Catholics and Sultans*, 88.

14. Another such institution, the Pontifical Urban University (*Urbaniana*), was named after its founder, Pope Urban VIII (1623–44). See Frazee, *Catholics and Sultans*, for full descriptions of the foundations of the various Roman Catholic institutions.

15. Timothy Ware, *Eustratios Argenti: A Study of the Greek Church under Turkish Rule* (Oxford: Clarendon Press, 1964), 31n3.

16. In fact, Charles Frazee entitled the second part of his work "The Golden Age of the Missions" (Frazee, *Catholics and Sultans*, 65–150).

17. Kallistos Ware, "Orthodox and Catholics in the Seventeenth Century: Schism or Intercommunion?" in *Schism, Heresy and Religious Protest*, ed. Derek Baker (Cambridge: Cambridge University Press, 1972), 265.

18. Ware, "Orthodox and Catholics in the Seventeenth Century," 265.

19. Ware, "Orthodox and Catholics in the Seventeenth Century," 265.

20. Ware, *Eustratios Argenti*, 21.

21. Ware, *Eustratios Argenti*, 25.

22. Ware, "Orthodox and Catholics in the Seventeenth Century," 265.

23. Ware, *Eustratios Argenti*, 27.

24. That is, Orthodox.

25. Haddad, "Constantinople over Antioch," 238.

26. Haddad, "Constantinople over Antioch," 235–38; see also Haddad, "Conversion of Eastern Orthodox Christians" and Constantin Panchenko, *Arab Orthodox Christians Under the Ottomans: 1516-1831*, trans. Brittany Pheiffer Noble and Samuel Noble (Jordanville, NY: Holy Trinity Seminary Press, 2016), 364–408, for a detailed analysis of the establishment of the *Unia* in Syria. The chief architect of the *Unia* was Euthymios al-Ṣaifī, metropolitan of Sidōn (1683–1723), who is said to have used relief from Orthodox canons on fasting and marriage impediments to satisfy "the quest for mundane advantage" and draw Orthodox into communion with Rome (Haddad, "Conversion of Eastern Orthodox Christians," 457). In 1724 the Patriarchate of Antioch became split between the Uniate Kyrillos Ṭânâs (1724–60), who had formally submitted to Rome, and the Orthodox Silvestros (1724–66), a Cypriot who was elected at Constantinople. According to Constantin Panchenko, the weakening of the Ottoman Empire, the strengthening of European influence, and the importance of religious and cultural factors explain the success of the *Unia*. These factors included educational advantages, learning, and the opportunity for spiritual renewal provided by Rome and not otherwise available for most Orthodox, (Constantin Panchenko, *Arab Orthodox Christians*, 407–8).

27. Haddad, "Constantinople over Antioch," 238.

28. For accounts of the eighteenth-century controversy over the efficacy of Roman Catholic baptisms, see Louis Petit, "L'entrée des Catholiques dans l'église orthodoxe," *Échos d'Orient* 5 (1899): 129–38; and Ware, *Eustratios Argenti*, 65–107.

29. Haddad, *Syrian Christians*, 72.

30. John Barrett, "International Politics, American Protestant Missions and the Middle East" (PhD diss., Baylor University, 2012), 33. On Protestant missionaries in the Ottoman empire, see also Mehmet Ali Doğan and Heather Jane Sharkey, eds., *American Missionaries and the Middle East: Foundational Encounters* (Salt Lake City: University of Utah Press, 2011); Ussama Makdisi, *Artillery of Heaven: American Missionaries and*

the Failed Conversion of the Middle East (Ithaca, NY: Cornell University Press, 2009); Heather Jane Sharkey, *American Evangelicals in Egypt: Missionary Encounters in an Age of Empire* (Princeton, NJ: Princeton University Press, 2008).

31. Barrett, "International Politics," 30–32, 33.

32. Rufus Anderson, *History of the Missions of the American Board of Commissioners for Foreign Missions to the Oriental Churches*, vol. 1 (Boston: Congregational Publishing Society, 1872), 1–2, as quoted in Barrett, "International Politics," 38.

33. H. H. Jessup, *The Greek Church and Protestant Missions* (New York, 1891), 6, 18, 22, as quoted in Haddad, *Syrian Christians*, 80.

34. Pieter Pikkert, "Protestant Missionaries to the Middle East: Ambassadors of Christ or Culture" (PhD diss., University of South Africa, 2006), 46.

35. Pikkert, "Protestant Missionaries," 47.

36. Barrett, "International Politics," 36.

37. Pikkert, "Protestant Missionaries," 47.

38. Pikkert, "Protestant Missionaries," 49.

39. Barrett, "International Politics," 35.

40. Paschalis Kitromilides, "Orthodox Identities in a World of Ottoman Power," in *The Balkans and the Eastern Mediterranean, 12th–17th Centuries, Proceedings of the International Symposium in Memory of D. A. Zakythinos, Athens, January 14–15, 1994* (Athens: National Hellenic Research Foundation, Institute for Byzantine Research, 1998), 4.

41. Paschalis Kitromilides, "'Balkan Mentality': History and Imagination," *Nations and Nationalism* 2 (1996): 171.

42. Kitromilides, "'Balkan Mentality,'" 177–78.

43. Paschalis Kitromilides, "From Orthodox Commonwealth to National Communities: Greek-Russian Intellectual and Ecclesiastical Ties in the Ottoman Era," in *Hellas-Russia: One Thousand Years of Bonds*, ed. Lily Macrakis (Athens: Διεθνές Ἐμπορικό Ἐπιμελητήριο, 1994), 4–5.

44. Kitromilides, "Orthodox Identities," 11; Paschalis Kitromilides, "The Ecumenical Patriarchate and the 'National Centre,'" in *Phanari 400 Years* (Istanbul: Ecumenical Patriarchate, 2001), 4–7.

45. Kitromilides, "Ecumenical Patriarchate," 6.

46. *Regulations in Effect of the Theological School in Halki of the Great Church of Christ in the Sacred Monastery of the Holy Trinity (1845)*, § 1.2. Life at the school was controlled under regulations issued in various editions beginning in 1845. A stauropegial monastery is directly subject to the cognizance of a patriarchate rather than the local bishop.

47. During Ecumenical Patriarch Iōakeim III's first reign (1878–84), a short-lived attempt was made to establish an additional year of study.

48. Kōnstantinos Typaldos-Iakōvatos (1795–1867) was the first headmaster of the School (1844–60) as well as a professor of theology and philosophy. Beginning in 1848 he was metropolitan of the titular see of Stauroupolis (located in the region of western Anatolia).

49. *Regulations (1845)*, § 4.1: "In time, they wish that classes in Hebrew (sacred), Arabic, Armenian, Turkish, and one of the modern languages, as well as ecclesiastical music, might be added in due order."

50. Ἀπόστολος Μέξης, *Ἡ ἐν Χάλκῃ Ἱερὰ Θεολογικὴ Σχολή, Ἱστορικὰ Σημειώματα (1844-1935)* (Κωνσταντινούπολις: Φαζιλέτ, 1933), 67–68. According

to Μέξης, "The complete lack of instruction books was a great impediment to the instruction of thorough learning of Slavonic" (p. 69), and consequently, the patriarchal printing press published works produced by the professors at the Theological School, including a Slavonic grammar by Iōannēs Dēmētriadēs in 1850 and a chrestomathy by Neophytos Rylliōtēs in 1854.

51. Essey, "Saint Raphael Hawaweeny," 338–39. St. Raphael was born Rafla ibn Mikha'il ibn Jirjis al-Hawaweeny and given the name Raphael most likely after being tonsured a monk in 1879.

52. *Regulations of the Theological School in Halki of the Great Church of Christ (1874)*, § 6.37. The regulations of 1867 were renewed in 1874 and were in force during St. Raphael's tenure as a student (see Appendix 3 for the translated text).

53. *Regulations of the Theological School in Halki,* § 6.42.

54. *Regulations of the Theological School in Halki,* § 6.38.

55. *Regulations of the Theological School in Halki,* § 6.42.

56. *Regulations of the Theological School in Halki,* § 6.43.

57. *Regulations of the Theological School in Halki,* § 15.98.

58. *Regulations of the Theological School in Halki,* §§ 16.102, 16.103, 16.105.

59. *Regulations of the Theological School in Halki,* § 18.118.

60. *Regulations of the Theological School in Halki,* § 17.108.

61. *Regulations of the Theological School in Halki,* § 18.117.

62. *Regulations of the Theological School in Halki,* § 17.106.

63. *Regulations of the Theological School in Halki,* § 12.85.

64. *Regulations of the Theological School in Halki,* §§ 5.25, 5.27.

65. *Regulations of the Theological School in Halki,* § 5.29.

66. *Regulations of the Theological School in Halki,* §§ 5.30, 12.86.

67. *Regulations of the Theological School in Halki,* § 7.45.

68. *Regulations of the Theological School in Halki,* § 11.78. The regulations do not provide details on the direction of the thesis, other than the approval of its subject and presentation to the headmaster. The headmaster Archimandrite Germanos Grēgoras was also a professor of dogmatics at the time and may have exercised a significant influence on the thesis. Likely, the archimandrite experienced adversarial relationships between Orthodox and Western Christians at the Holy Places when directing the School of the Holy Cross under the Patriarchate of Jerusalem (1858–62), but his theological approach and thought are not known due to an absence of publications, except for a minor study dealing with the patriarch of Alexandria, Meletios I Pēgas (1590–1604). The regulations dealing with the oral and written examinations for the diploma make no mention of the thesis.

69. *Regulations of the Theological School in Halki,* § 11.83, emphasis in the original text.

70. Stavro Skendi, "Language as a Factor of National Identity in the Balkans of the Nineteenth Century," *Proceedings of the American Philosophical Society* 119 (1975): 186–89; Slobodan G. Markovitch, "Patterns of National Identity Development among the Balkan Orthodox Christians during the Nineteenth Century," *Balcanica* 44 (2013): 219–22; Peter Mackridge, *Language and National Identity in Greece, 1766–1976* (Oxford: Oxford University Press, 2009).

71. The number of such quotations and their systematic use to address points of argumentation appear to suggest the use of a florilegium of extracts from patristic writings.

72. Ἀντώνιος, Ἀρχιμανδρίτης, *Δογματικὴ θεολογία τῆς 'Ορθοδόξου Καθολικῆς καὶ Ἀνατολικῆς Ἐκκλησίας*, trans. Θεόδωρος Βαλλιάνος (Athens: Τύποις Χ. Νικολαΐδου Φιλαδελφέως, 1858); Φιλάρετος, Μητροπολίτης Μόσχας, *Χριστιανικὴ κατ' ἔκτασιν κατήχησις τῆς ὀρθοδόξου, καθολικῆς καὶ ἀνατολικῆς ἐκκλησίας / ἐξετασθεῖσα μὲν καὶ ἐγκριθεῖσα ὑπὸ τῆς Ἁγιωτάτης Διοικούσης Συνόδου, καὶ ἐκδοθεῖσα Ρωσσιστὶ πρὸς δημόσιον ἐν τοῖς σχολείοις παράδοσιν, καὶ πρὸς χρῆσιν ἁπάντων τῶν ὀρθοδόξων Χριστιανῶν, Μεταφρασθεῖσα δὲ καὶ τύποις ἐκδοθεῖσα κατ' ἐπιταγὴν τῆς αὐτῆς Ἁγίας Διοικούσης Συνόδου* (Odessa: Ἐκ τῆς Τυπογραφίας τοῦ Α. Βράουν καὶ Συντρ., 1848); Μακάριος Μόσχας, *Εἰσαγωγὴ εἰς τὴν ὀρθοδόξον θεολογίαν*, trans. Νικόλαος Σπ. Παπαδόπουλος, 2 vols. (Leipzig: Geisekke and Dervient, 1858–61).

73. For a discussion of Voulgarēs, see Stephen K. Batalden, *Catherine II's Greek Prelate: Eugenios Voulgaris in Russia, 1771–1806* (Boulder, CO: East European Monographs, 1982).

74. Claude Fleury, *Histoire ecclésiastique*, 36 vols. (Paris: Pierre Emery, Saugrain l'aîne, and Pierre Martin, 1719–68); Heinrich Klee, *Katholische Dogmatik*, 3rd ed. (Mainz: Kirkheim, Schott und Thielmann, 1844); Heinrich Klee, *Lehrbuch der Dogmengeschichte*, 2 vols. (Mainz: Kirkheim, Schott und Thielmann, 1836–37); Johann Adam Möhler, *La symbolique, ou, Exposition des contrariétés dogmatiques entre les catholiques et les protestants d'après leurs confessions de foi publiques*, trans. F. Lachat, 2 vols. (Brussels: La société nationale pour la propagation des bons livres, 1838); Nicolas-Sylvestre Bergier and Pierrot, abbé, *Dictionnaire de théologie dogmatique, liturgique, canonique et disciplinaire*, 4 vols. in 2 pts. (Paris: J.-P. Migne, 1850). On the influence of Möhler, see Judith Schaefer, *The Evolution of a Vow: Obedience as Decision Making in Communion* (Berlin: Lit Verlag, 2008), 100–1.

75. Less than eight years prior to St. Raphael's matriculation, a serious incident at the School took place, indicative of the adversarial relationship with the Roman Catholic Church, which resulted in major changes in administration, including the replacement of the headmaster. According to the account of Basileios Antōniadēs (1851–1932), a student and later a professor at the School ("A Page from My Studies," *Ὀρθοδοξία* 2 [1927]: 125–29):

> Visitation of our school and its library was always accessible and without special formalities for those who wished—not even the ones who came from the Latin clergy were excluded; neither the authorities nor the students of the School ever thought that Western priests and monks might also come for the purpose of proselytizing for the *Unia*. And nevertheless it appears that such a purpose was not foreign to them when visits of the colleagues of the aforementioned clergyman took place during the years 1871–1872; and they found such a courteous and sincere reception among the guileless students that he [Vanuteli] encouraged them to also cast baits for catching as many as they could. And their baits were certainly enticing ones, for example, that they send them to Italy and Rome for more advanced and comfortable studies and provide them a future much more bright than could be hoped for among us. It is no wonder that they found among the sixty to seventy students at least a few who paid close attention to the suggestions and promises, and indeed three also even proceeded with secret understandings.

After the discovery of the activity, which included the "capture" of three students about to leave the School as Roman Catholic proselytes, Antōniadēs describes the strength of feeling engendered by the incident:

> But a distress and indignation of another type took possession of us who were not up to this time participants in the commotion, an anger against those authors of the truly painful events—how those clergymen of the Western church, who came in sheep's clothing to the School and were considered worthy of every sincere courtesy and welcome, had so behaved and acted, and had been able to act like ravenous wolves for this very reason—and we decided without delay to send immediately a bitter letter to the author himself, as we thought, Vanuteli, with bitter complaints regarding such conduct. It was decided to write the letter in Latin.

"Vanuteli" is most likely Vincenzo Cardinal Vannutelli (December 5, 1836–July 9, 1930), who became a priest in 1860; was consecrated as a bishop in 1880; and was created a cardinal in 1889, which was announced publicly in 1890. He would have been ninety years of age and the oldest living cardinal on December 5, 1926, as Antōniadēs observes. Vannutelli's career involved work in seminary faculties and the Roman curia. In 1872 he was working in the Vatican Secretariat of State and was given foreign postings. He served as apostolic vicar of Constantinople from January 23, 1880, until December 22, 1882. Among his accomplishments was his major contribution to the development of the 1917 Code of Roman Catholic Canon Law.

76. Homer, *Odyssey* 9.51.

77. Dt. 32:7.

78. 1 Cor. 11:34.

79. 2 Jn. 1:12.

80. 2 Thes. 2:15.

81. Mt. 18:20.

82. Jn. 14:16; 16:13.

83. Irenaeus, *Against Heresies* 4.36.1.

84. Rom. 10:15.

85. His reign dates (1620–23, 1623–33, 1633–34, 1634–35, 1637–38) reflect the instability of the patriarchate during this period.

86. For general coverage of the Council of Jerusalem and Dositheos II, see Norman Russell, "From 'Shield of Orthodoxy' to 'Tome of Joy': The Anti-Western Stance of Dositheos II of Jerusalem," in *Orthodox Constructions of the West*, ed. George Demacopoulos and Aristotle Papanikolaou (New York: Fordham University Press, 2013), 71–82.

87. In this connection, the question may be explored whether this expertise factored in the Russian Holy Synod's 1895 canonical release of St. Raphael from his position following graduation (as an instructor of Arabic and anti-Islamic polemic at the Kazan Theological Academy) to serve the Syrian community in North America.

Overview of the Translation

THE FOLLOWING TRANSLATION IS BASED on a transcription of the handwritten Greek text contained in the archives of the Theological School in Halki of the Great Church of Christ. The transcription appears in the appendix. The abbreviations of modern and ancient sources used in the thesis are retained and are listed with corresponding full bibliographical information in the appendix as well. Footnotes were sparsely used in the original writing and are differentiated from any explanatory notes added to the translation.

The first page of the translation gives the appearance of a title page, but is actually a description of its contents and subject, most likely used for its archiving. The general description of the subject appearing on this page—"Theological Thesis Concerning Sacred Tradition and Its Undeniable Authority"—was also most likely the one used to obtain the required approval of the headmaster prior to beginning work on the thesis. The actual title—"The True Significance of Sacred Tradition and Its Great Worth"—appears on page 3 of the thesis.

In general, conventional English spellings are used for place names and ancient authors. Names of modern persons along with certain objects and concepts will be transliterated. Capitalizations of theological terms and institutions generally follow those of the original text. The page numbering for the translation and the transcribed text of the thesis correspond to the handwritten pages of the original. The select bibliography lists the most available sources for St. Raphael's life.

Select Bibliography on St. Raphael Hawaweeny

Essey, Basil. "Saint Raphael Hawaweeny, Bishop of Brooklyn: 'The Good Shepherd of the Lost Sheep in America.'" In *The Orthodox Christian World*, edited by Augustine Casiday, 338–44. London: Routledge, 2012.

Essey, Basil, et al. *Our Father among the Saints, Raphael, Bishop of Brooklyn, "Good Shepherd of the Lost Sheep in America."* Englewood, NJ: Antakya Press, 2000.

Gabriel, Antony. *The Ancient Church on New Shores: Antioch in North America.* Self-published, 2012.

Garrett, Paul D. "The Life and Legacy of Bishop Raphael Hawaweeny." In *The First One Hundred Years: A Centennial Anthology Celebrating Antiochian Orthodoxy in North America*, edited by George S. Corey. Englewood, NJ: Antakya Press, 1995.

———. "Envoy from Antioch: The life and Ministry of Bishop Raphael Hawaweeny." *Again* 16, no. 4 (December 1993): 6–9.

———. "Pascha, 1901." *The Word* 28, no. 4 (April 1984): 15–16.

PART 2

THEOLOGICAL THESIS CONCERNING SACRED TRADITION AND ITS UNDENIABLE AUTHORITY

By
Hierodeacon Raphael M. Hawaweeny
In the Theological School at Halki

On May 1, 1886

"Brethren, stand fast and hold firm to the traditions that you were taught whether by word or our letter." (2 Thes. 2:15)

"Of the dogmas and preaching that are preserved in the Church, some we possess from written teaching, others we have received from the tradition of the Apostles that was preserved for us in secret; both of which have the same force in relation to right belief." (Basil the Great, *To Amphilochius concerning the Holy Spirit* 27)

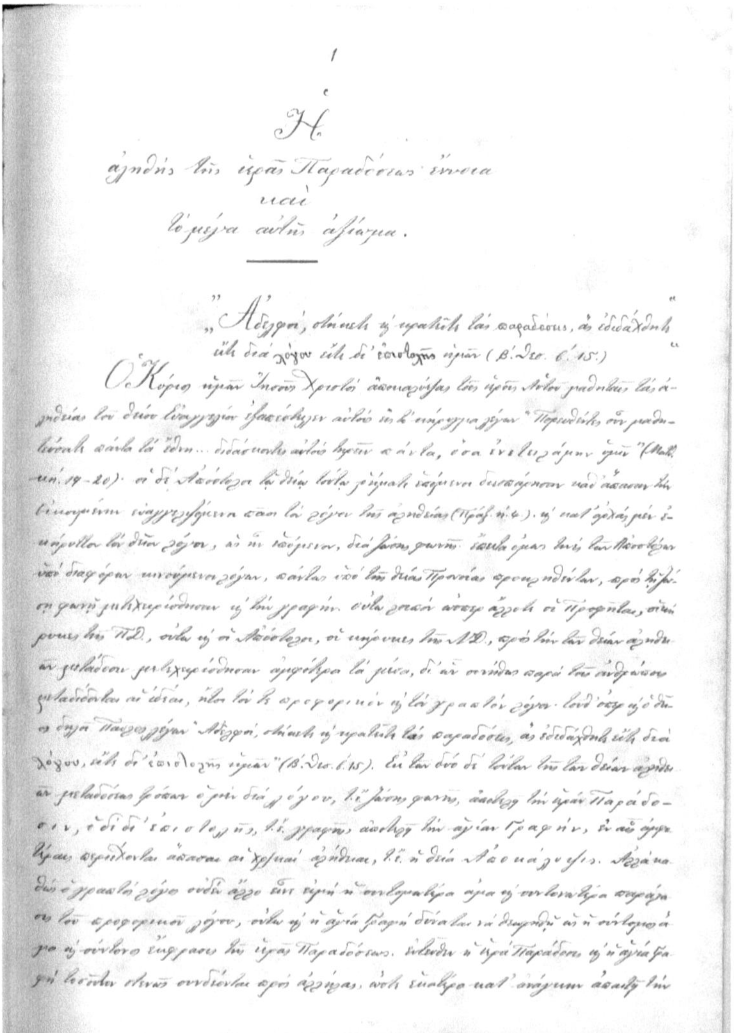

The True Significance of Sacred Tradition and Its Great Worth }1

"Brethren, stand fast and hold firm to the traditions that you were taught whether by word or our letter." (2 Thes. 2:15)

OUR LORD JESUS CHRIST, when revealing to His sacred disciples the truths of His divine gospel, sent them forth, saying to them in proclamation, "Going, therefore, make disciples of all the nations . . . teaching them to observe all things, whatever I commanded you" (Mt. 28:19–20). The Apostles who obeyed this divine command scattered throughout the entire world, proclaiming to all the word of truth (Acts 8:4). And from the beginning they preached the divine word, as was expected, by a living voice. However, thereupon some of the Apostles, motivated by various reasons, which were caused completely by divine providence, in addition to the living voice, also used writing. In this way, then, just as the Prophets, the heralds of the Old Testament, formerly did, so also the Apostles, the heralds of the New Testament, for the transmission of the divine truths made use of both means by which ideas often are transmitted by men, namely the spoken and written word, the very thing that also the divine Paul makes known, saying, "Brethren, stand fast and hold firm to the traditions that you were taught whether by word or our letter" (2 Thes. 2:15). Of these two ways of transmitting divine truths, the one by word, that is, living voice, constitutes sacred Tradition, [and] the other

by letter, that is, writing, constitutes holy Scripture, in both of which all Christian truth, that is, divine revelation, is contained. But just as the written word is nothing other than the more brief and at the same time more constant representation of the spoken word, so also holy Scripture can be viewed as the brief and at the same time constant expression of sacred Tradition. Hence sacred Tradition and holy Scripture are thus very closely
tied to one another, so that each by necessity requires the }other, and the }2
absence of one in these important points is detrimental to the other. In this way, when holy Scripture is disregarded, sacred Tradition runs the danger of distortion because then the human can be mixed up easily with the divine, the profane with the holy, and truth with falsehood. On the other hand, when sacred Tradition is removed, holy Scripture is subject to many misinterpretations because when holy Scripture is left to each one's free understanding and interpretation, a certain strange diversity within the one and same Christian teaching can hence result. Nevertheless, and after all these improper consequences that come from the one-sided acceptance of sacred Tradition or of holy Scripture, unfortunately there was no lack of men in the Church who followed the one or the other side already from these first centuries of Christianity, such as the followers of the many-headed Gnostic heresy and other heretics. But in order that we pass over such heretics that appeared in more ancient times, whose remains or even names that scarcely survive today set forth before us shining evidence of their false teachings, come, let us now examine the more modern and at the same time more important of the two aforesaid one-sided heresies: I speak of the papists and the Protestants. Whereas the Orthodox Christian who freely searches the Scriptures subjects his individual precarious interpretation to the certain judgment of the universal Church, "taking captive," according to the divine Paul, "every thought to the obedience of Christ" (2 Cor. 10:5), on the other hand the papist who is prevented from the free search of the Scriptures blindly follows papist traditions in many fables, so resting his conscience upon the so-called infallible judgments of the Roman pontifex as the supreme interpreter of holy Scripture, and the Protestant who, basing himself only on his individual conscience, interprets the Scriptures in a completely arbitrary way. Thus papism, which centers in this manner all ecclesiastical life in one sole person, the pope, established in Rome a religious, so to speak, oracle, in whom the apostolic Traditions, distorted in many ways and confused with human

nonsense, are presented as incontestable writ of divine origin! The Protestant, who also rejected sacred Tradition along with this papist prattle, was deprived of any firm basis in the interpretation of holy Scripture and so, one-sidedly following Scripture, dismembered the one Church into so many parts,

> As many as the leaves and flowers multiply in spring![1]

}Because papism, thus impelled by an uncivilized spirit and centraliza- }3
tion, mixes the human with the divine for the attainment of this very aim and so distorts and falsifies sacred Traditions, Protestantism, spurred on by a tendency to struggle against these arrogant claims of papism, stumbled into the opposite excess of indiscipline and decentralization, completely rejecting sacred Traditions as human writ. On account of this, come, let us discuss certain brief points concerning sacred Tradition, demonstrating on the one hand its true significance against the papists who distort it, and on the other hand its great worth against the Protestants who reject it.

A.

> For the time is coming when they will not bear with sound teaching, but, having itching ears, they will accumulate for themselves teachers to suit their own lusts, and will turn away from listening to the truth, and wander into myths. (2 Tim. 4:3–4)

Just as every science has incontestable principles upon which it is based, and defined authorities by which its truth is derived, so also theology, the very science of sciences, has as an undisputed principle upon which it is grounded, and a most clear source by which its divine truth is undeniable: divine revelation, namely, the word of God. But this word of God was revealed to us, as we saw, in two manners, by word of mouth and in writing, that is, through sacred Tradition and holy Scripture, for both of which God Himself assigned the holy Orthodox Church of Christ to be the faithful guardian and infallible interpreter. In other words, sacred Tradition and holy Scripture, taken together and when interpreted by the infallible voice of the universal Orthodox Church, constitute one and the same

source of Orthodox Christian theology. When understanding things in this manner, it follows that every Christian ought to observe sacred Tradition like holy Scripture, and explain this identically as the Orthodox universal Church understands and holds this fast. In saying these things, we do not at all mean that, when interpreting at will the teaching transmitted to it by word of mouth, the Church is able to add to or subtract anything from this—as the papist Church maliciously does this for support of its various innovations—but on the contrary ought, when maintaining sacred Tradition clear and intact, to transmit it to the faithful undiminished and unadulterated, as the Orthodox Church truly does. Consequently, }in }4
order that we have as clear, distinct, and exact an understanding as possible of true sacred Tradition, just as the true Orthodox Church of Christ views and preserves it, we are bound to examine: (1) the true content of sacred Tradition, (2) its true sources, (3) its true characteristic marks, and (4) its true treasury and certain protection.

1.

The word *tradition* (παράδοσις), which is derived from "to be handed over" (παρα-διδόναι), denotes according to its primary meaning not only the practice of being handed over or being entrusted to someone, but also the very thing being handed over. According to its theological understanding, it means in general everything that our Lord Jesus Christ handed over through His holy Apostles to the Church by word of mouth or in writing (2 Thes. 2:15). However, particularly and especially in theology, only the unwritten word of God is called "tradition" and in distinction to that by writing, which is called "Scripture." Consequently, sacred Tradition, which is a complementary source of the Christian religion, is the unwritten word that is handed over by the Savior through the Apostles to the Church and recorded in large measure by the holy Fathers. Sacred Tradition is twofold, divine and human. And the divine is that of which God Himself is author, and which generally the sacred Luke means when saying that Jesus after the Resurrection "presented Himself to the Apostles . . . for forty days appearing to them and speaking things concerning the kingdom of God" (Acts 1:2–3).[2] Such a thing is, for example, the manner of celebrating the mysteries, as the Apostle Paul bears witness concerning the mystery of the divine Eucharist when saying

to the Corinthians (1 Cor. 11:23), "For I received from the Lord what also I handed over to you." Human tradition is what was delivered over by men. It is distinguished into apostolic, ecclesiastical, and purely human. The first of these has its origin from the Apostles themselves, who are viewed not as heralds of divine laws or as stewards of holy mysteries, but as shepherds of the faithful and bishops of the Churches. [This is] because in the first case the tradition is sacred, such as when the Apostle Paul states, "To those who have married I enjoin, not I but the Lord" (1 Cor. 7:10), but in the second occasion the tradition is purely apostolic when the same Apostle says, "But to the rest I say, not the Lord" (ibid., 7:12). Such purely apostolic traditions are, for example, the holy and great Lent and in general }all the }5
remaining regulations, of which the Apostolic Canons treat. Ecclesiastical tradition is that which has its source from the successors of the Apostles and afterward. Such ecclesiastical traditions are, for example, the sign of the Cross, prayer toward the East, [and] generally the tradition concerning all ecclesiastical ceremony, order, and teaching, as well as all commonly received Christian customs, which the Apostle Paul implies when saying, "But if anyone is disposed to be contentious, we do not have such a custom nor do the churches of God" (1 Cor. 11:16). Finally, human tradition is clearly that which men handed over having neither mission nor authority in the Church. Such are, for example, the teaching concerning the primacy of the pope and generally all the innovations of the papal Church and other heretical, erroneous beliefs. However, let us note that because the Apostles handed over nothing that they did not receive or know from the Lord Himself (2 Pt. 1:16; 1 Jn. 1:1–3), and the successors of the Apostles taught nothing that they were not taught or that they did not hear from the Apostles (Ignatius in Eusebius, *Church History* 3.16; Polycarp, in ibid., 4.14; Irenaeus, *Against Heresies*, 3.3; etc.); on account of this we can certainly view and without distinction call divine and apostolic both the apostolic and generally received ecclesiastical traditions. However, distinguishing in this respect the divine or apostolic Traditions from the purely ecclesiastical, inasmuch as our Church ascribes absolute authority to the first, as also to holy Scripture itself, and to the ecclesiastical relatively and with limits, on account of this, the apostolic Traditions not only necessarily must be preserved by the entire Orthodox Church, but also doctrines can certainly be based on them. These ecclesiastical ones by necessity also must be preserved, but only things inasmuch as it seems good to the same Church (see

"Concerning Tradition" in Εὐγένιος Βούλγαρης, *Θεολογικόν*; *Πηδάλιον*, p. 388, n. 3; and "Tradition" in Nicolas Bergier, *Dictionnaire de théologie*).

2.

Accordingly, in this manner, the Apostles, as the sacred Chrysostom also says, "hand over not everything by letter, but also many things in unwritten form" (*Homily 4 on 2 Thes.*), but these things that were handed over in unwritten form by the Apostles to the Church from the beginning, as Basil the Great, the mouth of truth, bears witness; on account of the uninitiated "our fathers guarded [these unwritten traditions] in a silence not meddled with and examined out of curiosity, when they learned well that the sacred things of the mysteries are preserved through silence" (*Concerning the Holy Spirit* 27). After these times, however, on the one hand, for faithful transmission }and observance of these divine truths, }6
and on the other hand, for effective struggle against false teachings, many things of that hidden and secret teaching, i.e., of sacred Tradition, the divinely illuminated Fathers and teachers of the Church memorialized in their own writings, interpreting through them, unfolding and more accurately laying down, the doctrines and preaching of the faith in relation to the theological questions that arose on each occasion. Thus what was from the beginning transmitted only through the mouth of the Apostles to the Church was stored up, completely by divine economy, in numerous blessed writings, some of which unfortunately were lost; many, however, also fortunately survived until the present. Such writings, out of which as from most pure springs we draw the sweet and at the same time salutary streams of many doctrines and proclamations of the faith, are the following: (1) The most ancient symbols, namely those brief confessions of faith that are generally accepted as authoritative by the entire Church. Many such symbols existed in various local Churches during the first three centuries of Christianity [and were] usually diverse in letter, though unanimous in spirit. But all these ancient symbols, because they had been drawn up by particular persons or only some Churches, were not in common use by the entire Church, until when during the fourth century the Church universally replaced them through the Symbol of Faith drawn up at Nicaea and completed at Constantinople, which then acquires irrefutable authority, inasmuch indeed it contains in summary the whole of the teaching of

the Orthodox faith certainly by the words themselves, for the most part from holy Scripture. Henceforth, to this day, the Orthodox Church also recognizes this alone as a universal symbol, rejecting the two other symbols falsely viewed by both the papists and Protestants as likewise universal, the so-called Apostolic,[3] concerning which very correctly Mark Eugenikos answered the Latins in Florence, saying, "We neither have, nor do we know a symbol of the Apostles" (Sylvester Syropoulos, *History of the Council in Florence*, section 6, chap. 6), and the false Athanasian (or *quicumque*), which is just an obscure work of the papist Church.[4] (2) The Apostolic Canons, which always not only by the local Churches, but also by the whole Church, were viewed as prototypes and examples that all the Fathers of the Church and all holy councils, both local and ecumenical, followed. But if also the respect that they received already during the first centuries of Christianity compels us to believe }unhesi- }7
tatingly in their divine origin, nevertheless still we cannot accept that these Apostles themselves transmitted them in writing, because then they would have been immediately placed from the beginning in the canon of books of the New Testament. But we can accept that the immediate successors of the Apostles, orally receiving them, recorded them in the order and form that they survive in until today, and there are πε΄ (= 85) canons in number and they contain the traditions of the Apostles concerning various questions that relate to church administration and good order. (3) The ancient liturgies, some of which go back until the very times of the Apostles, namely, the Liturgy of the Apostle James. Their ancient origin and uninterrupted use from that time until the present in all the Churches of both the East and West witnesses to their worth and importance. In these liturgies, which we can view as the most authoritative safeguards of the apostolic Tradition, many doctrines of faith are confessed and honored. (4) The most ancient martyrologies, namely, those of Ignatius the God-bearer, St. Polycarp, and certain others composed by men not only contemporary, but also eyewitnesses. In these martyrologies there exist many truths of the Christian faith that have been set forth, which unreservedly those inspired martyrs confessed in the name of Christ. Inasmuch as these martyrologies are authentic, all the more they were read in public in the common assemblies for prayer of the faithful after their preceding diligent investigation and confirmation by the bishop of the place of the martyrdom.

(5) The decisions and canons[(1)] of the holy councils, both the eight ecumenical and the nine local ones[(2)] confirmed by the latter. First, this source is very precious because our holy Church together attributed absolute authority to the ecumenical councils, in which the entire Church, gathered together, makes decisions under the care of the Holy Spirit who "abides in it forever" and "guides it to all truth" (Jn. 14:16; 16:13), for which reason they begin their decisions according to the example of the
holy Apostles }always by the words "it seemed good to the Holy Spirit }8
and to us" (Acts 15:18).[5] Second, because during the time of these councils, those divinely illuminated Fathers and teachers of the Church who gathered from everywhere and acted unanimously introduced nothing new into the faith or life, but when defending the ancients things existing in Scripture and Tradition against various heresies, decided and confirmed on the basis of Tradition rather than Scripture, because heretics also defended themselves when maliciously misinterpreting through Scripture; for which reason, all those who reject the councils of the Fathers and their traditions that are in harmony with divine revelation and piously preserved by the Orthodox Church are excommunicated from the Orthodox Church (see the ceremony of the Sunday of Orthodoxy). (6) The writings of all the ancient Fathers of the Church, in harmony with holy Scripture and the sacred Traditions that are preserved and in use in the whole Church. They either composed special confessions for proof of their own correct faith before the Church, namely, these are the expositions of the faith of St. Athanasius, Pope Pelagius, and many others; elucidated the concise doctrines of the faith for teaching of the faithful, just as, for example, the catechesis of Cyril of Jerusalem, the theology of John of Damascus, and very numerous other homilies and commentaries on holy Scripture; or wrote various apologies and refutations against pagans, heretics, and schismatics. The authority of the holy Fathers is beyond doubt only in subjects of divine revelation, and indeed then only when perfect

(1) The decisions being discussed concern doctrines, the canons or regulations, the administration, and the good order of the Church. [—St. Raphael]

(2) The seven ecumenical councils are Nicaea (325), Constantinople (381), Ephesus (431), Chalcedon (451), Constantinople (553), Constantinople (680), and Nicaea (787); Penthektē, which was held in Constantinople (692), is supplementary. The nine local councils are Carthage (256), Ancyra (315), Neocaesarea (315), Gangra (340), Antioch (341), Sardica (347), Laodicaea (364), Constantinople (394), Carthage (418). Outside of these there exist also two other councils that were assembled during the reign of the sacred Photius, Prōtodeutera (861) and Constantinople (879). [—St. Raphael]

unanimous agreement prevails among them. In this case, the authority of the Fathers is incontestable, we say, not only because, as flourishing in different places and times going back until the Apostles themselves, they represent their own local Churches, and consequently their accord also shows the agreement of the Churches themselves; but also, on the one hand, on account of the sanctity of their lives, which they spent in most rigorous apostolic simplicity and plainness, and on the other hand, owing to their ardent zeal for the Orthodox faith, for the sake of which they endured persecutions, tortures, and a myriad of other hardships; and finally, also on account of the purity of their divinely illuminated mind, which also naturally has been endowed with many spiritual gifts, they could not impart teachings except those consistent with divine revelation. For which reason also many of them were proclaimed by the whole Church either implicitly or explicitly as universal teachers and pillars of Orthodoxy, and in addition they also were adorned with various epithets analogous to their spiritual gifts, namely, for example, divine, God-bearing, }Godly-wise, God-speaking, Theologian, Great, Golden-mouthed, }9
Christ-speaking, and so forth. Consequently, when rightly having these things, the holy Fathers can be viewed as trustworthy witnesses of the true Tradition (see the *Ἐπιστολὴν τῶν τεσσάρων Πατριαρχῶν τῆς Ἀνατολῆς*, article 12), for which reason all those who reject the councils of the Fathers and their Traditions that are in harmony with divine revelation and piously preserved by the Orthodox Church are excommunicated from the Orthodox Church (see the ceremony of the Sunday of Orthodoxy). (7) A source of sacred Tradition is also the various customs and practices that have been received from time immemorial in common use throughout the universal Church. These are: (a) sacred times, namely, feasts, fasts, prayers, and so forth; (b) sacred places, namely, altars, tables, and generally the whole temple with all of its particulars; and (c) sacred services and other church rites and ceremonies. (8) As a final source of sacred Tradition, we can observe the witness of the most ancient heresies, which truly distorted certain proofs of orthodox teaching, on account of which they were also condemned by the Church, but when separated preserved many things safe and unadulterated. On this account, then, even they, on the one hand negatively, and on the other positively, can be of use for us as witnesses of the true apostolic Tradition (compare Μακάριος, *Εἰσαγωγὴ εἰς τὴν ὀρθοδόξον θεολογίαν*; and Ἀντώνιος, *Δογματικὴ θεολογία Εἰσαγωγή*).

3.

And these are the various sources of sacred Tradition, which nevertheless are not all also entirely immaculate and pure, but in some of them there exist many things that can by no means be called apostolic. Hence it follows that certain particular characteristic marks are required for a correct discernment of apostolic Traditions from those that are not. There exist such characteristic marks, on the one hand, that are internal or negative, through which we know what are not true apostolic Traditions, and on the other hand, external or positive, through which we know the true apostolic Traditions. And the first ones are: (1) the agreement of apostolic Tradition with itself because as the word of God it cannot contain anything contradictory; (2) its agreement with other Traditions unquestionably apostolic because the Apostles, since they have the mind of Christ, cannot be contradictory to one another, and much more [not] to themselves; and (3) its agreement with holy Scripture because the one who is the cause of both is one and the same, the Holy Spirit. One must see that deciding whether a certain tradition is or is not in accord with Scripture is neither proper for one, as the papist Church is asserting, or for many, because everyone is subject to error, but }to the holy Church in general, which the }10
Holy Spirit itself "guides to all truth" and which Paul calls "a pillar and bulwark of the truth" (Jn. 16:13; 1 Tim. 3:15), and for which reason all those who reject the councils of the Fathers and their Traditions that are in harmony with divine revelation and piously preserved by the Orthodox Church are excommunicated from the Orthodox Church (see the ceremony of the Sunday of Orthodoxy). The second ones, namely, external or positive characteristic marks of sacred Tradition, are the three designated by Vincent, bishop of Lérins (who flourished during the fifth century), namely, the things "*quod ubique* (what everywhere), *quod semper* (what always), *quod ab omnibus* (what by all) *creditum est* (was believed)" (see *Commonitorium pro Catholicae fidei antiquitate et universitate adversus profanas omnium haereticorum novitates* 3). The very thing that shows the apostolicity of whatever tradition demonstrates: (1) Its catholicity, i.e., that tradition is truly apostolic which was and is commonly received as such by the whole Orthodox Church, although it does not exist in Scripture either at all or under the form preserved by the Church. Because everything the Catholic Orthodox Church preserves and believes, without doubt

it received from those "who from the beginning become eyewitnesses and servants of the Word" (Lk. 1:2), therefore also the Apostle Paul states that the Church of God "was built upon the foundation of the Apostles and Prophets, Jesus Christ Himself being the chief cornerstone" (Eph. 2:20), [and] thus it becomes clear that whatever the Orthodox Church of Christ in general professes, this it received from the Apostles and Prophets themselves either in writing or by word of mouth; therefore, also by necessity, it bears in itself the seal of truth. "One must not," St. Irenaeus states, "seek from others the truth, which is easily received from the Church because the Apostles have deposited all things of truth in it as if in a rich storehouse so that all who might wish may receive from it a drink of life, for it is the entrance of life" (*Against Heresies* 3.4.1). (2) Its antiquity, i.e., that tradition is truly apostolic which can be traced back to apostolic times. This very thing Irenaeus also shows when saying, "If there might be controversy concerning any average question for anyone, must one not depart to the most ancient Churches, in which the Apostles dwelled, and take from them what is certain and clear concerning the question under discussion?" (*Against Heresies* 3.4.1; compare 3.3.1). (3) The agreement concerning it, i.e., that tradition is truly apostolic concerning which, if not all, at least most of the Fathers and teachers of the Church during the first five centuries are in agreement, because such united agreement of
them is, so }to speak, the Lydian stone of truly apostolic Traditions, the }11
very thing also that Tertullian says: "*Quod apud multos unum invenitur, non est erratum, sed traditum*" (*On the Sacrament of the Incarnation of the Lord* 82), namely, "Whatever is found the same by many, this was not contrived, but was handed over" (compare Μακάκιος, *Εἰσαγωγὴ εἰς τὴν ὀρθοδόξον θεολογίαν*, Παπιστ. ἐλέγχ., pt. 1, § 12; and "Tradition" in Nicolas Bergier, *Dictionnaire de théologie*).[6]

4.

Such being the case, it now remains for us to also point out that rich storehouse in which the Apostles, according to St. Irenaeus, "deposited all things of truth." In other words, it remains for us to examine which of the two Churches already divided and in conflict, I speak of the Eastern and the Western, is the true treasury and certain protection of sacred Traditions. The papist Church, which separated from the one, holy, catholic,

and apostolic Orthodox Church of Christ through condemnations, which the Lord knows, confidently asserts that the apostolic Church of Rome is a true treasury of the truly apostolic Traditions; the infallible representative of Christ on earth, the key-keeping Pope, is the faithful guardian of them! (see Heinrich Klee, *Lehrbuch der Dogmengeschichte*, "Concerning Tradition," § 2). But if one might open the impartial history of the Church, it will be observed that the Western Church that walked together modestly and steadfastly with the Eastern Church until about the ninth century, which [the Western Church] certainly, according to the witness of Sozomen, "regulating itself purely by the doctrines of the Fathers, wished to avoid quarrels and prattle concerning these things" (*Church History* 3.12[7]), from that time, because it no longer prospered, by the conceit of Lucifer becoming arrogant, inasmuch as viewing itself as more senior among equal sisters, and diverging from the royal road that up to then it walked along, it took the one leading to innovations, making use of every means licit and illicit in order that it might also drag the chaste sister, the Eastern Church, with it into the abyss of false belief into which it had fallen! In this manner, proportionately to her ambitious proclivities, advancing from error to error in spiritual and worldly affairs, it has left nothing unshaken, nothing without innovation, nothing without perversion—neither doctrines, nor mysteries, nor customs—but it spoiled and distorted everything written and unwritten! In truth, time lacks even to simply enumerate the shameless innovations of the papist Church, which both church and civil history report with horror, but lest I appear to say unsubstantiated things, let it be permitted for me that I make a brief
}comparison of the present-day so-called papist Church with our Ortho- }12
dox Church, or rather with itself, when at one time, being in agreement in everything with our own Church, it was called an orthodox Church of Rome, because nothing more disinterested and impartial than history can demonstrate for us which of the two discussed Churches is the faithful and true guardian of sacred Traditions. And first, when studying the history of church hierarchy, we see that whereas the ancient Roman Church viewed the bishop of Rome as simply a spiritual and only an administrative leader of the West, the papist Church views him as both an absolute spiritual and worldly leader of Christianity as a whole, contrary to both Scripture (Mt. 20:26; Lk. 22:26) and Tradition (First Ecumenical Council, canon 6). Whereas the ancient Roman Church viewed the hierarch of

Rome as *primus inter pares* (= first among equals) and as subject to the decisions of ecumenical councils, to which also the Apostle Peter submitted himself (Gal. 2:11), the papist Church views him as *summus pontifex* (= supreme hierarch) and, when placed above the councils, honors and venerates him as the infallible (oh the folly!) representative (!) of God upon earth, contrary both to Scripture (Mt. 20:26, 27; Eph. 2:20) and Tradition (Apostolic Canon 34; First Ecumenical Council, canon 6; Second Ecumenical Council, 2 and 4; Sixth [Ecumenical Council], 36; etc.). (Compare Φ. Βαφείδης, *Ἐκκλησιαστικὴ Ἱστορία*, vol. 2, § 130.) But second, let us also open the history of divine doctrines and mysteries and let us see if the papist Church feared these. But alas! The papacy also overturned these things because whereas the orthodox Roman Church taught that the Holy Spirit proceeds from the Father while anathematizing any addition or subtraction in the Symbol of Faith, the papist Church not only teaches the *Filioque* (= and from the Son), but also adds it in the Symbol of Faith (see Φ. Βαφείδης, *Ἐκκλησιαστικὴ Ἱστορία*, vol. 2, § 130) contrary to Scripture (Jn. 55:26[8]) and Tradition (all of the ecumenical councils and all of the Fathers of the Western and Eastern Church until the ninth century). Whereas the orthodox Roman Church celebrated baptism by triple immersion, the papist one introduced infusion and sprinkling, contrary both to Scripture (Mk. 1:10; Acts 8:36–39; Rom. 6:4; Col. 2:12) and Tradition (Apostolic Canon 50; Second Ecumenical Council, 7; Sixth, 45; paradoxically, also compare Klee, *Dogmatik*, 3:129). Whereas the orthodox Roman Church immediately after holy baptism celebrated the mystery of chrismation, the papist one celebrates it not just by the bishop
alone, but also after }the child reaches seven to twelve years of age, }13
calling it *confirmatio* (= confirmation), contrary both to Scripture (Acts 8:14–17; 19:2–6) and Tradition (Council of Laodicea, canon 48; Dionysius the Areopagite, *Ecclesiastical Hierarchy* 7; Cyril of Jerusalem, *Catechetical Lecture* 18.33). Whereas the orthodox Roman Church celebrated the divine Eucharist with leavened bread, the papist one celebrates it with unleavened, contrary both to Scripture (Mt. 26:26; Mk. 14:22; Lk. 24:30–35; Jn. 6:35, 41, 48, 51, 58; Acts 2:42–46; 20:7; 1 Cor. 10:16; 11:20) and Tradition (Justin, *Apology* 1.66; Irenaeus, *Against Heresies* 4.18; Cyril of Jerusalem, *Mystagogic Catechesis* 4.1–6; Ambrose, *On the Sacrament of the Incarnation of the Lord* 4.4). Whereas the orthodox Roman Church invoked God that He might hallow the offered gifts when

blessing them with the sign of the Cross, the papist one recites simply and historically the words of institution ("this is My body" and "this is My blood"), being of the opinion that by them and by only displaying the holy gifts, they are hallowed and transubstantiated, contrary clearly to apostolic and divine Tradition (see the Liturgy of the Apostle James and in general the ancient liturgies of the Orthodox; and compare also Irenaeus, *Against Heresies* 4.24; Origen, *Against Celsus* 8; Cyril of Jerusalem, *Mystagogic Catechesis* 1.7, 3.3, 5.7; Basil, *Concerning the Holy Spirit* 27; Augustine, *On the Trinity* 3.4; etc.). Finally, whereas the orthodox Roman Church provided this fearful mystery to all the faithful without exception and under both species, the papist one not only deprived small children of it contrary to apostolic Tradition (Apostolic Constitutions 8.13; Dionysius the Areopagite, *Ecclesiastical Hierarchy* 7.11; Cyprian, *Testimonies against the Jews* 3.25; Augustine, *On the Merits and Remission of Sins and on the Baptism of Infants* 1.20; and others), but also dared to exclude all the laity from communion of the precious blood of Christ, contrary both to Scripture (which expressly commands, "Drink of it, all of you" [Mt. 27:27;[9] Mk. 14:23]) and Tradition (all of the seven ecumenical councils and ancient Fathers of the Church). Whereas the orthodox Roman Church viewed the penances imposed in the mystery of repentance as having a simple correcting effect on the one repenting, the papist one, misunderstanding the true meaning of this mystery, not only subdivided it into three, namely, into *contritionem* (= contrition), *confessionem* (= confession), and *satisfactionem* (= satisfaction), but also views the penances as having an effect propitiatory of the divine justice that is offended by the sin of the one repenting, and as if this did not suffice, it added, on the one hand, that by virtue of the authority given to it from God to bind and loose, it can release from these penances the one repenting through pardoning absolutions, which are bestowed from the inexhaustible treasury that it possesses of excess merits earned not only by Christ, but also the saints (!!!); and on the other hand, that these absolutions work }even after death to emancipate the one who happened to die }14
under the burden of penances from the punishment of purifying fire (!!!). The papist Church teaches all these things contrary both to Scripture (Lk. 15:18, 19; 18:13; 2 Cor. 7:10; 1 Pt. 4:8; Acts 10:43; 4:12; Heb. 7:25) and Tradition (Cyprian, *On the Lapsed* 30; Basil, *On Isaiah* 15; John Chrysostom, *Homily on 2 Tim.* 6.3). But let us proceed further: whereas

the orthodox Roman Church prescribed celibacy as obligatory only for bishops (according to canon 12 of the Ecumenical Council in Trullo), the papist one imposed it on all clergy in general, both great and small, contrary both to Scripture (Eph. 5:31–32; 1 Tim. 4:3) and Tradition (Apostolic Canon 5; Sixth Ecumenical, canons 13 and 18; Carthage, 4 and 33; Gangra, 1, 4, and 14). Whereas the orthodox Roman Church permitted the dissolution of marriage in the case of spousal infidelity, the papist one views it as completely indissoluble, contrary both to Scripture (Mt. 5:32) and Tradition (Neocaesarea, canon 8; Carthage, 115; Basil, canons 9, 21, 39, and 48; Sixth, canon 87). Finally, whereas the orthodox Roman Church celebrated unction both by priests and for any sick [person] whatsoever, the papist one celebrates it only by the bishop and only for those who are dying as a last anointing (= *extrema unctio*), contrary both to Scripture (Jas. 5:14, 15) and Tradition (Chrysostom, *Concerning the Priesthood* 3.6; Cyril of Alexandria, *Encomium on Holy Mary the Theotokos* 6.13). In general, regarding these innovations of the papist Church concerning the mysteries, see Φ. Βαφείδης, *Ἐκκλησιαστικὴ Ἱστορία*, vol. 2, § 192 and § 194; Δημήτριος Βερναρδάκης, *Ἱερα Κατήχησις*, "Concerning the Mysteries"; and Γρηγόριος, *Ἡ φωνὴ τῆς Ὀρθοδοξίας*. But after these doctrines and mysteries had finally undergone such change and alteration in the papist Church, what must one understand regarding the other apostolic and church customs? Perhaps papism left these undisturbed? Not at all, because whereas the orthodox Church of Rome forbade fasting or kneeling on the Sabbath, breaking the fast on Wednesday or Friday, eating blood or clotted blood or any other impure thing, using any musical instrument whatsoever in the churches, venerating statues or unwritten images, ordaining more than one priest during one and the same liturgy, offering every day more than one sacrifice on the same altar, shaving hair or the beard and much more the mustache—whereas, I say, all these things and many such others, on account of good order and decorum, the ancient orthodox Church of Rome forbade, as identically the orthodox Eastern Church does up to the present day, on the other hand, the papist Church does not only simply allow all these things, }but also }15
imposes strictly many of them, completely contrary to the purely apostolic and church Tradition of which was decreed, "Let the ancient customs prevail" (First Ecumenical Council, canon 6). In general, concerning such innovations of the papist Church, see Εὐγένιος Βούλγαρης, *Κατὰ*

Λατίνων Στηλιτευτικὴ Ἐπιστολή; Γρηγόριος, *Ἡ φωνὴ τῆς Ὀρθοδοξίας*; and *Πηδάλιον*. Consequently, after also explaining such things of papism, let any impartial man tell us which of the two said Churches is the true treasury and certain protection of sacred Traditions, or as Irenaeus said, “the rich storehouse in which the Apostles have deposited all things of truth”: the papist Church, which innovated so much and greatly from 1054 until the present day, or the orthodox Eastern Church, which neither added or subtracted nor altered a jot or tittle from the divine deposit handed over to it from apostolic times until the present day?

B.

> Therefore take heed to yourselves and all the flock . . . for I know this, that after my departure fierce wolves will come among you, not sparing the flock, and from among yourselves will arise men speaking perverted things, in order to drag away the disciples after them. (Acts 20:28–30)

While the great pontiffs of Rome who draw their inspiration from the soul-corrupting love of power subverted both divine and human doctrines and so, deviating altogether from the royal road, dragged with themselves during the gloomy darkness of the Middle Ages all the peoples of the West into the dreadful abyss of most impious innovations, suddenly, as from a light of the renaissance of letters that began to shine in the West already during the fifteenth century, some, being enlightened, observed both with fear and trembling that they were being brought to a precipice; therefore, also immediately after discontinuing their destructive march, they decided that, if possible, with the leaders who seduced them they would return with all speed to that royal road from which they deviated. But their mischievous guides, the haughty pontiffs of Rome, becoming intoxicated with much conceit, could no longer regain their senses from their lethargy, but every day constructing new paths, they fabricated new claims, which they had received from supposed ancient traditions, and so increased day }by day the power of }16
despotism and tyranny, hastening their march to the abyss of spiritual destruction. Hence those wretched servants of revived letters, finally seeing that thus they cried vainly when protesting against the excessive

papist claims, shook off the burdensome yoke of papist tyranny and in this manner decided that they would alone return to that ancient royal road. But the infants! Instead of joining among themselves to seek what leads without confusion to the royal road, on the contrary, while taking the road completely opposite to the spiritual despotism of Rome, they went to the other extreme of spiritual anarchy and religious mob rule. Consequently, these Protestants who discarded all tradition and church legislation submit Scripture as the sole source of Christian faith; all the same when each of them interprets [Scripture] arbitrarily, without sacred Tradition, he is basing his religious conviction upon his individual conscience.(1) Thus, when utterly destroying any unity in faith, they surpassed the papists, preceding them into the abyss of spiritual destruction! And it is true that in the orthodox Eastern Church, holy Scripture is considered first and by nature a source of the revelation of the full Christian religion; therefore also not only does the tendency prevail on its part to base whatever question of faith firstly and above all on holy Scripture, but [the Church] even holds that there is not one valid doctrine that is not contained in Scripture either in word or in spirit (see Cyril of Jerusalem, *Catechetical Lectures* 16.2). Nevertheless, holy Scripture is still not viewed by [the Church] as the sole and sufficient source of the Christian religion, but requires for its completion and explanation sacred Tradition, which has the same authority (see Chrysostom, *Homily 4 on 2 Thes.* 2.15; and Basil, *Concerning the Holy Spirit* 27. 2). But let us, who already showed the true meaning of sacred Tradition against the papists who maliciously distorted it, now show its great worth contrary to the Protestants (Προτεσταντῶν) who reject it, that is, the "Protesting ones" (Διαμαρτυρομένων), demonstrating its great worth: (1) in the history of divine revelation and clear witness of the Fathers, (2) in the voice of the universal Church and the unanimous witness of all its ancient Fathers and teachers, and (3) in }the indispensable use of sacred Tradition for }17
correct discernment of the authenticity, canonicity, and inspiration of sacred books; for their true comprehension, understanding, and interpretation; and finally for any true knowledge not contained in Scripture, most indispensable still to both faith and Christian life.

(1) Of all the Protestants, the Anglican Church alone preserved a portion of Orthodoxy because it accepted the Tradition of the first five centuries, i.e., the first five ecumenical councils. [—St. Raphael]

1.

If one wishes to open the sacred books of holy Scripture, one sees immediately at the beginning that this inspired Scripture witnesses that the first man who began to record the revelations of God to man is the God-seer Moses (Dt. 31:9, 24). Consequently, from Adam until Moses, namely, during an interval of nearly four thousand years (from 5508 to 1609), true faith in God was certainly not otherwise preserved and transmitted except by word of mouth, that is, by tradition. But even after the means of transmission of divine revelations through writing was introduced from Moses onward, did the means of transmission by living voice from father to son cease in any way? By no means. Moses himself, who already recorded in writing the law of God, when finding himself close to death, exhorts the Israelites in this manner: "Remember the days of old, understand generation from generation: ask your father, and he shall proclaim to you; your elders, and they shall tell you" (Dt. 32:7) and not "Read only the law written by me" because Moses knew that without the clear and detailed tradition of their fathers, the Israelites could not understand the simple memorials written by him (see ibid., 6:20, 21). But if we will advance even until this royal era also of the Prophets, in addition to Scripture we also find tradition. Thus the prophet and king David says, "I will open my mouth in parables; I utter riddles from the beginning, as much as we heard and these things we learned, also our fathers described to us . . . that another generation might know, sons will be born, rise, and announce these things to their sons" (Ps. 77:2, 3, 6). The Prophet Joel says to the elders of Israel, "You will declare on their behalf to your children, and your children to their children, and their children to another generation" (1:3). Thus in this manner, these two means of transmission of divine revelation proceeded parallel to one another, i.e., one of tradition and the other of Scripture, throughout the entire duration of the Judaic kingdom until the coming }of our Lord and God and Savior Jesus Christ. Before }18
we otherwise leave the synagogue and come to the church, let us see what the Protestants who reject Tradition say in response to what was discussed. They often begin by bringing forward Deuteronomy 4:2, "You shall not add to the word which I command you." Nevertheless, we respond to them with sacred Augustine (*On John*, chap. 79) saying that in this passage Moses forbids the addition of anything detrimental and repugnant to

what was written, and not the addition of things profitable and in agreement with what was written, because otherwise how were the Prophets added after Deuteronomy? But let us come now to the Christian era. Sacred history witnesses unerringly that the original means of transmission of the Christian faith was chiefly and from the beginning the living voice, that is, tradition, by which also Christian conscience was formed in the first place and those who believed in the divine word formed the Christian Church. Our Lord Jesus Christ Himself, who preached the gospel of salvation only by word of mouth, wrote nothing either concerning His life or concerning His teachings, but only attended to the foundation of His holy Church also through a living voice, and in addition, while living in an intimate relationship with His disciples and instructing them in the things concerning His mission, sent them forth, saying to them in proclamation, "Going, therefore, make disciples of all the nations . . . teaching them to observe all things, whatever I commanded you" (Mt. 28:19), and, for faithful and exact transmission of this divine teaching, when filling them with the Holy Spirit on the day of Pentecost, [He] also promised that He would be with them "always until the close of the age" (Mt. 28:20). The Apostles who obeyed this divine command scattered everywhere in order to preach the divine word while all following the same means of teaching from the beginning, that is, by living voice, but then some of them and their disciples, thus only a certain number, motivated by various reasons, wrote some brief memorials of their particular teaching by word of mouth. Thus Matthew, for example, wrote his Gospel at the request of the Palestinian Christians with whom he lived from the beginning [and] who desired that they might have the teaching in writing (Eusebius, *Church History* 3.24). Luke also then wrote a Gospel and the Acts of the Apostles for Theophilus (Lk. 1:4; Acts 1:1). Paul wrote his various letters on occasion for various reasons. And finally, the
other }sacred authors wrote for other circumstances and causes, as a }19
result of which their sacred writings also did not become immediately known to the entire Church. That these sacred authors did not record everything they taught by a living voice, this is shown firstly in this: the Apostle Paul, in his Epistle to the Hebrews (6:1), promises that after arriving he will set the Church's matters in order and teach them "concerning repentance from dead works, faith in God, teaching concerning baptism, laying on of hands, resurrection of the death, and eternal judgment,"

which we find set forth in not one other letter of his. Consequently, these things [were what] the same one [Paul], after arriving, taught them by a living voice only. The Apostle Jude reports a tradition concerning the Archangel Michael, i.e., that he, "when disputing with the devil, argued concerning the body of Moses" (9), which nevertheless is mentioned nowhere by holy Scripture. But also in Acts (20:35) the words of the Lord "It is more blessed to give than to receive" are presented, which nevertheless are not contained in the Gospels. Second, these sacred authors themselves also expressly make this known. Thus the Apostle Paul says to the Corinthians (1 Cor. 11:34), "About the remaining things, when I come, I will give direction," and again the Apostle John makes this known more plainly when saying in Second John 12,[10] "Having many things to write to you, I did not wish to use paper and ink, but I hope to come to you and speak face to face," and in Third John 13,[11] "I had many things to write, but I do not wish to write to you by ink and pen, but I hope to immediately see you and will speak to you face to face" (compare also Jn. 20:31–32; 21:25). And on the one hand, it is true that without doubt according to divine economy the sacred Scriptures were handed down to the Church, because the Christian conscience that was formed through preaching by word of mouth must have taken also an external form that preserved it from anything foreign threatening its purity, but it is likewise also true that the Apostles did not have the duty to write, for which reason also the majority of them wrote nothing at all, and nevertheless, they also not only successfully preached the word of God everywhere, but also established Churches, many of which until the beginning of the third century and after, as true history reveals, knew nothing outside of sacred Tradition (see Irenaeus, *Against Heresies* 3.42). But were not also the various nations that were Christianized after the third century, inasmuch as they did not have their own translation of holy Scripture, confined only to sacred Tradition? But even after translations took place, was Scripture obtainable?
}Very far from it. The history of the discovery of the printing press evi- }20
dences that during the course of fifteen centuries the sacred Bible, as also any writing in general at that time, was so precious that scarcely a few copies existed in each Church or even in the houses of wealthy patrons of the arts. Consequently, all the remaining Christians were confined to the teaching of the Church, only by which were the doctrines and preaching of the faith also taught. However, who would dare to call into question

true faith and salvation for so many millions of Christians? But outside of history, also holy Scripture itself evidences both the existence and the great meaning of sacred Tradition with very clear words. Thus the sacred Luke clearly acknowledges that he writes his Gospel according to the oral tradition of the Apostles. He states, "Inasmuch as many have undertaken to draw up a narrative concerning the matters that have taken place among us, just as those who have been eyewitnesses and servants of the word delivered them to us, it also seemed good to me, etc." (Lk. 1:1–2). Above all, the Apostle Paul, writing in his First Epistle to the Corinthians (11:2), states, "And I praise you, brethren, that you remember me in all things and keep the traditions as I have delivered them to you," in which passage he clearly means oral traditions, because he now writes for a first time to the Corinthians, but in the Second Epistle to the Thessalonians (2:15), he writes, "Therefore, brethren, stand fast and hold firm to the traditions that you were taught whether by word or our letter." There are two certain noteworthy points in this passage: (1) on the one hand that Paul orders the observance of traditions by the Thessalonians, while they had already in hand his two epistles; and (2) that clearly Paul ascribes the same worth and meaning to both holy Scripture and sacred Tradition. Paul brings this second point into view still more when ordering them elsewhere, "In the name of our Lord Jesus Christ, that you keep away from every brother who walks in a disorderly way and not according to the tradition that they received from us" (ibid., 3:6). The same Apostle again writes to Timothy in First Timothy 6:20, "O Timothy, guard the deposit [and not: my epistles only], avoiding profane chatter and opposing tenets of falsely named knowledge," and in Second Timothy 1:13, "You have a pattern of sound
words that in }faith and love in Christ Jesus you have heard from me [and }21
not: which I wrote to you]" and "What you heard from me [and not: what I write to you] before many witnesses, entrust these things to faithful men who will also teach others" (ibid., 2:2). What is at the same time more clear and true than these witnesses inspired by God? Nevertheless, the Protestants, when doing everything possible that they might attack the authority of sacred Tradition, protest, bringing forward the passage of St. Paul, who says, "But even if we or an angel of heaven should preach a gospel to you besides what we preached to you, let him be anathema. As we have previously said, also now again I say, if anyone preaches to you a gospel besides that which you received, let him be anathema" (Gal.

1:8–9). But they do not know that their very opposition turns against them because Paul in this passage dissuades the Galatians from the acceptance not of unwritten traditions, which on the contrary in many places in his epistles he recommends fervently, but of the false teachings of certain deceivers "who wish to pervert the gospel of Christ" (ibid., 1:7), for which reason also he does not say, "If anyone preaches a gospel to you besides what we wrote," but "besides what we preached" and "besides that which you received." But rather, Paul preached the word of God to the Galatians by a living voice (because they did not have another epistle from him), and the Galatians received from his mouth the gospel of salvation, the very thing that we call Tradition. But the detractors of the sacred Traditions protest and again bring forward a passage from Revelation (22:18): "If anyone adds to them, God will add upon him plagues described in this book," but they lack the discernment that this sacred Apostle, who, instead of "writing by ink and paper," [and who] prefers always "to speak face to face," does not prohibit sacred Traditions by this passage, but the insertion of one's own teachings as divine words into holy Scripture, the very thing that was characteristic of many false teachers at that time (and yet also of many heresies today, exactly as the splintering heresies of the Protestants do).

2.

Aside from holy Scripture, the voice of the one, holy, catholic, and apostolic Church declares manifestly the great worth of sacred Tradition, which, as coming from the holy Apostles and through them from our Lord Jesus Christ Himself, its most holy head, is not limited by place or time,
but, }being eternal in the midst of the ages, serves as a constant witness }22
of the truth. Its catholicity, inspiration, and infallibility are supported by the Lord's very words, which lack error. He states, "For where there are two or three gathered in my name, there I am in the midst of them" (Mt. 18:20); "I am with you always until the close of the age" (ibid., 28:20); "I will pray to the Father, and He will give you another counselor, that He may be with you forever, the Spirit of Truth" (Jn. 14:16); and "When the Spirit of truth comes, He will guide you into all the truth" (Jn. 16:13). Thus the voice of such a Church—namely, the unanimous agreement of all the holy Fathers who gathered in both the seven ecumenical and the nine local

councils—manifestly witnesses to the great worth of sacred Tradition because also in these councils, as we saw, orthodox doctrines were defined and the heretical ones were refuted on the basis of Tradition rather than Scripture. Consequently, the Fathers of the Seventh Ecumenical Council in their seventh act stated, "We preserve without innovation the traditions that have been prescribed in writing and by word of mouth" (calling the use of them a royal road), and state in their first canon, "We embrace the divine canons with gladness, and confirm whole and unshaken the regulation of them [the canons] that was set forth by the wholly blessed Apostles, the trumpets of the Spirit, both the six ecumenical councils and the local ones that were assembled for setting forth such regulations, and our holy Fathers. For all who were also enlightened by one and the same Spirit determined what was fitting." Nevertheless, even after all these things, while defiling themselves when intemperately protesting against sacred Traditions, they dare to accuse such a Church, which saved the divine deposit pure and intact, of corrupting the true Christian faith! But if this had been the case and the Church in fact fell from the truth (God forbid the blasphemy!), as these rash men allege, then, let us ask them, where are those divine promises of the Savior that he will be with [the Church] "always until the close of the age" and that "He will send to it the spirit of truth that He might guide it to all the truth," and so on? Oh! The great audacity and folly of these imprudent men!

But in addition to the voice of the universal Church, }the witness of all }23
the Church's holy Fathers, teachers, and other ecclesiastical writers also confirms the great authority of sacred Tradition, whose great importance not only all Orthodox and the papists proclaim, but which also many of the Protestants themselves understand and acknowledge. And in the first place, let us see the testimony of the renowned apostolic Fathers, who, as direct disciples and successors of the Apostles, know better than anyone genuine apostolic teaching. Thus Ignatius the God-bearer, as Eusebius of Caesarea testifies (*Church History* 3.36), "exhorted the parishes in each city in which he stayed . . . he encouraged them to hold fast to the Tradition of the Apostles, which he regarded necessary to be given fixed form for certainty, when witnessing [to the Tradition] in writing at that time." The sacred martyr Polycarp also encouraged the same things, as his disciple Irenaeus gives testimony, saying, "In the time of Anicetus, when he stayed in Rome, he turned many from the aforementioned heretics to the Church

of God, while preaching that this one and only truth was received from the Apostles, which was handed over by the Church" (*Against Heresies* 3.3). Papias acknowledges that aside from the divine Scriptures, he also received certain other true teachings from the Apostles: "Not from books," he adds, "did I receive so much to benefit me, as from a voice living and enduring" (Eusebius, *Church History* 3.39). Finally, Dionysius the Areopagite states, "Therefore we accept as clearly necessary for man's salvation the divine law, prophetic ordinances, and the evangelic commands in the Apostolic Constitutions and sacred unwritten traditions of the Church, the transgressors of which are called heretics" (*Concerning Ecclesiastical Hierarchy* 1). During the second century Hegesippus, as Eusebius testifies (*Church History* 4.22), when visiting many cities and eparchies everywhere, found the same genuine apostolic teaching: "Therefore he collected the unerring tradition of apostolic preaching in five books with the most simple style of writing" (Eusebius, *Church History* 4.8). St. Irenaeus, when refuting the heretics by Tradition rather than by Scripture, states to them, "Anyone who wishes to see the truth is able to see in every Church the apostolic Tradition that is known to the entire world" (*Against Heresies* 3.3). During the third century Tertullian not only exhorts holding apostolic Traditions, but also through them he principally confutes }the false beliefs of the }24
heretics. See what he says: "Apostolos Domini habemus auctores, qui nec ipsi quidquam ex suo arbitrio, quod inducerent, elegerunt, sed acceptam a Christo disciplinam fideliter nationibus adsignaverunt"[12] (*On the Prescription of Heretics* 6). Clement of Alexandria says, "But those who preserve the true Tradition of blessed teaching directly from the holy Apostles John, James, and Paul, being handed on from father to son (but a few similar to fathers), came by God's will to us also to deposit those ancestral and apostolic seeds" (*Stromata* 1.1.11–12). Origen, the father of criticism, states, "Therefore, because the apostolic tradition must be preserved, which is handed over in the order of succession from the Apostles and exists in our Churches to the present day, only this truth must be accepted that differs in no respect from ecclesiastical and apostolic Tradition" (*On First Principles*, preface, 2). St. Cyprian states, "It is easy for pious and simple souls both to avoid falsehood and to find the truth, for at the same time that we turn to the source of divine Tradition, falsehood is destroyed" (*Epistle 63*). Finally, during the fourth century the greatest and most illustrious Fathers and teachers of the Church flourished. I deem sufficient for the silencing

of the enemies of sacred Tradition that we cite only the testimony of three Fathers concerning this, the very ones, though, who all the ages view as the three greatest illuminators of the Christian firmament: I speak of Basil the Great, Gregory the Theologian, and John Chrysostom. And Basil the Great states the following: "Of the dogmas and preaching that are preserved in the Church, some we possess from written teaching, others we have received from the Tradition of the Apostles that was preserved for us in secret; both of which have the same force in relation to right belief. And no one will speak against these, no one who has even at least a little experience of the institutions of the Church. For if we were to attempt to reject unwritten customs, as not having great value, we might be negligent in these principal customs, injuring the Gospel [and] instead turning the preaching into a mere word. For example, to take the first and most general custom, who taught in writing those who have trusted in the name of our Lord Jesus Christ to seal themselves by the sign of the Cross? What writing taught us to turn toward the East during prayer? }Which of the }25
saints has left us in writing the words of the invocation at the displaying of the bread of the Eucharist and the cup of blessing? For we are certainly not content with what the Apostle or the Gospel has recorded, but we both proclaim and say other words that have great importance to the mystery, which we receive from unwritten teaching. By which writings do we bless the water of baptism, the oil of the chrism, and above all the very one being baptized? Is it not by silent and mystical tradition? What then? What written word taught the very anointment of the oil? From where is man baptized thrice? But from what Scripture are many customs of baptism, such as the renunciation of Satan and his angels? Do they not come from this unpublished and secret teaching, which our fathers guarded in a silence not meddled with and examined out of curiosity?" (*Concerning the Holy Spirit* 27). Gregory the Theologian states, "[Julian], seeing that our reasoning is strong, both in doctrines and in testimonies from above . . . but still greater and more well known in the types of the Church that have been handed down and preserved at present, that not even this might remain without guile, what does he plot, and what does he do?" (*First Invective against Julian* 110), and elsewhere, "Preserving the good deposit, which we received from the Fathers while worshiping Father, Son, and Holy Spirit, knowing the Father in the Son, the Son in the Spirit, in whom we have been baptized, in whom we have believed, to whom we

have sworn allegiance" (*Oration* 6.22).[13] Finally, the sacred Chrysostom, who comments on the passage Second Thessalonians 2:15, states, "Hence it is clear that they [the Apostles] did not hand over everything by letter, but many things also equally by word of mouth, and both the former and latter are trustworthy. Therefore we also believe that the Tradition of the Church is trustworthy. It is a tradition; seek nothing further" (*Homily 4 on 2 Thes.*).

Yet after all this clear and most enlightening testimony of the Fathers and teachers of the Church, the Protestants, apart from attempting to destroy the Traditions, oppose us with the testimony of certain Fathers who apparently reject sacred Traditions. First, Irenaeus, they say, when struggling against the Gnostics and especially the Marcionites, rejects traditions by what he says to them: "Legite diligentius id quod ab apostolis est Evangelium nobis datum, et legite diligenitius prophetas, et invenietis . . .
om}nem doctrinam Domini nostri praedictam in ipsis" (*Against Heresies* }26
4.36.1), that is, "Read carefully the Gospel given to us by the Apostles and the Prophets, and you will find in them . . . all the aforementioned teaching of our Lord," but how much this Father is unjustly slandered! Because in this text Irenaeus not only is not rejecting sacred Traditions, but also on the contrary defends and fortifies them against the false traditions of falsely called knowledge. He encourages the Marcionites in the reading of the Gospels and Prophets not because he does not also accept sacred Tradition (which on the contrary, as we saw, he both accepts and recommends to others), but because he wishes to show to the aforementioned heretics that both the Old Testament and New Testament are works of the same God, the very thing these heretics denied. Therefore he also says to them to read with care both the Gospels and Prophets that they might be persuaded regarding the full agreement of both Testaments because Irenaeus in the above text rejects not sacred Traditions, but those false and erroneous teachings that the Marcionites contended the Lord Himself secretly handed over to certain chosen disciples in order that they would reveal them only to those able to understand and preserve them; the same one [Irenaeus] points this out in what he states a little further above: "For even if the Apostles knew certain hidden mysteries that they taught the perfect privately and secretly from the rest, above all they would teach these to those whom they also entrusted the Churches themselves" (*Against Heresies* 3.3.1). Consequently, with good reason struggling against the

Marcionites, St. Irenaeus rejects their false traditions, which all are contrary to both holy Scripture and sacred Tradition. But also Jerome, they say, in his writings against Helvidius (*Against Helvidius* 19) rejects all tradition, saying, "Sed ut haec quae scripta sunt, non negamus, ita ea quae non sunt scripta, renuimus," which is, "Just as we do not deny what has been written, so we do not accept what has not been written," and elsewhere (*On Mt. 23:35–36*) he states, "Hoc quia de scripturis non habet auctoritatem, eadem facilitate comtemnitur, qua probatur," which is, "What is not confirmed by the Scriptures is easily condemned, as it is also fabricated," but how this Father also is slandered maliciously! Because when Jerome says these things, he means not the sacred }Traditions, the }27
observance of which he recommends in many of his writings, but the false and groundless prattle of the Helvidians, for example, that Christ was issued from the virgin womb foul as other infants, that Zacharias the son of Barachias was father of John the Baptist, and other such lies. But also Cyril of Jerusalem, they say, preaching concerning the Holy Spirit, dismisses sacred Tradition, recommending only holy Scripture. The passage is this: "You will absolutely not believe even me who says these things to you, if you do not receive proof from the divine Scriptures of what is announced" (*Catechetical Lecture* 4.17). But does any prudent man who reads this passage (let him also thus be isolated) wish to draw the absurd conclusion that St. Cyril rejects sacred Traditions? Because besides the fact that the sacred Traditions agree in everything with holy Scripture, the sacred Cyril also spoke this text when having before him an audience obedient to his words in everything, and consequently he did not at all fear that they would dispute with him the soundness of interpretation that was being given by him to various scriptural passages. Whereas if he had other audiences, for instance, Arians or Pneumatomachoi, who certainly would have disputed with him the meaning of all passages of Scripture or would bring other texts against him, then how would St. Cyril otherwise be able to prove to them the true meaning of the scriptural passages being misinterpreted by them except through Tradition? But does not the sacred Cyril recommend sacred Traditions also in many places elsewhere in his catechetical lectures? (see *Catechetical Lecture* 4.35).

When the Protestants altogether unjustly and maliciously slander these and other ancient writers and teachers of the Church, they seek that they might reject the authority of the sacred Traditions as supposed human

ordinances and nothing more! But here we ought to observe for the truth's sake that not all Protestants reject all the sacred Tradition, but whereas some, when rejecting all the sacred Traditions in general, altogether shamelessly attack our holy Fathers, others who conduct themselves somewhat more moderately contend that only the traditions of the first four centuries are true apostolic Traditions. And the former justify their absurd animosity against the holy Fathers }when saying that those ancient }28
Fathers of the Church were gullible men, easily duped and completely devoid of discerning knowledge, who, while very involved in Platonic philosophy, which in many ways they sought to reconcile with Christianity, deviated from correct Christian teaching, either accepting many dubious works as genuine or falling into other errors and fallacies, as, for example, that God and the angels are corporeal, that Christ lived on earth more than forty years, that Christ will rule over the earth a thousand years before the second coming, that Pascha must be celebrated on the fourteenth of Nisan, and such things. Hence, they say, Tradition, when corrupted, became a source of new doctrines and teachings not at all contained in Scripture. When responding to these things, we observe: (1) That if the Fathers in fact were so ignorant and duped, so that they corrupted the true Christian faith, then the Apostles themselves blundered, who established such successors in the Church! Then the promises of the Lord that He will be with the Church "always" and that the Holy Spirit Himself "will guide it in all the truth" remained unaccomplished! Then, finally, also our salvation itself is doubtful! (2) In fact, if those Fathers, out of a lack of discerning knowledge, accepted certain dubious works as genuine, then, let us ask, how are we able to affirm concerning the authenticity of the Scriptures that we have today? But if (3) indeed those Fathers fell into certain erroneous ideas, which, let us ask, such erroneous idea of whatever Father is viewed in the Church as an apostolic tradition? Were the Chiliasts, the Quartodecimans, and in general also all those heretical opinions that were contrary either to holy Scripture or sacred Tradition not condemned? That the Fathers could fall into error, this we do not deny. But the question is whether these certain erroneous ideas then became accepted in the Church as apostolic Traditions, and whether consequently the authentic apostolic teaching was adulterated or corrupted by and under the Fathers. We maintain that the Fathers not only did not adulterate or corrupt the apostolic teaching, but neither were they able to adulterate or

distort it: (1) Because those Fathers and shepherds of the Church who
taught publicly the doctrines of the faith, what is more while, in the assem-
blies of Christians, from childhood }being taught the Christian faith, }29
either hearing even the Apostles themselves or their successors, were not
only unable to distort the apostolic teaching, but neither [did they] invol-
untarily deviate from it. Because if even one dared ever to introduce
something foreign into the teaching of the Apostles, such a person after a
first and second warning was viewed by the Church as a heathen and was
driven out of its precinct. The fate of Paul of Samosata, Sabellius, Arius,
Nestorius, Eutyches, Dioscorus, and the remaining heresiarchs is known.
How impartial the Church was in the defense of the divine deposit, of
which it was appointed guardian and defender from God, its condemna-
tion of men otherwise distinguished and of genius shows, such as Theo-
dore of Mopsuestia, Apollinaris of Laodicea, and the most admirable of
all, Origen Adamantius. (2) The Fathers, we say, were unable to distort the
apostolic teaching because, when fighting against the heretics who mali-
ciously misinterpreted and distorted holy Scripture, they appealed, in wit-
ness of the true meaning of Scripture, to the apostolic Tradition, which the
heretics who were unable, as in the case of Scripture, to distort and misin-
terpret, [and so they] fled for refuge in various sophisms and philosophi-
cal arguments, sometimes accusing the Apostles of ignorance, other times
the Fathers of a bad understanding of apostolic teaching! Thus, how in the
midst of such fearsome enemies could those holy Fathers and teachers
distort even one single doctrine of the Christian faith? Hence many of the
Protestants, understanding the indisputable authority of sacred Traditions,
decide that Tradition is necessary, but are able to follow with certainty
only the Tradition of the first three or four centuries because they say that
during the first four centuries of Christianity all things were fresh, when
no corruption had yet entered the Church, and the Christian faith was still
limited to a few doctrines, the very thing that was not also preserved
during subsequent times, during which the pure apostolic Tradition was
altered and the doctrines were multiplied. But when responding to Protes-
tants who maintain such things, immediately from the beginning let us ask
them: what are these new doctrines that they say were created after the
fourth century? By any chance do they view as a creation of new doctrines
the explanation and formulation of the content of divine revelation in rela-
tion to the theological questions that arose on occasion? }[This is] another }30

way, then, that they much deceive themselves, confusing the essential with the secondary and what is constant and always the same with the accidental and mutable as the occasion arises. However, not at all confusing explanation with creation, we maintain that the Church, which preaches to all nations in all centuries the gospel of salvation, when preserving the essence and spirit of the apostolic teaching, is able to set forth Christian truths and adapt correspondingly to the needs of various epochs. And this is very natural and logical because what ought the Church to have done when on this side Nestorius and Dioscorus arose, confusing the unconfused and separating the inseparable, and on the other side the faithful who, terrified in the face of this vile teaching of the heretics, were shaken in their faith and driven into confusion? Should the Church have permitted these heretics to sow freely the tares of their soul-destroying teaching, or, rooting out the tares, ought it immediately to define more rigorously and formulate more clearly Christian teaching? The Church did the second. But when doing this, did it prescribe something new or contrary to the sacred Tradition of the first four centuries? When defining, for example, the consubstantiality of the Son and His God-manhood (τὸ θεάνθρωπον), were whole new doctrines introduced?[14] God forbid! But let us also now come to the second part of the objection, i.e., that the true apostolic Tradition was altered during the fourth century and corrupted. But let us leave aside on the one hand the Fathers' ardent zeal in support of apostolic Traditions, and on the other hand the faithful's great devotion to them. Let us only ask our opponents this: how was it possible for the "apostolic Tradition known to the entire world" (Irenaeus) to be changed and corrupted generally in every local Church, many of which the Apostles established and sealed by their blood? Was not even one Church among these able to remain faithful to the apostolic teaching? But then one must admit either of the two as true by necessity: either that the true Church of Christ failed for many centuries, as the Protestant reformers maintain, though this very thing is completely absurd and contrary to the divine promises of the Savior (Mt. 28:20; Jn. 16:13); or that the Church of Christ never failed, and then the Protestants who assert that they returned to the authentic apostolic teaching are telling lies }(compare "Concerning }31
Tradition" in Εὐγένιος Βούλγαρης, *Θεολογικόν*; "Concerning Tradition in the teachings of the Fathers" in K. Κοντογόνης, *Πατρολογίαν*; and "Tradition" in Nicolas Bergier, *Dictionnaire de théologie*; and others).

3.

Even if what was said up to now demonstrates not only the great worth of sacred Tradition, but also its equal honor and equal force to holy Scripture, nevertheless it remains for us now that we show also both the fact that sacred Tradition is so necessary, and consequently its worth is so great, that without it the holy Scripture alone is unable to express the full and true spirit of Christianity. In other words, the undeniable authority of sacred Tradition demonstrates at length its absolute necessity first for the correct solution of various questions that relate to the authenticity and inspiration of the sacred books of Scripture, second for the true interpretation and comprehension of holy Scripture, and third for the knowledge of certain truths not contained in the Scripture but necessary to faith and Christian life.

And first, the impartial history of the Church from the apostolic times themselves until the present witnesses to the absolute necessity of sacred Tradition for the accurate separation of authentic and inspired books of holy Scripture from pseudepigraphal and apocryphal ones. Already the scholar Origen, as Eusebius relates (*Church History* 6.25), when speaking concerning the sacred books of the New Testament, states, "as having learned by Tradition concerning the four Gospels, which alone are incontrovertible in the Church of God under heaven." But also Eusebius himself says that he distinguished the canonical sacred books from [among] the received [books] by using as a canon ancient Tradition (*Church History* 3.25). Nevertheless, the adversaries of sacred Tradition think that this question of the authenticity and inspiration of sacred books is solved—according to some—if we take common sense as a guide, and according to others [if we take] holy Scripture itself. But either is mistaken dreadfully because if for an instant we accept common sense alone as a guide, then we would never have full certainty either concerning the authenticity or concerning the inspiration of the sacred books of Scripture. Because when the point in question is their authenticity, }since the ancient lists }32
of sacred books are, as it is known, very rich, this is why reason relied upon alone in these cases cannot decide with unquestionable certainty that these books are genuine and those are apocryphal. When the point in question is their inspiration, likewise reason can establish nothing except at most the excellence of scriptural teaching, but even this again only with probability. Add also the point that human reason left to itself leads

to many absurdities because then each man, when examining at will the sacred books of Scripture, can accept as authentic and inspired those that agree with his point of view, and reject as apocryphal the ones opposed. History affords this perfect example for us: the head of the Protestant heresy himself, Luther, who dared to reject many books of holy Scripture as apparently apocryphal. Thus the rash man discarded six books from the New Testament alone, namely, the Epistle of James, the Second Epistle of Peter, the Second and Third Epistles of John, the Epistle of Paul to the Hebrews, and the Revelation of John! (see Moehler, *Symbolique*, vol. 2, chap. 5, § 41). What do we think about the rationalists, who have only common sense as a guide when leaving unassailable not one book of holy Scripture? (see A. Δ. Κυριακός, *Δοκίμιον Ἐκκλ. ἱστ.*, 402). But if, second, we accept Scripture itself as a guide for knowledge of both the authenticity and inspiration of the sacred books, again we do not attain what is being sought because on the one hand we find no evidence in holy Scripture concerning the canon and the authenticity of the books that constitute it, and on the other hand, concerning inspiration there exist certain texts such as these: 2 Timothy 3:16 and 2 Peter 1:20, but these relate either only to the Old Testament, to certain books from it, or even to only certain passages. But granted even that there exist certain ones that relate to the entire Scripture, these still contain no certain and undeniable proof as evidence of Scripture concerning itself. Moreover, how many doubts are raised when Scripture is referring to itself? Thus the inexactitude of many manuscripts, the obscurity of ancient languages, the variety of translations, the change of habits and customs, the grammatical details, and many other things only give us suspicions and doubts concerning the authenticity and inspiration of holy Scripture, whereas if we take as a guide the authentic apostolic }Tradition, all these difficulties are easily }33
resolved. Therefore many of the Protestants who understood these absurdities, to which the two aforementioned principles lead, were compelled to admit that the question of both the authenticity and inspiration of the sacred books cannot otherwise be resolved except through the witness of the ancient Fathers of the Church, because, they say, those Fathers always compared the different copies of the holy Scripture with the manuscripts publicly read in the Church and so judged concerning their authenticity or not. But because those Fathers are trustworthy when the point in question is the authenticity and inspiration of the sacred books of Scripture,

why, let us ask, are they not trustworthy when the point in question is sacred Traditions, which themselves also were preached and celebrated in public? How, we say, can the holy Fathers of the Church be of use to us as trustworthy witnesses when the point in question is the written word of God, but when the point in question concerns the unwritten word of God they are not trustworthy? This is irrational and completely absurd.

Second, the absolute need of sacred Tradition for the unerring interpretation and comprehension of holy Scripture: (1) Sacred history shows [this] clearly when teaching that not only the Lord "interpreted for his disciples in all the Scriptures the things concerning himself" (Lk. 24:27), but also the Apostles themselves often interpreted for the faithful the books of the Old Testament (Acts 2:25ff.; 8:30–35), commanding them to adhere to holy Scripture as much as also to sacred Traditions (2 Thes. 2:15), because of which also the Church of Christ, from these apostolic times until the present holding fast to the sacred Traditions, declares with a loud voice that "Tradition is necessary for direction in the correct comprehension of holy Scripture, in the correct accomplishment of the mysteries and preservation of the sacred services in the purity of their first arrangement" ("Concerning sacred Tradition and holy Scripture," *Ἐκτεταμ. Χρ. Κατηχ. τῆς ὀρθ. Ἐκκλ.*). (2) Scripture itself also shows the absolute need of sacred Tradition for correct interpretation of holy Scripture. Many mysterious things incomprehensible to the human mind exist in it, such as the supernatural mysteries of the Holy Trinity, of the divine Incarnation, and so forth; [and] also many things incomprehensible and difficult to understand, as also the Apostle Peter himself found when reading the epistles of
the Apostle }Paul (2 Pt. 3:16); and finally other things that have been set }34
forth very succinctly, either being mentioned only in the form of allusions or being contained in other truths that can be inferred only by syllogisms, such as points regarding the virginity of the Theotokos, the invocation of the saints and angels, the state of souls after death, infant baptism, and many other matters. How can we correctly understand and explain in an Orthodox manner all these remaining matters if we do not call upon sacred Tradition that has divine authority for our assistance? For this reason, very rightly the sacred Epiphanius expressed himself, saying, "One must have tradition, for not everything can be received from the divine Scripture, for which cause the holy Apostles handed over things in writing and in tradition" (*Against Heresies* 61:6). And nevertheless, [among] our

opponents, instead of this guide that has been given by God in the interpretation of holy Scripture, some just desire reason only as a guide, others holy Scripture itself, and finally others some external divine illumination. But we say that each of these three guides, when so isolated without sacred Tradition, leads us to dangerous conclusions that threaten our salvation itself, because: (1) As regards human reason, we do not deny that it can and ought to have a part in interpretation of holy Scripture, but on the condition that it is always subject to divine reason, and when it proves not only useful to us, but also frequently indispensable. However, we do not accept it as the sole guide, first because human reason—because it is so subject to many changes, so that often all it thinks true today, the following day it views this as false—on account of this, when taken as a guide in the interpretation of the holy Scriptures, leads to many interpretations that contradict one another; and second, also because finite human reason can only interpret with certainty the truths accessible by it in Scripture, whereas it will either interpret the supernatural and mysterious truths at pleasure or reject [them] as incomprehensible. The Socinians, who issue from the bosom of Protestantism, indeed appeal to reason—[they] who, having common sense as a sole guide, called into dispute the truth of any doctrine inaccessible to reason, because of which finally they rejected the miracles as impossible and the mysteries as incomprehensible! Next came }the Quakers, who declared that, reason being sufficient for us, we }35
do not have a need for divine revelation! (see Α. Δ. Κυριακός, *Δοκίμιον Ἐκκλ. ἱστ.*, 395 and 396–97). (2) As regards those who say that one must interpret the Scripture by Scripture, we respond to them that indeed interpreting unclear passages of Scripture by more clear ones is indeed even a most necessary canon of sacred interpretation, but it is not also the only guide in the interpretation of Scripture because Scripture as written certainly cannot prevent us from giving one such or another meaning to its various texts. But on the contrary, and history is witness [to this], we see that all, both orthodox and heterodox, assert that each finds their own teaching in it. Who, then, among so many that contradict one another when interpreting holy Scripture can declare with certainty that this or that interpretation is the correct one? As far as we are concerned, there is one Ariadne's thread that guides us safely in the labyrinth of these diverse interpretations of holy Scripture: sacred Tradition, which came from the beginning down to our times.[15] (3) Finally, as regards those who suggest

internal enlightenment as the only guide in the correct interpretation of holy Scripture, we affirm also these things: that although we do not deny that, just as in the practice of any good, so also in the interpretation of holy Scripture we have need of enlightenment from above (Jas. 1:17; 2 Jn. 2:27), and the sacred Chrysostom states, "For those who search there is need of radiance from above, that they might find what is being sought, and keep what is pursued" (*On Psalm 119*), still we do not accept that this internal enlightenment is sufficient and always a certain guide in the interpretation of holy Scripture because this internal illumination is mysterious and incomprehensible, [and so] any odd sort of person, when interpreting the Scripture according to his subjective ideas, can spread his own twaddle as divine words or even finally end in the complete dismissal of the holy Scriptures. History is witness, which presents us with the Swedenborgians, who assert that they receive divine illumination and internal revelations. They concluded that because the Holy Spirit immediately enlightens us, we do not have a need for Scripture! (see Α. Δ. Κυριακός, *Δοκίμιον Ἐκκλ. ἱστ.*, 398). But even after all these absurd matters, the Protestants, like shortsighted ones under the fog of their own heresy and unable }to see the bright shining light of the truth, resist by producing the }36
text of the Apostle Paul, who says, "But to each is given the manifestation of the Spirit for benefit" (1 Cor. 12:7), but what a distortion and misinterpretation of scriptural passages! Because in this passage Paul speaks concerning the various gifts of the Holy Spirit, which being both many and varied, all things are not also provided to all, but "to one is given a word of wisdom through the Spirit, and to another a word of knowledge by the same Spirit, and to another faith," and so forth (ibid., 12:8–11). And so also the Spirit does not bestow the gift of comprehension and interpretation of holy Scripture to all, but to those He wishes. He wished to bestow this to the God-bearing Fathers, from whom by Tradition from on high we receive the true mind of the holy Fathers.

Finally, third, [Tradition's] absolute necessity for knowledge of certain truths, which are not contained in holy Scripture but are essential to the faith and the Christian life, demonstrates the great worth of sacred Tradition. Such truths are both historical and teleturgical [and] concern fasting, feasts, the construction of temples, the use of sacred vestments, and certain other subjects, all of which form particular lessons of theology, i.e., liturgy, church archaeology, and canon law, due to which their great

significance in our Church is also demonstrated. But the Protestants who have as a maxim “Anything not mentioned in Scripture is a human regulation” reject the aforesaid truths as alleged mere contrivances of the sacred Fathers, but what ingratitude of these Protestants toward our holy Fathers! While on the one hand they [the Protestants] condemn them [the Fathers] as introducers of new doctrines and teachings, on the other hand they [the Fathers] interpret the Scripture, enlightening their [the Protestants’] eyes, which are shortsighted from the fog of heresy, by the light of their [the Fathers’] divine writings. But the foolishness of the Protestants advances even further, unfortunately. While on the one hand they violate the sacred Traditions of the Apostles as alleged human regulations, on the other hand they place themselves truly under the yoke of human regulations, which they follow with blind eyes as divine commandments! Because each Protestant, whether he is a Lutheran, Calvinist, or a follower of another Protestant heresy, when taking in hand the holy Scripture, finds in it exactly that very teaching that from childhood he heard from his parents and was
taught by his teachers; and [he finds] the heresy }in which he was born }37
and brought up, [and by which he] was saturated. Hence each Protestant heresy also has its own symbolic books, namely, its dogmatic traditions, which its leader created and formulated, and which he obligates each of their members to observe just as some deposit given by God, according to which also he ought to interpret holy Scripture and regulate his life! What, then, did the Protestants do when contending that they reformed the Church? While trampling on the sacred Traditions of the Apostles, they followed after traditions of men, such as the Lutherans, the Zwinglians, and others—of men who, according to the evidence of major historians (Fleury, *Hist. Eccles.* [Paris, 1724], vol. 25, p. 476), not out of pious zeal but on account of their own passions proclaimed themselves apostles of the reformed Churches! But on what authority did they attempt the reform of the Church? The divine teaching demands a divine mission: “How can they preach unless they are sent?” (Rom. 1:15).[16] What, then, are the distinctive marks of their divine mission? Disobedience toward the shepherds and teachers appointed in the Church by Christ Himself through His Apostles (Heb. 13:7; Lk. 10:16); contempt for the Church established on earth by Christ Himself through His Apostles (Mt. 18:17); violation of the unwritten word of God, namely, of sacred Tradition (2 Thes. 2:15); and other worse feats—behold the true distinctive marks, or rather, odious

stigmas, of these false apostles! Hence the Protestants, when having called upon only Scripture, or rather, its letter, shout out in their conceit and say, "Where does Scripture enjoin the sealing of oneself by the sign of the Cross, praying toward the East, blessing the water of baptism and the oil of chrism, and the remaining church regulations and rites in general?" But let it be permitted for us that also we shall ask these self-conceited ones who, "claiming to be wise, became foolish" (Rom. 1:22): "Where does Scripture prohibit the sign of the Cross, prayer toward the East, the blessing of both the water of baptism and the oil of chrism, and all the remaining traditions observed in the Church in general?" But, oh, false teachers and "those who are experts in their own estimation" (Is. 5:21),
}tell us: "How, while on the one hand do you reject the sacred Traditions }38
for the reason that they do not exist in Scripture, on the other hand you accept and observe others although [they are] not contained in Scripture, such as the observance of Sunday, the feast of Pascha, infant baptism, and other such matters?" (compare in general Μακάκιος, *Εἰσαγωγὴ εἰς τὴν ὀρθοδόξον θεολογίαν*, pt. 2, "Concerning Tradition"; "Concerning Tradition" in Εὐγένιος Βούλγαρης, *Θεολογικόν*; and "Tradition" in Nicolas Bergier, *Dictionnaire de théologie*; and others).

But lest we still speak further at length with these quarreling men, who "wandered away into vain discussion, wishing to be teachers of the law without understanding either what they say or what they assert" (1 Tim. 1:7),[17] we complete this, our theological thesis, with the most true and at the same time most clear witness of our holy Church concerning the true meaning of sacred Tradition and its great and undeniable worth: "Every foul heresy accepts the divine Scripture, but, when using metaphors, ambiguities, and sophistries of human wisdom, misinterprets it, confusing the unconfused, and trifling with what ought not to be trifled with. For if it were otherwise, [with] each man holding a different opinion concerning it on a daily basis, the Catholic Church would not be presently by grace of Christ a Church, which holds one opinion concerning faith, which always believes both in the same way and identically, but would be divided into innumerable parts and subject to heresies; and neither [would it] be the holy Church, pillar and mainstay of the truth, both without defect or wrinkle, but would be the Church of those who act wickedly, which that of the heretics has become, as it appears, without doubt—[the heretics] who are not ashamed to learn from the Church and then to repudiate it wickedly.

Consequently, we also believe the witness of the Catholic Church to be no less than that which the divine Scripture holds, for one and the same Holy Spirit being the author of both, it is completely equal to be taught by the Scripture and by the Catholic Church. It is possible, then, for any man who therefore speaks of his own accord to sin, deceive, and be deceived, but it is entirely impossible for the Catholic Church—because, never having spoken or speaking of its own accord, but by the Spirit of God (who also enriches a teacher ceaselessly forever)—to sin or completely deceive or be deceived, but it is like the divine Scripture, having undiminished and eternal authority" }(see *Ἐπιστολὴν τῶν τεσσάρων Πατριαρχῶν τῆς* }39
Ἀνατολῆς, article 2).

End.

Written
in the Theological School
at Halki

On
May 1,
1886

Raphael M., hierodeacon
from Damascus

NOTES

1. Homer, *Odyssey* 9.51.
2. The citation should be Acts 1:3.
3. That is, the Apostles' Creed.
4. That is, the Athanasian Creed. The term in Latin should be *quicunque*.
5. The citation should be Acts 15:28.
6. The Lydian stone is a touchstone or standard for comparison.
7. The reference should be to 3.13.2.
8. The citation should be Jn. 15:26.
9. The reference should be to Mt. 26:27.
10. The citation should be 2 Jn. 1:12.
11. The citation should be 3 Jn. 1:13–14.
12. "We have the Apostles of the Lord as our authorities, who not even themselves chose to introduce anything on their own authority, but faithfully handed on to the nations the rule received from Christ" (Herbert Bindley, trans., *Tertullian on the Testimony of the Soul and on the Prescription of Heretics* [London: SPCK, 1914], 43).
13. PG 35:749C. For the entire work, see *Λόγος* 6, *Ειρηνικός* Α', *ἐπὶ τῇ ἑνώσει τῶν μοναζόντων, μετὰ τὴν σιωπὴν, ἐπὶ παρουσία τοῦ πατρὸς αὐτοῦ* (PG 35:722A–752C).
14. The use of the term *God-manhood* (τὸ θεάνθρωπον) refers to the two natures of Christ—human and divine—in hypostatic union.
15. Ariadne, a figure from classical mythology, gave wool thread to Theseus to navigate the labyrinth after killing the Minotaur.
16. The citation should be Rom. 10:15.
17. The citation should be 1 Tim. 1:6–7.

APPENDIX 1

Sources Used by St. Raphael

ANCIENT AUTHORS

Ambrose	*On the Sacrament of the Incarnation of the Lord*
Augustine	*On John*
Augustine	*On the Merits and Remission of Sins and on the Baptism of Infants*
Augustine	*On the Trinity*
Basil the Great	*Concerning the Holy Spirit*
Basil the Great	*On Isaiah*
Clement of Alexandria	*Stromata*
Cyprian	*Epistle 63*
Cyprian	*On the Lapsed*
Cyprian	*Testimonies against the Jews*
Cyril of Alexandria	*Encomium on Holy Mary the Theotokos*
Cyril of Jerusalem	*Catechetical Lectures*
Cyril of Jerusalem	*Mystagogic Catecheses*
Dionysius the Areopagite	*Ecclesiastical Hierarchy*
Eusebius	*Church History*
Gregory the Theologian	*First Invective against Julian*
Gregory the Theologian	*Oration 6*
Homer	*Odyssey*
Irenaeus	*Against Heresies*
Jerome	*Against Helvidius*
Jerome	*On Matthew*
John Chrysostom	*Concerning the Priesthood*
John Chrysostom	*Homily 4 on 2 Thes.*
John Chrysostom	*Homily on 2 Tim.*
John Chrysostom	*On Psalm 119*
Justin	*Apology*

Origen	*Against Celsus*
Origen	*On First Principles*
Sozomen	*Church History*
Sylvester Syropoulos	*History of the Council in Florence*
Tertullian	*On the Prescription of Heretics*
Vincent of Lérins	*Commonitorium pro Catholicae fidei antiquitate et universitate adversus profanas omnium haereticorum novitates*

MODERN AUTHORS

Ἀντώνιος, *Δογματικὴ θεολογία Εἰσαγωγή*	Ἀντώνιος, Ἀρχιμανδρίτης, *Δογματικὴ θεολογία τῆς 'Ορθοδόξου Καθολικῆς καὶ Ἀνατολικῆς Ἐκκλησίας*, trans. Θεόδωρος Βαλλιάνος (Athens: Τύποις Χ. Νικολαΐδου Φιλαδελφέως, 1858).
Γρηγόριος, *Ἡ φωνὴ τῆς Ὀρθοδοξίας*	Γρηγόριος, Μητροπολίτης Χίου τοῦ Βυζαντίου, *Ἡ φωνὴ τῆς Ὀρθοδοξίας* (Chios: Ἐκ τῆς Τυπογραφίας Κ. Μ. Προκίδου, 1863).
Δημήτριος Βερναρδάκης, *Ἱερα Κατήχησις*	Δημήτριος Βερναρδάκης, *Ἱερα Κατήχησις* (Constantinople: Ἐκ τοῦ Τυπογραφείου Ἀ. Κορομηλά, 1872).
Ἐκτεταμ. Χρ. Κατηχ. τῆς ὀρθ. Ἐκκλ.	Φιλάρετος, Μητροπολίτης Μόσχας, *Χριστιανικὴ κατ᾽ἔκτασιν κατήχησις τῆς ὀρθοδόξου, καθολικῆς καὶ ἀνατολικῆς ἐκκλησίας / ἐξετασθεῖσα μὲν καὶ ἐγκριθεῖσα ὑπὸ τῆς Ἁγιωτάτης Διοικούσης Συνόδου, καὶ ἐκδοθεῖσα Ρωσσιστὶ πρὸς δημόσιον ἐν τοῖς σχολείοις παράδοσιν, καὶ πρὸς χρῆσιν ἁπάντων τῶν ὀρθοδόξων Χριστιανῶν, Μεταφρασθεῖσα δὲ καὶ τύποις ἐκδοθεῖσα κατ' ἐπιταγὴν τῆς αὐτῆς Ἁγίας Διοικούσης Συνόδου* (Odessa: Ἐκ τῆς Τυπογραφίας τοῦ Α. Βράουν καὶ Συντρ., 1848).
Ἐπιστολὴν τῶν τεσσάρων Πατριαρχῶν τῆς Ἀνατολῆς	*Τὰ ἐν τῇ ἐν Ἱεροσολύμοις συνόδῳ πρακτικὰ μετὰ τῆς ὁμολογίας ταύτης ἀποτελοῦσιν ἕν τι ὅλον, ἔργον τοῦ αὐτοῦ συγγραφέως, τοῦ Δοσιθέου, Πατριάρχου Ἱεροσολύμων, κατὰ τὴν αὐτὴν ἐποχὴν συντεθὲν* (1672).
Εὐγένιος Βούλγαρης, *Θεολογικόν*	Εὐγένιος Βούλγαρης, *Θεολογικόν* (Venice: Τύποις τοῦ Χρόνου, 1872).

Εὐγένιος Βούλγαρης, *Κατὰ Λατίνων Στηλιτευτικὴ Ἐπιστολή*	Εὐγένιος Βούλγαρης, *Βιβλιάριον κατὰ Λατίνων ἔχον ὄνομα ἐγκύκλιος ἐπιστολή* (Constantinople: Χριστόφορος Ἀρτίνος, 1796).
Φ. Βαφείδης, *Ἐκκλησιαστικὴ Ἱστορία*	Φιλάρετος Βαφείδης, *Ἐκκλησιαστικὴ Ἱστορία ἀπὸ τοῦ Κυρίου ἡμῶν Ἰησοῦ Χριστοῦ μέχρι τῶν καθ' ἡμᾶς χρόνων*, 2 vols. (Constantinople: Τύποις Σ. Ι. Βουτυρά, 1884–86).
Fleury, *Hist. Eccles.*	Claude Fleury, *Histoire ecclésiastique*, 36 vols. (Paris: Pierre Emery, Saugrain l'aîne, and Pierre Martin, 1719–68).
Klee, *Dogmatik*	Heinrich Klee, *Katholische Dogmatik*, 3rd ed. (Mainz: Kirkheim, Schott und Thielmann, 1844).
Klee, *Lehrbuch Dogmengeschichte*	Heinrich Klee, *Lehrbuch der Dogmengeschichte*, 2 vols. (Mainz: Kirkheim, Schott und Thielmann, 1836–37).
Κ. Κοντογόνης, *Πατρολογίαν*	Κωνσταντίνος Κοντογόνης, *Φιλολογικὴ καὶ κριτικὴ ἱστορία τῶν ἀπὸ τῆς Α' μέχρι τῆς Η' ἑκατονταετηρίδος ἀκμασάντων ἁγίων τῆς Ἐκκλησίας Πατέρων, καὶ τῶν συγγραμμάτων αὐτῶν*, 2 vols. (Athens: Σ. Κ. Βλαστοῦ, 1851–53).
Κυριακός, *Δοκίμιον ἐκκλησιαστικῆς ἱστορίας*	Αναστάσιος Διομήδης-Κυριακός, *Δοκίμιον ἐκκλησιαστικῆς ἱστορίας : χάριν τῶν περὶ τὴν θεολογίαν σπουδαζόντων* (Athens, 1878).
Μακάκιος, *Εἰσαγωγὴ εἰς τὴν ὀρθοδόξον θεολογίαν*	Μακάκιος Μόσχας, *Εἰσαγωγὴ εἰς τὴν ὀρθοδόξον θεολογίαν*, trans. Νικόλαος Σπ. Παπαδόπουλος, 2 vols. (Leipzig: Geisekke and Dervient, 1858–61).
Moehler, *La Symbolique*	Johann Adam Möhler, *La symbolique, ou, Exposition des contrariétés dogmatiques entre les catholiques et les protestants d'après leurs confessions de foi publiques*, trans. F. Lachat, 2 vols. (Brussels: La société nationale pour la propagation des bons livres, 1838).
Nicolas Bergier, *Dictionnaire de théologie*	Nicolas-Sylvestre Bergier and Pierrot, abbé, *Dictionnaire de théologie dogmatique, liturgique, canonique, et disciplinaire*, 4 vols. in 2 (Paris: J.-P. Migne, 1850).
Πηδάλιον	Νικόδημος ὁ Ἁγιορείτης, *Πηδάλιον*, 2nd ed. (Athens, 1841).

APPENDIX 2

Transcription of the Handwritten Greek Text

Θέσις Θεολογικὴ
περὶ τῆς
Ἱερᾶς Παραδόσεως καὶ τοῦ ἀναντιρρήτου αὐτῆς κύρους

ὑπὸ Ῥαφαὴλ Μ. Ἀουαΐνου Ἱεροδιακόνου
Ἐν τῇ κατὰ Χάλκης Θεολογικῇ Σχολῇ

Τῇ 1ῃ Μαΐου 1886

“᾿Αδελφοί, στήκετε καὶ κρατεῖτε τὰς παραδόσεις, ἃς ἐδιδάχθητε εἴτε διὰ λόγου εἴτε δι᾿ἐπιστολῆς ἡμῶν” (Β.΄ Θεσ. β΄. 15).

“Τῶν ἐν τῇ Ἐκκλησίᾳ πεφυλαγμένων δογμάτων καὶ κηρυγμάτων, τὰ μὲν ἐκ τῆς εγγράφου διδασκαλίας ἔχομεν, τὰ δὲ ἐκ τῆς τῶν Ἀποστόλων παραδόσεως διασωθέντα ἡμῖν ἐν μυστηρίῳ παρεδεξάμεθα, ἅπερ ἀμφότερα τὴν αὐτὴν ἰσχὺν ἔχει πρὸς τὴν εὐσέβειαν” (Βασιλ. τὸν Μεγ. *πρὸς Ἀμφιλόχιον περὶ Ἁγίου Πνεύμ.* κεφ. κζ΄).

Ἡ ἀληθὴς τῆς ἱερᾶς Παραδόσεως ἔννοια καὶ τὸ μέγα αὐτῆς ἀξίωμα.[1]

"Ἀδελφοί, στήκετε καὶ κρατεῖτε τὰς παραδόσεις, ἃς ἐδιδάχθητε εἴτε διὰ λόγου εἴτε δι᾽ἐπιστολῆς ἡμῶν" (Β.΄ Θεσ. β΄. 15)

Ὁ ΚΎΡΙΟΣ ἩΜΩΝ ἸΗΣΟΥΣ ΧΡΙΣΤῸΣ ἀποκαλύψας τοῖς ἱεροῖς Αὐτοῦ μαθηταῖς τὰς ἀληθείας τοῦ θείου Εὐαγγελίου ἐξαπέστελεν αὐτοὺς εἰς τὸ κήρυγμα λέγων "Πορευθέντες οὖν μαθητεύσατε πάντα τὰ ἔθνη . . . διδάσκοντες αὐτοὺς τηρεῖν πάντα, ὅσα ἐνετειλάμην ὑμῖν" (Ματθ. κη΄. 19–20)˙ οἱ δὲ Ἀπόστολοι τῷ θείῳ τούτῳ ῥήματι ἑπόμενοι διεσπάρησαν καθ᾽ἅπασαν τὴν οἰκουμένην εὐαγγελιζόμενοι πᾶσι τὸν λόγον τῆς ἀληθείας (Πραξ. η΄. 4)˙ καὶ κατ᾽ἀρχὰς μὲν ἐκήρυττον τὸν θεῖον λόγον, ὡς ἦν ἑπόμενον, διὰ ζώσης φωνῆς˙ ἔπειτα ὅμως τινὲς τῶν Ἀποστόλων ὑπὸ διαφόρων κινούμενοι λόγων, πάντως ὑπὸ τῆς θείας Προνοίας προκληθέντων, πρὸς τῇ ζώσῃ φωνῇ μετεχειρίσθησαν καὶ τὴν γραφήν˙ οὕτω λοιπὸν ὥσπερ ἄλλοτε οἱ Προφῆται, οἱ κήρυκες τῆς Π.Δ., οὕτω καὶ οἱ Ἀπόστολοι, οἱ κήρυκες τῆς Κ.Δ., πρὸς τὴν τῶν θείων ἀληθειῶν μετάδοσιν μετεχειρίσθησαν ἀμφότερα τὰ μέσα, δι᾽ὧν συνήθως παρὰ τοῖς ἀνθρώποις μεταδίδονται αἱ ἰδέαι, ἤτοι τὸν τε προφορικὸν καὶ τὸν γραπτὸν λόγον˙ τουθ᾽ὅπερ καὶ ὁ θεῖος δηλοῖ Παῦλος λέγων, "Ἀδελφοί, στήκετε καὶ κρατεῖτε τὰς παραδόσεις, ἃς ἐδιδάχθητε εἴτε διὰ λόγου, εἴτε δι᾽ἐπιστολῆς ἡμῶν" (Β΄. Θεσ. β΄. 15)˙ Ἐκ τῶν δύο δὲ τούτων τῆς τῶν θείων ἀληθειῶν μεταδόσεως τρόπων ὁ μὲν διὰ λόγου, τ.ἔ. ζώσης φωνῆς,

ἀποτελεῖ τὴν ἱερὰν Παράδοσιν, ὁ δὲ δι᾽ἐπιστολῆς, τ.ἔ. γραφῆς, ἀποτελεῖ τὴν ἁγίαν Γραφήν, ἐν αἷς ἀμφοτέραις περιέχονται ἅπασαι αἱ χριστιανικαὶ ἀλήθειαι, τ. ἔ. ἡ θεία Ἀποκάλυψις. Ἀλλὰ καθὼς ὁ γραπτὸς λόγος οὐδὲν ἄλλο εἶνε εἰμὴ ἡ συντομωτέρα ἅμα καὶ συντονωτέρα παράστασις τοῦ προφορικοῦ λόγου, οὕτω καὶ ἡ ἁγία Γραφὴ δύναται νὰ θεωρηθῇ ὡς ἡ σύντομος ἅμα καὶ σύντονος ἔκφρασις τῆς ἱερᾶς Παραδόσεως˙ ἐντεῦθεν ἡ ἱερὰ Παράδοσις καὶ ἡ ἁγία Γραφὴ τοσοῦτον στενῶς συνδέονται πρὸς ἀλλήλας, ὥστε ἑκατέρα κατ᾽ἀνάγκην ἀπαιτεῖ τὴν }ἑτέραν, ἡ δ᾽ἔλλειψις }2
τῆς μιᾶς εἰς αὐτὰ τὰ καίρια ζημιοῖ τὴν ἄλλην˙ οὕτω παρορωμένης τῆς ἁγίας Γραφῆς ἡ ἱερὰ Παράδοσις διατρέχει τὸν κίνδυνον τῆς διαστροφῆς διότι τότε εὐκόλως δύναται ν᾽ἀναμιχθῇ τὸ ἀνθρώπινον μετὰ τοῦ θείου, τὸ βέβηλον μετὰ τοῦ ἁγίου καὶ τὸ ἀληθὲς μετὰ τοῦ ψευδοῦς˙ τοὐναντίον δέ, τῆς ἱερᾶς Παραδόσεως αἰρομένης ἡ ἁγία Γραφὴ ὑπόκειται εἰς πλείστας ὅσας παρερμηνείας˙ διότι τότε ἀφιεμένης τῆς Γραφῆς εἰς τὴν ἐλευθέραν ἑνὸς ἑκάστου ἀντίληψιν καὶ ἑρμηνείαν δύναται ἐντεῦθεν νὰ προέλθῃ τερατώδης τις ποικιλία ἐν τῇ μιᾷ καὶ τῇ αὐτῇ Χριστιανικῇ διδασκαλίᾳ˙ ἐν τούτοις καὶ μεθ᾽ ὅλας τὰς ἀτόπους ταύτας συνεπείας τὰς ἐκ τῆς μονομεροῦς ἀποδοχῆς τῆς ἱερᾶς Παραδόσεως ἢ τῆς ἁγίας Γραφῆς προσερχομένας δὲν ἔλειψαν δυστυχῶς ἀπ᾽αὐτῶν ἤδη τῶν πρώτων τοῦ Χριστιανισμοῦ αἰώνων ν᾽ἀναφαίνονται ἐν τῇ Ἐκκλησίᾳ ἄνδρες τὴν μίαν ἢ τὴν ἄλλην μονομέρειαν ἀκολουθοῦντες, οἷοι οἱ τῆς πολυκεφάλου Γνωστικῆς αἱρέσεως ὀπαδοὶ καὶ οἱ λοιποὶ αἱρετικοί˙ ἀλλ᾽ ἵνα παραλίπωμεν τοὺς ἐν ἀρχαιοτέροις χρόνοις ἀναφανέντας τοιούτους αἱρετικούς, ὧν τὰ μόλις σωζόμενα σήμερον λείψανα ἢ καὶ μόνα ὀνόματα πρόκεινται ἡμῖν λαμπρότητα τῶν ψευδῶν αὐτῶν διδασκαλῶν μαρτύρια, φέρε νῦν θεωρήσωμεν τοὺς νεωτέρους ἅμα καὶ σπουδαιοτέρους τῶν ῥηθεισῶν δύο μονομερειῶν ἀντιπροσώπους, τοὺς Παπιστὰς λέγω καὶ τοὺς Διαμαρτυρομένους. Ἐνῷ ὁ ὀρθόδοξος Χριστιανὸς ἐλευθέρως τὰς Γραφὰς ἐρευνῶν καθυποτάσσει τὴν ἐπισφαλῆ ἀτομικὴν αὐτοῦ κρίσιν εἰς τὴν ἀσφαλῆ τῆς Οἰκουμενικῆς Ἐκκλησίας γνώμην "αἰχμαλωτίζων," κατὰ τὸν θεῖον Παῦλον, "πᾶν νόημα εἰς τὴν ὑπακοὴν τοῦ Χριστοῦ" (Β΄. Κορ ι᾽. 5), τοὐναντίον ὁ μὲν Παπιστὴς ἀπειργόμενος τῆς ἐλευθέρας τῶν Γραφῶν ἐρεύνης τυφλῶς ἀκολουθεῖ τὰς ἐν πολλοῖς μυθώδεις Παπικὰς παραδόσεις ἐπαναπαύων οὕτω τὴν συνείδησιν αὐτοῦ ἐπὶ τῶν δῆθεν ἀλαθήτων ἀποφάσεων τοῦ Ῥωμαίου Ποντίφικος ὡς τοῦ ὑπάτου τῆς ἁγίας Γραφῆς ἑρμηνέας, ὁ δὲ Διαμαρτυρόμενος μόνον ἐπὶ τῆς ἀτομικῆς αὐτοῦ συνειδήσεως στηριζόμενος ὅλως αὐθαιρέτως ἐρευνᾷ τὰς Γραφάς. Ὁ μὲν

λοιπὸν Παπισμὸς συγκεντρῶν οὕτως ἅπασαν τὴν Ἐκκλησιαστικὴν ζωὴν ἐν ἑνὶ καὶ μόνῳ προσώπῳ, τῷ Πάπᾳ, ἵδρυσεν ἐν Ῥώμῃ θρησκευτικόν, οὕτως εἰπεῖν, χρηστήριον, ἐν τῷ ὁποίῳ αἱ Ἀποστολικαὶ Παραδόσεις πολυειδῶς διαστρεφόμεναι καὶ ἀνθρωπίνοις ὕθλοις συμφυρόμεναι παρίστανται ὡς ἀναντίλεκτα θείας καταγωγῆς ἐντάλματα! ἡ δὲ Διαμαρτύρησις σὺν ταῖς Παπικαῖς ταύταις τερθρείαις καὶ τὰς ἱερὰς ἀπορρίψασα Παραδόσεις ἐστερήθη σταθερᾶς τινος ἐν τῇ ἑρμηνείᾳ τῆς ἁγίας Γραφῆς βάσεως καὶ οὕτω μονομερῶς τὴν Γραφὴν ἀκολουθήσασα κατεμέλισε τὴν μίαν Ἐκκλησίαν εἰς τοσαύτας,

Ὅσα τε φύλλα καὶ ἄνθεα γίγνεται ὥρῃ!

}Ἐπειδὴ λοιπὸν ὁ μὲν Παπισμὸς ἐκ πνεύματος ἀπολυτισμοῦ καὶ }3
συγκεντρώσεως ὠθούμενος ἀναμιγνύει πρὸς ἐπίτευξιν τοῦ σκοποῦ αὐτοῦ τούτου τὸ ἀνθρώπινον μετὰ τοῦ θείου καὶ οὕτω διαστρέφει καὶ νοθεύει τὰς ἱερὰς Παραδόσεις, ἡ δὲ Διαμαρτύρησις ἐκ τάσεως πρὸς καταπολέμησιν τῶν ὑπερφιάλων τούτων τοῦ Παπισμοῦ ἀξιώσεων οἰστρηλατουμένη ἐξωλίσθησεν εἰς τὴν ἀντίθετον ὑπερβολὴν τῆς ἀνυποταξίας καὶ ἀποκεντρώσεως ἀπορρίψασα ὅλως τὰς ἱερὰς Παραδόσεις ὡς ἀνθρώπινα ἐντάλματα, διὰ τοῦτο φέρ᾽ εἴπωμεν βραχέα τινὰ περὶ τῆς ἱερᾶς παραδόσεως καταδεικνύοντες ἀφ᾽ ἑνὸς μὲν τὴν ἀληθῆ αὐτῆς ἔννοιαν ἀπέναντι τῶν διαστρεβλούντων αὐτὴν Παπιστῶν, ἀφ᾽ ἑτέρου δὲ τὸ μέγα αὐτῆς ἀξίωμα ἀπέναντι τῶν ἀπορριπτόντων αὐτὴν Προτεσταντῶν.

Α΄.

Ἔσται καιρὸς ὅτε τῆς ὑγιαινούσης διδασκαλίας οὐκ ἀνέξονται, ἀλλὰ κατὰ τὰς ἐπιθυμίας τὰς ἰδίας ἑαυτοῖς ἐπισωρεύσουσι διδασκάλους κνηθόμενοι τὴν ἀκοήν, καὶ ἀπὸ μὲν τῆς ἀληθείας τὴν ἀκοὴν ἀποστρέψουσιν, ἐπὶ δὲ τοὺς μύθους ἐκτραπήσονται. (Β΄. Τιμοθ. δ΄. 3–4).

Καθὼς πᾶσα ἐπιστήμη ἔχει ἀναντιρρήτους ἀρχάς, ἐφ᾽ ὧν στηρίζεται, καὶ ὡρισμένας πηγάς, ἐξ ὧν τὰς ἀληθείας αὐτῆς ἀρύεται, οὕτω καὶ ἡ Θεολογία, ἡ ἐπιστήμη αὕτη τῶν ἐπιστημῶν, ἔχει ὡς ἀναντίλεκτον ἀρχήν, ἐφ᾽ ἧς ἑδράζεται, καὶ καθαρωτάτην πηγήν, ἐξ ἧς τὰς θείας αὐτῆς ἀληθείας ἀπαρνέται, τὴν θείαν Ἀποκάλυψιν, ἤτοι τὸν λόγον τοῦ θεοῦ·

ἀλλ᾽ὁ λόγος οὗτος τοῦ θεοῦ ἀπεκαλύφθη ἡμῖν, ὡς εἴδομεν, κατὰ δύο τρόπους, προφορικῶς καὶ γραπτῶς, τ.ἔ. διὰ τῆς ἱερᾶς Παραδόσεως καὶ τῆς ἁγίας Γραφῆς, ὧν ἀμφοτέρων φύλαξ πιστὸς καὶ ἑρμηνευτὴς ἀλάθητος ἐτάχθη ὑπ᾽αὐτοῦ τοῦ θεοῦ ἡ ἁγία τοῦ Χριστοῦ Ὀρθόδοξος Ἐκκλησία˙ ἄλλως εἰπεῖν ἡ ἱερὰ Παράδοσις καὶ ἡ ἁγία Γραφὴ ὁμοῦ λαμβανόμεναι καὶ ὑπὸ τῆς ἀλαθήτου φωνῆς τῆς Οἰκουμενικῆς Ὀρθοδόξου Ἐκκλησίας ἑρμηνευόμεναι ἀποτελοῦσι μίαν καὶ τὴν αὐτὴν τῆς ὀρθοδόξου Χριστιανικῆς θεολογίας πηγήν. Τούτων οὕτως ἐχόντων ἕπεται ὅτι πᾶς Χριστιανὸς ὀφείλη καθάπερ τὴν ἁγίαν Γραφήν, οὕτω καὶ τὴν ἱερὰν Παράδοσιν νὰ φυλάττῃ καὶ ἑρμηνεύῃ ἀπαραλλάκτως ὥσπερ ἐννοεῖ αὐτὴν καὶ διακατέχει ἡ ὀρθόδοξος Οἰκουμενικὴ Ἐκκλησία˙ ταῦτα ὅμως λέγοντες οὐδόλως ἐννοοῦμεν ὅτι ἡ Ἐκκλησία δύναται τὴν παραδοθεῖσαν αὐτῇ προφορικὴν διδασκαλίαν κατὰ τὸ δοκοῦν ἑρμηνεύουσα νὰ προσθέσῃ τι εἰς αὐτὴν ἢ ν᾽ ἀφαιρέσῃ, ὡς κακοβούλως τοῦτο πράττει ἡ Παπικὴ Ἐκκλησία πρὸς ὑποστήριξιν τῶν διαφόρων αὐτῆς καινοτομιῶν, ἀλλ᾽ἀπεναντίας ὀφείλει καθαρὰν καὶ ἀλώβητον τὴν ἱερὰν φυλάττουσα Παράδοσιν νὰ μεταδιδῷ αὐτὴν τοῖς πιστοῖς ἀπαραμείωτον καὶ ἀνόθευτον, ὡς ἀληθῶς πράττει τοῦτο ἡ Ὀρθόδοξος Ἐκκλησία. Ὅθεν }ἵνα ἔχωμεν }4
ὅσον ἔνεστι σαφῆ, εὐκρινῆ καὶ ἀκριβῆ τῆς ἀληθοῦς ἱερᾶς Παραδόσεως ἔννοιαν, καθάπερ θεωρεῖ αὐτὴν καὶ φυλάττει ἡ ἀληθὴς τοῦ Χριστοῦ ὀρθόδοξος Ἐκκλησία, ὀφείλομεν ἵνα καταμάθωμεν α΄.) Τὸ ἀληθὲς τῆς ἱερᾶς Παραδόσεως περιεχόμενον, β᾽.) Τὰς ἀληθεῖς αὐτῆς πηγάς, γ᾽.) Τὰ ἀληθῆ αὐτῆς χαρακτηριστικὰ γνωρίσματα, καὶ δ᾽.) Τὸ ἀληθὲς αὐτῆς ταμεῖον καὶ ἀσφαλὲς φυλακτήριον.

α΄.

Ἡ λέξις παράδοσις ἐκ τοῦ παρα-διδόναι παραγομένη κατὰ μὲν τὴν κυρίαν αὐτῆς σημασίαν δηλοῖ οὐ μόνον τὴν πρᾶξιν τοῦ παραδιδόναι ἢ ἐμπιστεύεσθαί τινί τε, ἀλλὰ καὶ τὸ παραδιδόμενον αὐτό˙ κατὰ δὲ τὴν θεολογικὴν αὐτῆς ἐκδοχὴν σημαίνει καθόλου μὲν πᾶν ὅ,τι ὁ Κύριος ἡμῶν Ἰ. Χριστὸς διὰ τῶν ἁγίων αὐτοῦ Ἀποστόλων παρέδωκε τῇ Ἐκκλησίᾳ ἀγράφως ἢ ἐγγράφως (Β΄. Θεσ. β᾽. 15)˙ ἰδίᾳ ὅμως καὶ ἐξαιρέτως παράδοσις ἐν τῇ θεολογίᾳ καλεῖται μόνον ὁ ἄγραφος τοῦ θεοῦ λόγος πρὸς διάκρισιν καὶ ὑπὸ τοῦ γραπτοῦ, ὅστις καλεῖται Γραφή˙ κατὰ ταῦτα ἡ ἱερὰ παράδοσις, οὖσα συμπληρωματικὴ τῆς Χριστιανικῆς Θρησκείας πηγή, εἶνε ὁ ἄγραφος τοῦ θεοῦ λόγος ὁ ὑπὸ τοῦ Σωτῆρος διὰ τῶν Ἀποστόλων

τῇ Ἐκκλησίᾳ παραδοθεὶς καὶ ὑπὸ τῶν ἁγίων Πατέρων κατὰ μέγα μέρος ἀναγραφείς. Διττὴ δ' εἶνε ἡ ἱερὰ Παράδοσις, θεία καὶ ἀνθρωπίνη˙ καὶ θεία μὲν εἶνε ἐκείνη, ἧς ἀρχηγὸς εἶνε αὐτὸς ὁ θεός, καὶ ἣν γενικῶς δηλοῖ ὁ ἱερὸς Λουκᾶς λέγων ὅτι ὁ Ἰησοῦς μετὰ τὴν Ἀνάστασιν "παρέστησεν ἑαυτὸν τοῖς Ἀποστόλοις . . . δι' ἡμερῶν τεσσαράκοντα ὀπτανόμενος αὐτοῖς καὶ λέγων τὰ περὶ τῆς βασιλείας τοῦ Θεοῦ" (Πραξ. α'. 2–3)˙ τοιαύτη εἶνε π.χ. ὁ τρόπος τῆς τελέσεως τῶν μυστηρίων ὡς μαρτυρεῖ ὁ Ἀπ. Παῦλος περὶ τοῦ μυστηρίου τῆς θείας Εὐχαριστίας λέγων τοῖς Κορινθίοις (Α'. ια'. 23) "'Εγὼ παρέλαβον ἀπὸ τοῦ Κυρίου, ὃ καὶ παρέδωκα ὑμῖν". Ἀνθρωπίνη δὲ παράδοσις εἶνε ἡ παρ' ἀνθρώπων παραδοθεῖσα˙ διακρίνεται δ' αὕτη εἰς Ἀποστολικήν, Ἐκκλησιαστικὴν καὶ καθαρῶς ἀνθρωπίνην˙ τούτων ἡ μὲν πρώτη ἔχει τὴν ἀρχὴν παρ' αὐτῶν τῶν Ἀποστόλων θεωρουμένων οὐχὶ ὡς κηρύκων τῶν θείων νόμων ἢ ὡς οἰκονόμων τῶν ἁγίων μυστηρίων, ἀλλ' ὡς ποιμένων τῶν πιστῶν καὶ ἐπισκόπων τῶν Ἐκκλησιῶν˙ διότι ἐν μὲν τῇ πρώτῃ περιπτώσει ἡ παράδοσις εἶνε θεία, οἵα ἡ τοῦ Ἀπ. Παύλου λέγοντος "Τοῖς δὲ γεγαμηκόσι παραγγέλλω, οὐκ ἐγώ, ἀλλ ' ὁ Κύριος" (Α'. Κορ. ζ'. 10), ἐν δὲ τῇ δευτέρᾳ περιστάσει ἡ παράδοσις εἶνε καθαρῶς Ἀποστολική, οἵα ἡ τοῦ αὐτοῦ Ἀποστόλου λέγοντος "τοῖς δὲ λοιποῖς ἐγὼ λέγω, οὐχὶ ὁ Κύριος" (αὐτόθι. ζ'. 12). Τοιαῦται καθαρῶς Ἀποστολικαὶ παραδόσεις εἶνε π.χ. ἡ ἁγία καὶ μεγάλη Τεσσαρακοστὴ καὶ πᾶσαι ἐν γένει
}αἱ λοιπαὶ διαταγαί, περὶ ὧν διαλαμβάνουσιν οἱ Ἀποστολικοὶ κανόνες. }5
Ἐκκλησιαστικὴ δὲ παράδοσις εἶνε ἡ παρὰ τῶν διαδόχων τῶν Ἀποστόλων καὶ ἐφεξῆς τὴν ἀρχὴν ἔχουσα˙ τοιαῦται δ' ἐκκλησιαστικαὶ παραδόσεις εἶνε π.χ. τὸ σημεῖον τοῦ Σταυροῦ, ἡ κατ' Ἀνατολὰς προσευχή, ἅπασα ἐν γένει ἡ περὶ τῆς Ἐκκλησιαστικῆς ἀκολουθίας, τάξις καὶ διδασκαλία ὡς καὶ πᾶσαι αἱ κοινῶς παραδεδεγμέναι Χριστιανικαὶ συνήθειαι, ἃς ὑποδηλοῖ ὁ Ἀπ. Παῦλος λέγων "Εἰ δὲ τις δοκεῖ φιλόνεικος εἶναι, ἡμεῖς τοιαύτην συνήθειαν οὐκ ἔχομεν, οὐδὲ αἱ ἐκκλησίαι τοῦ Θεοῦ" (Α'. Κορ. ια'. 16)˙ καθαρῶς τέλος ἀνθρωπίνη παράδοσις εἶνε ἐκείνη, ἣν παρέδοσαν ἄνθρωποι μήτε ἀποστολὴν μήτε κῦρος ἐν τῇ Ἐκκλησίᾳ ἔχοντες˙ τοιαῦται εἶνε π.χ. ἡ περὶ τοῦ πρωτείου τοῦ Πάπα διδασκαλία καὶ πᾶσαι καθόλου αἱ καινοτομίαι τῆς Παπικῆς Ἐκκλησίας καὶ τῶν ἄλλων αἱρετικῶν αἱ κακοδοξίαι. Σημειωτέον ὅμως ὅτι ἐπειδὴ οἱ μὲν Ἀπόστολοι οὐδὲν παρέδοσαν, ὃ μὴ ἀπ' αὐτοῦ τοῦ Κυρίου παρέλαβον ἢ εἶδον (Β'. Πετρ. α'. 16. Α'. Ιωάν. α'. 1–3), οἱ δὲ τῶν Ἀποστόλων διάδοχοι οὐδὲν ἐδίδαξαν, ὃ μὴ παρ' αὐτῶν τῶν Ἀποστόλων ἐδιδάχθησαν ἢ ἤκουσαν (Ἰγνάτ. παρ' Εὐσεβίῳ *Ἐκκλ. ἱστ.* γ'. 36. Πολύκαρπ. *αὐτόθι* δ'. 14. Εἰρην. *Κατὰ αἱρ.* γ'.

3, κτλ.), διὰ τοῦτο τάς τε Ἀποστολικὰς καὶ τὰς κοινῶς παραδεδεγμένας Ἐκκλησιαστικὰς παραδόσεις δυνάμεθα ἀσφαλῶς νὰ θεωρήσωμεν καὶ ἀδιαφόρως νὰ ὀνομάσωμεν Θείας ἢ Ἀποστολικάς˙ διακρίναντας ὅμως αἱ θεῖαι ἢ Ἀποστολικαὶ παραδόσεις ἀπὸ τῶν καθαρῶς Ἐκκλησιαστικῶν κατὰ τοῦτο, καθ' ὅσον εἰς μὲν τὰς πρώτας ἀποδίδωσιν ἡ ἡμετέρα Ἐκκλησία ἀπόλυτον κῦρος, οἷον καὶ εἰς αὐτὴν τὴν ἁγίαν Γραφήν, εἰς δὲ τὰς Ἐκκλησιαστικὰς σχετικὸν καὶ περιωρισμένον˙ διὰ τοῦτο αἱ μὲν Ἀποστολικαὶ οὐ μόνον κατ' ἀνάγκην ὑφ' ἁπάσης τῆς ὀρθοδόξου Ἐκκλησίας δέον ἵνα φυλάττωνται, ἀλλὰ καὶ δόγματα δύνανται ἀσφαλῶς ἐπ' αὐτῶν νὰ στηρίζωνται˙ αἱ δὲ Ἐκκλησιαστικαὶ κατ' ἀνάγκην μὲν καὶ αὗται φυλακτέαι, ἀλλὰ μόνα ἐφ' ὅσον τῇ αὐτῇ Ἐκκλησίᾳ δοκεῖ (ὅρα *Θεολογικὸν* Βουλγ. περὶ παραδόσεως. *Πηδάλιον* ἐκδ. β΄. ἐν Ἀθήν. 1841 σελ. 388 σημ. 3. καὶ Bergier, *Λεξικὸν τῆς θεολ.* ἐν λέξει "Tradition").

β΄.

Οὕτω λοιπὸν οἱ Ἀπόστολοι, ὡς λέγει καὶ ὁ ἱερὸς Χρυσόστομος, "οὐ πάντα δι᾽ἐπιστολῆς παρεδίδοσαν, ἀλλὰ πολλὰ καὶ ἀγράφως" (*ὁμιλ. δ.΄εἰς τὴν Β.΄ Θεσ.*)˙ ἀλλὰ τὰ ἀγράφως ταῦτα ὑπὸ τῶν Ἀποστόλων τῇ Ἐκκλησίᾳ παραδοθέντα κατ᾽ἀρχὰς μέν, ὡς μαρτυρεῖ τὸ στόμα τῆς ἀληθείας Βασίλειος ὁ Μέγας, ἕνεκα τῶν ἀμυήτων "ἀπολυπραγμονήτῳ καὶ ἀπεριεργάστῳ σιγῇ οἱ πατέρες ἡμῶν ἐφύλαξαν, καλῶς ἐκεῖνοι δεδιδαγμένοι, τῶν μυστηρίων τὰ σεμνὰ σιωπῇ διασώζεσθαι" (*περί Ἁγ. Πν.* κζ΄.), μετὰ ταῦτα ὅμως, τὸ μέν, πρὸς πιστὴν τῶν θείων τούτων ἀληθειῶν μετάδοσιν }καὶ τήρησιν, τὸ δέ, πρὸς ἀποτελεσματικὴν τῶν }6
ψευδοδιδασκαλιῶν καταπολέμησιν, πολλὰ τῆς ἀδημοσιεύτου ἐκείνης καὶ ἀπορρήτου διδασκαλίας, τῆς ἱερᾶς δηλ#. Παραδόσεως, κατέθεντο οἱ θεοφώτιστοι τῆς Ἐκκλησίας Πατέρες καὶ διδάσκαλοι ἐν τοῖς ἑαυτῶν συγγράμμασιν ἑρμηνεύοντες δι᾽αὐτῶν, ἀναπτύσσοντες καὶ ἀκριβέστερον ὁρίζοντες τὰ τῆς πίστεως δόγματα καὶ κηρύγματα ἐν σχέσει πρὸς τὰ ἑκάστοτε ἀναφυόμενα θεολογικὰ ζητήματα˙ οὕτω δὲ τὰ κατ᾽ἀρχὰς μόνον διὰ στόματος ὑπὸ τῶν Ἀποστόλων τῇ Ἐκκλησίᾳ παραδοθέντα ἀπεθησαυρίσθησαν, θείᾳ πάντως οἰκονομίᾳ, ἐν πλείστοις ὅσοις συγγράμμασιν, ὧν τινα μὲν δυστυχῶς ἀπωλέσθησαν, πολλὰ ὅμως καὶ μέχρι σήμερον εὐτυχῶς διεσώθησαν. Τοιαῦται δὲ συγγραφαί, ἐξ ὧν ὡς ἐκ καθαρωτάτων πηγῶν ἀρυόμεθα τὰ γλυκέα ἅμα καὶ σωτηριώδη νάματα πολλῶν τῆς πίστεως δογμάτων καὶ κηρυγμάτων εἶνε αἱ ἑξῆς˙ 1.) Τὰ

ἀρχαιότατα σύμβολα, ἤτοι αἱ σύντομοι ἐκεῖναι τῆς πίστεως ὁμολογίαι, αἵτινες κοινῶς παρ᾽ἁπάσῃ τῇ Ἐκκλησίᾳ εἶνε παραδεδεγμέναι˙ τοιαῦτα δὲ σύμβολα ὑπῆρχον πολλὰ ἐν ταῖς διαφόραις ἐπὶ μέρους Ἐκκλησίαις τῶν τριῶν πρώτων τοῦ Χριστιανισμοῦ αἰώνων διάφορα μὲν ὡς ἐπὶ τὸ πολὺ κατὰ γράμμα, συμφωνότατα ὅμως κατὰ πνεῦμα˙ ἀλλὰ πάντα τὰ ἀρχαιότατα ταῦτα σύμβολα ὡς ὑπὸ ἰδιαιτέρων προσώπων ἢ μερικῶν μόνον Ἐκκλησιῶν συντεταγμένα δὲν ἦσαν ἐν κοινῇ παρ᾽ ἁπάσῃ τῇ Ἐκκλησίᾳ χρήσει, μέχρις οὗ κατὰ τὸν δ΄^{ον} αἰῶνα οἰκουμενικῶς ἡ Ἐκκλησία συνελθοῦσα ἀντικατέστησαν αὐτὰ διὰ τοῦ ἐν Νικαίᾳ συνταχθέντος καὶ ἐν Κωνσταντινουπόλει συμπληρωθέντος Συμβόλου τῆς πίστεως, ὅπερ δὴ κέκτηται κῦρος ἀκαταμάχητον, ἅτε δὴ ἐν ἐπιτομῇ ἅπασαν περιέχων τὴν τῆς ὀρθοδόξου πίστεως διδασκαλίαν δι᾽αὐτῶν δὴ ὡς τὸ πολὺ τῶν τῆς ἁγίας Γραφῆς λέξεων˙ ἐντεῦθεν ἡ ὀρθόδοξος Ἐκκλησία τοῦτο καὶ μόνον ἀναγνωρίζει μέχρι τῆς σήμερον ὡς Οἰκουμενικὸν σύμβολον ἀπορρίπτουσα τὰ ψευδῶς ὑπό τε τῶν Παπιστῶν καὶ τῶν Προτεσταντῶν ὡς Οἰκουμενικὰ ἐπίσης θεωρούμενα δύο ἕτερα σύμβολα, τὸ Ἀποστολικὸν λεγόμενον, περὶ οὗ πάνυ ὀρθῶς Μάρκος ὁ Εὐγενικὸς ἀπεκρίθη ἐν Φλωρεντιᾷ τοῖς Λατίνοις εἰπὼν "Ἡμεῖς οὔτε ἔχομεν, οὐδὲ εἴδομεν σύμβολον τῶν Ἀποστόλων" (*Ἰστ. τῆς ἐν Φλωρ. Συν.* ὑπὸ Σ. Συροπόλου τμῆμα στ΄. κεφ. 6), καὶ τὸ ψευδαθανασιανὸν (ἢ *quicumque*), ὅπερ ἐστὶ σκοταῖον ἔργον τῆς Παπικῆς Ἐκκλησίας. 2.) οἱ Ἀποστολικοὶ κανόνες, οἵτινες ἀείποτ᾽οὐ μόνον ὑπὸ τῶν ἐπὶ μέρους Ἐκκλησιῶν, ἀλλὰ καὶ ὑφ᾽ἁπάσης τῆς Ἐκκλησίας ἐθεωρήθησαν ὡς πρότυπα καὶ παραδείγματα, ἅπερ κατηκολούθησαν πάντες οἱ τῆς Ἐκκλησίας Πατέρες καὶ πᾶσαι αἱ ἅγιαι Σύνοδοι, αἵ τε Τοπικαὶ καὶ αἱ Οἰκουμενικαί˙ ἀλλ᾽εἰ καὶ τὸ σέβας, ὅπερ ἀπελάμβανον οὗτοι κατὰ τοὺς πρώτους ἤδη τοῦ Χριστιανισμοῦ αἰῶνας, ἀναγκάζει ἡμᾶς νὰ πιστεύσωμεν }ἀδιστάκτως εἰς τὴν θείαν αὐτῶν καταγωγήν, ἐν τούτοις ὅμως δὲν }7 δυνάμεθα νὰ παραδεχθῶμεν ὅτι αὐτοὶ οὗτοι οἱ Ἀπόστολοι ἐγγράφως αὐτοὺς παρέδοσαν, διότι τότε ἤθελον εὐθὺς ἐξ ἀρχῆς καταταχθῆ ἐν τῷ κανόνι τῶν βιβλίων τῆς Κ.Δ., ἀλλ᾽ ὅτι οἱ ἄμεσοι τῶν Ἀποστόλων διάδοχοι προφορικῶς αὐτοὺς παραλαβόντες κατέγραψαν ἐν ᾗ σήμερον σῴζονται τάξει καὶ μορφῇ εἶνε δὲ οἱ κανόνες οὗτοι πε΄(= 85) τὸν ἀριθμὸν καὶ περιέχουσι τὰς παραδόσεις τῶν Ἀποστόλων περὶ διαφόρων ζητημάτων τὴν Ἐκκλησιαστκὴν διοίκησιν καὶ εὐταξίαν ἀφορώντων. 3.) αἱ ἀρχαῖαι λειτουργίαι, ὧν τινες ἀνέρχονται μέχρι τῶν χρόνων αὐτῶν τῶν Ἀποστόλων, οἷα ἡ λειτουργία τοῦ Ἀποστόλου Ἰακώβου˙ τὴν ἀξίαν αὐτῶν καὶ σπουδαιότητα ἐπιμαρτυρεῖ ἥ τε ἀρχαία αὐτῶν καταγωγὴ καὶ ἡ ἔκτοτε

μέχρι τῆς σήμερον ἀδιάλειπτος αὐτῶν χρῆσις ἐν πάσαις ταῖς Ἐκκλησίαις τῆς τε Ἀνατολῆς καὶ τῆς Δύσεως· ἐν ταύταις δὲ ταῖς λειτουργίαις, ἃς δυνάμεθα νὰ θεωρήσαμεν ὡς τὸ κυριώτατον τῆς Ἀποστολικῆς Παραδόσεως φυλακτήρια, ὁμολογοῦνται καὶ πρεσβεύονται πολλὰ τῆς πίστεως δόγματα. 4.) Τὰ ἀρχαιότατα μαρτυρολόγια, οἷα τὰ τοῦ θεοφόρου Ἰγνατίου, τοῦ ἁγίου Πολυκάρπου καὶ ἄλλων ἅτινα συνεγράφησαν ὑπ᾿ἀνδρῶν οὐ μόνον συγχρόνων, ἀλλὰ καὶ αὐτοπτῶν· ἐν τοῖς μαρτυρλογίοις τούτοις ὑπάρχουσιν ἐκτεθειμέναι πολλαὶ τῆς Χριστιανικῆς πίστεως ἀλήθειαι, ἃς παρρησίᾳ οἱ ἔνθεοι ἐκεῖνοι μάρτυρες ὑπὲρ τοῦ ὀνόματος τοῦ Χριστοῦ ὡμολόγουν· ταῦτα δὲ τὰ μαρτυρολόγια εἶνε τοσούτῳ μᾶλλον ἀξιόπιστα, καθ᾿ ὅσον ἀνεγινώσκοντο δημοσίᾳ ἐν ταῖς κοιναῖς πρὸς προσευχὴν συνάξεσι τῶν πιστῶν μετὰ προηγουμένην ἐπιμελῆ αὐτῶν ἔρευναν καὶ ἐπικύρωσιν ὑπὸ τοῦ ἐπισκόπου τοῦ τόπου τοῦ μαρτυρίου. 5.) οἱ ὅροι καὶ οἱ κανόνες(1) τῶν ἁγίων Συνόδων τῶν τε ἑπτὰ Οἰκουμενικῶν καὶ τῶν ὑπ᾿αὐτῶν ἐπικυρωθεισῶν ἐννέα Τοπικῶν(2)· αὕτη δὲ ἡ πηγὴ εἶνε λίαν πολύτιμος, πρῶτον μέν, διότι ἡ ἁγία ἡμῶν Ἐκκλησία ἐπὶ τὸ αὐτὸ ἀποδίδωσιν ἀπόλυτον κῦρος ταῖς Οἰκουμενικαῖς Συνόδοις, ἐν αἷς ἅπασα ἡ Ἐκκλησία ἐπὶ τὸ αὐτὸ συνερχομένη ἀποφαίνεται ὑπὸ τὴν ἐπιστασίαν τοῦ Ἁγ. Πνεύματος τοῦ "μένοντος ἐν αὐτῇ εἰς τὸν αἰῶνα" καὶ "ὁδηγοῦντος αὐτὴν εἰς πᾶσαν τὴν ἀλήθειαν" (Ἰωάν. ιδ΄. 16. καὶ ιστ΄. 13)· διὸ καὶ αὗται κατὰ τὸ παράδειγμα τῶν ἁγίων Ἀποστόλων }ἄρχονται τῶν }8
ὅρων αὐτῶν πάντοτε διὰ τῶν λέξεων "ἔδοξε τῷ Πνεύματι τῷ Ἁγίῳ καὶ ἡμῖν" (Πράξ. ιε΄. 18)· δεύτερον δέ, διότι ἐπὶ τῶν Συνόδων τούτων οἱ θεοφώτιστοι ἐκεῖνοι τῆς Ἐκκλησίας Πατέρες καὶ διδάσκαλοι πανταχόθεν συνερχόμενοι καὶ ὁμοφώνως ἐνεργοῦντες οὐδὲν νέον οὔτε ἐν τῇ πίστει οὔτε ἐν τῷ βίῳ εἰσῆγον, ἀλλὰ τὰ ἀρχαῖα τὰ ἔν τε τῇ Γραφῇ καὶ Παραδόσει ὑπάρχοντα ὑπερασπίζοντες ἀπέναντι τῶν διαφόρων αἱρετικῶν καθόριζον καὶ ἐπεκύρουν ἐπὶ τῇ βάσει τῆς Παραδόσεως μᾶλλον ἢ τῆς Γραφῆς· διότι διὰ τῆς Γραφῆς κακοβούλως παρερμηνευομένης ἠμύνοντο καὶ οἱ αἱρετικοί· διὸ καὶ ἀφορίζονται τῆς ὀρθοδόξου Ἐκκλησίας πάντες οἱ

(1). Οἱ μὲν λεγόμενοι ὅροι ἀφορῶσι τὰ δόγματα, οἱ δὲ κανόνες ἢ διατάξεις τὴν τῆς Ἐκκλησίας διοίκησιν καὶ εὐταξίαν.

(2). Αἱ μὲν ἑπτὰ Οἰκ. Σύνοδοι εἶνε ἡ ἐν Νικαίᾳ (325), Κωνσταντινουπόλει (381), Ἐφέσῳ, (431), Χαλκηδόνι (451), Κωνσταντινουπόλει (553), Κωνσταντινουπόλει (680), καί Νικαίᾳ (787), προστιθεμένης τῆς ἐν Κωνσταντινουπόλει (692) συγκροτηθείσης Πενθέκτης· αἱ ἐννέα Τοπ. Σύνοδοι εἶνε ἡ ἐν Καρχηδόνι (256), Ἀγκύρᾳ (315), Νεοκαισαρείᾳ (315), Γάγγρᾳ (340), Ἀντιοχείᾳ (341), Σαρδικῇ (347), Λαοδικείᾳ (364), Κωνσταντινουπόλει (394), καὶ Καρθαγένῃ (418). Ἐκτὸς τούτων ὑπάρχουσι καὶ δύο ἕτεροι Σύνοδοι ἐπὶ τοῦ ἱεροῦ Φωτίου συγκροτηθεῖσαι, ἡ Πρωτοδευτέρα (861) καὶ ἡ ἐν Κωνσταντινουπόλει (879).

ἀπορρίπτοντες τὰς Συνόδους τῶν Πατέρων καὶ τὰς παραδόσεις αὐτῶν τὰς συνῳδοὺς τῇ θείᾳ Ἀποκαλύψει καὶ εὐσεβῶς ὑπὸ τῆς ὀρθοδόξος Ἐκκλησίας τηρουμένας (ὅρα Ἀκολουθ. τῆς Κυρ. τῆς ὀρθ.). 6.) Τὰ συγγράμματα πάντων τῶν ἀρχαίων τῆς Ἐκκλησίας Πατέρων, οἵτινες, συνῳδὰ τῇ ἁγίᾳ Γραφῇ καὶ ταῖς ἱεραῖς Παραδόσεσι ταῖς τηρουμέναις καὶ ἐν ἁπάσῃ τῇ Ἐκκλησίᾳ ἐν χρήσει οὔσαις, ἤ συνέγραψαν εἰδικὰς ὁμολογίας πρὸς ἀπόδειξιν τῆς ἑαυτῶν ὀρθῆς πίστεως ἐνώπιον τῆς Ἐκκλησίας, οἷαί εἰσιν αἱ ἐκθέσεις τῆς πίστεως τοῦ ἁγίου Ἀθανασίου, τοῦ Πάπα Πελαγίου καὶ ἄλλων πολλῶν, ἤ ἀνέπτυξαν τὰ συνεπτυγμένα τῆς πίστεως δόγματα πρὸς διδασκαλίαν τῶν πιστῶν, καθὼς εἶνε π.χ. αἱ κατηχήσεις Κυρίλλου Ἱεροσολύμων, ἡ θεολογία Ἰωάννου τοῦ Δαμασκηνοῦ καὶ πλεῖσται ἄλλαι ὁμιλίαι καὶ ἑρμηνεῖαι τῆς ἁγίας Γραφῆς, ἤ τέλος ἔγραψαν διαφόρους ἀπολογίας καὶ ἐλέγχοις κατ᾽ἐθνικῶν, Αἱρετικῶν καὶ Σχισματικῶν. Τὸ δὲ κῦρος τῶν ἁγίων Πατέρων εἶνε ἀναμφισβήτητον μόνον ἐν ἀντικειμένοις τῆς θείας Ἀποκαλύψεως, καὶ δὴ τότε μόνον, ὅταν ἐπικρατῇ παρ᾽αὐτοῖς τελεία ὁμόθυμος συμφωνία˙ ἐν τῇ περιστάσει ταύτῃ εἶνε ἀναντίρρητον, λέγομεν, τὸ κῦρος τῶν ἁγίων Πατέρων, οὐ μόνον διότι οὗτοι ὡς ἐν διαφόροις τόποις καὶ χρόνοις μέχρις αὐτῶν τῶν Ἀποστόλων ἀνερχομένοις ἀκμάσαντες παριστᾶσι τὰς ἑαυτῶν τοπικὰς Ἐκκλησίας, καὶ ἑπομένως ἡ συμφωνία αὐτῶν δηλοῖ καὶ τὴν τῶν Ἐκκλησιῶν αὐτῶν ὁμοφωνίαν, ἀλλὰ καὶ διότι, τὸ μέν, ἕνεκα τῆς ἁγιότητος τοῦ βίου αὐτῶν, ὃν ἐν αὐστηροτάτῃ Ἀποστολικῇ ἁπλότητι καὶ λιτότητι διήγαγον, τὸ δέ, διὰ τὸν ἔνθερμον αὐτῶν ζῆλον ὑπὲρ τῆς ὀρθοδόξου πίστεως, χάριν τῆς ὁποίας ὑπέστησαν καὶ διωγμοὺς καὶ βασάνους καὶ μυρίας ἄλλας ταλαιπωρίας, τὸ δὲ τέλος καὶ διὰ τὴν καθαρότητα τοῦ θεοφωτίστου αὐτῶν νοῦ τοῦ καὶ φύσει διὰ πολλῶν πνευματικῶν δώρων πεπροκισμένου, δὲν ἠδύναντο νὰ διδάσκωσιν εἰμὴ σύμφωνα τῇ θείᾳ Ἀποκαλύψει διδάγματα˙ διὸ καὶ πολλοὶ ἐξ αὐτῶν ὁμοφώνως παρ᾽ ἁπάσης τῆς Ἐκκλησίας ἀνεκηρύχθησαν εἴτε σιωπηλῶς εἴτε φανερῶς οἰκουμενικοὶ διδάκαλοι καὶ στύλοι τῆς ὀρθοδοξίας, πρὸς δὲ καὶ ἀναλόγως τῶν πνευματικῶν αὐτῶν χαρισμάτων ἐκοσμήθησαν διὰ διαφόρων ἐπιθέτων, οἷον π.χ. θεῖοι, θεοφόροι, }θεόσοφοι, θεορρήμονες, }9
θεολόγοι, μεγάλοι, Χρυσόστομοι, Χρυσορρήμονες, κτλ.˙ τούτων λοιπὸν οὕτως ἐχόντων δικαίως οἱ ἅγιοι Πατέρες δύνανται νὰ θεωρηθῶσιν ἀξιόπιστοι τῆς ἀληθοῦς Παραδόσεως μάρτυρες (ὅρα *ἐπιστ. τῶν 4 Πατριαρ.* ὅρον ιβ΄.)˙ διὸ καὶ ἀφορίζονται τῆς ὀρθοδόξου Ἐκκλησίας πάντες οἱ ἀπορρίπτοντες τὰς συνόδους τῶν Πατέρων καὶ τὰς παραδόσεις αὐτῶν τὰς συνῳδοὺς τῇ Θείᾳ Ἀποκαλύψει καὶ εὐσεβῶς ὑπὸ τῆς ὀρθοδόξου

Ἐκκλησίας τηρουμένας (ὅρα Ἀκολουθ. ἐν τῇ Κυρ. τῆς ὀρθ.). 7.) πηγὴ τῆς ἱερᾶς Παραδόσεως εἶνε καὶ τὰ διάφορα ἤθη καὶ ἔθιμα τὰ ἔκπαλαι ἐν κοινῇ χρήσει παρὰ τῇ οἰκουμενικῇ Ἐκκλησίᾳ παραδεδεγμένα˙ ταῦτα εἶνε α΄.) οἱ ἱεροὶ χρόνοι, οἷον ἑορταί, νηστεῖαι, προσευχαί, κτλ.˙ β΄.) οἱ ἱεροὶ τόποι, οἷον θυσιαστήρια, τράπεζαι, καὶ ὅλος ἐν γένει ὁ ναὸς μεθ᾽ ὅλων αὐτοῦ τῶν λεπτομερειῶν, καὶ γ΄.) αἱ ἱεροπραξίαι καὶ λοιπαὶ Ἐκκλησιαστικαὶ τελεταὶ καὶ ἱερουργίαι˙ 8.) ὡς τελευταίαν τῆς ἱερᾶς Παραδόσεως πηγὴν δυνάμεθα νὰ θεωρήσωμεν τὴν μαρτυρίαν τῶν ἀρχαιοτάτων αἱρέσεων, αἵτινες ναὶ μὲν διέστρεψάν τινα τῆς ὀρθοδόξου διδασκαλίας διδάγματα, δι᾽ ἃ καὶ κατεδικάσθησαν ὑπὸ τῆς Ἐκκλησίας, διετήρησαν ὅμως ἀποχωρισθεῖσαι πολλὰ σῷα καὶ ἀνόθευτα˙ διὰ τοῦτο δὴ καὶ αὗται, τὸ μὲν ἀρνητικῶς, τὸ δὲ θετικῶς, δύνανται νὰ χρησιμεύσωσιν ἡμῖν ὡς μάρτυρες τῆς ἀληθοῦς Ἀποστολικῆς Παραδόσεως (πρβλ. Μακαρίου *Εἰσαγωγ. εἰς τὴν ὀρθ. θεολ.* καὶ Ἀντωνίου *Δογμ. Θεολ. εἰσαγωγ.*).

γ΄.

Καὶ αὗται μὲν εἶνε αἱ διάφοροι τῆς ἱερᾶς Παραδόσεως πηγαί, αἵτινες ὅμως δὲν εἶνε πᾶσαι καὶ κατὰ πάντα ἄμιαντοι καὶ καθαραί, ἀλλ᾽ ἔν τισιν ἐξ αὐτῶν ὑπάρχουσι πολλὰ μηδόλως δυνάμενα κληθῆναι Ἀποστολικά˙ ἐντεῦθεν ἕπεται ὅτι πρὸς ὀρθὴν τῶν Ἀποστολικῶν Παραδόσεων ἀπὸ τῶν μὴ τοιούτων διάκρισιν ἀπαιτοῦνται ἰδιαίτερά τινα χαρακτηριστικὰ γνωρίσματα˙ τοιαῦτα δὲ χαρακτηριστικά γνωρίσματα ὑπάρχουσι, τὸ μέν, ἐσωτερικὰ ἢ ἀρνητικὰ, δι᾽ ὧν γνωρίζομεν τὰς μὴ ἀληθεῖς Ἀποστολικὰς Παραδόσεις, τὸ δέ, ἐξωτερικὰ ἢ θετικά, δι᾽ ὧν γνωρίζομεν τὰς ἀληθεῖς Ἀποστολικὰς Παραδόσεις. Καὶ τὰ μὲν πρῶτα εἶνε -1.) ἡ πρὸς ἑαυτὴν συμφωνία τῆς Ἀποστολικῆς Παραδόσεως˙ διότι αὕτη ὡς λόγος τοῦ θεοῦ δὲν δύναται νὰ περιέχῃ τι ἀντιφατικόν, 2.) ἡ συμφωνία αὐτῆς πρὸς ἄλλας ὁμολογουμένως Ἀποστολικὰς Παραδόσεις˙ διότι ὡς νοῦν Χριστοῦ ἔχοντες οἱ Ἀπόστολοι δὲν ἠδύναντο ν᾽ἀντιφάσκωσι πρὸς ἀλλήλους, πολλῷ δὲ μᾶλλον πρὸς ἑαυτούς, καὶ 3.) ἡ συμφωνία αὐτῆς πρὸς τὴν ἁγίαν Γραφήν˙ διότι ἀμφοτέρων αἴτιος εἶνε εἷς καὶ ὁ αὐτός, τὸ Πνεῦμα τὸ Ἅγιον. Ἰστέον δ᾽ ὅτι οὔτε ἑνί, ὡς ἡ Παπικὴ Ἐκκλησία διατείνεται, οὔτε πολλοῖς προσήκει τὸ ἀποφαίνεσθαι περὶ τοῦ ἐὰν παράδοσίς τις συνᾴδῃ πρὸς τὴν Γραφὴν ἢ ἀπᾴδῃ, διότι ἕκαστος ὑπόκειται τῇ πλάνῃ,
ἀλλὰ }τῇ ἁγίᾳ καθόλου Ἐκκλησίᾳ, ἣν αὐτὸ τὸ Πνεῦμα τὸ Ἅγιον "ὁδηγεῖ }10
εἰς πᾶσαν τὴν ἀλήθειαν" καὶ ἣν ὁ Παῦλος καλεῖ "στύλον καὶ ἑδραίωμα

τῆς ἀληθείας" (Ἰωάν. ιστ΄. 13 καὶ Α΄. Τιμ. γ΄. 15)˙ διὸ καὶ ἀφορίζονται τῆς ὀρθοδόξου Ἐκκλησίας οἱ ἀπορρίπτοντες τὰς Συνόδους τῶν Πατέρων καὶ τὰς παραδόσεις αὐτῶν τὰς συνῳδοὺς τῇ θείᾳ Ἀποκαλύψει καὶ εὐσεβῶς ὑπὸ τῆς ὀρθοδόξου Ἐκκλησίας τηρουμένας (Ἀκολ. ἐν Κυρ. τῆς ὀρθ.). Τὰ δὲ δεύτερα, ἤτοι ἐξωτερικὰ ἢ θελικὰ τῆς ἱερᾶς Παραδόσεως χαρακτηριστικὰ γνωρίσματα, εἶνε τὰ ὑπὸ τοῦ Βικεντίου Ἐπισκόπου Λερίνης (Vincent de Lerins ἀκμάσαντος κατὰ τὴν ε΄ην ἑκατονταετηρίδα) ὑποδεικνυόμενα τρία, ἤτοι τὰ "*quod ubique* (ὅπερ πανταχοῦ), *quod semper* (ὅπερ πάντοτε), *quod ab omnibus* (ὅπερ ὑπὸ πάντων) *creditum est* (ἐπιστεύθη)" (ὅρα *Tract. pro cath. fid. ant. et. univ.* c. III)˙ τουθ' ὅπερ δηλοῖ ὅτι τὸ Ἀποστολικὸν οἱασδήποτε παραδόσεως ἀποδείκνυσι 1.) ἡ καθολικότης αὐτῆς˙ ἐκείνη δηλ.# ἡ παράδοσις εἶνε ἀληθῶς Ἀποστολική, ἥτις ἦν καὶ ἔστι κοινῶς παραδεδεγμένη ὡς τοιαύτη ἐν ἁπάσῃ τῇ ὀρθοδόξου Ἐκκλησίᾳ, καίτοι δὲν ὑπάρχει ἐν τῇ Γραφῇ εἴτε οὐδόλως εἴτε ὑφ' ἣν μορφὴν φυλάττει αὐτὴν ἡ Ἐκκλησία˙ διότι πᾶν ὅ, τι φυλάττει καὶ πιστεύει ἡ Καθολικὴ ὀρθόδοξος Ἐκκλησία, τοῦτο ἀναμφιβόλως παρέλαβεν παρ' αὐτῶν "τῶν ἀπ' ἀρχῆς αὐτοπτῶν καὶ ὑπηρετῶν γινομένων τοῦ λόγου" (Λουκ. α΄. 2.)˙ διὸ καὶ ὁ Ἀπ. Παῦλος λέγει ὅτι ἡ Ἐκκλησία τοῦ θεοῦ "ἐποικοδομήθη ἐπὶ τῷ θεμελίῳ τῶν Ἀποστόλων καὶ Προφητῶν, ὄντος ἀκρογωνιαίου αὐτοῦ Ἰησοῦ Χριστοῦ" (Ἐφεσ. β΄. 20)˙ ὁπόθεν δῆλον γίνεται, ὅτι πᾶν ὅ, τι πρεσβεύει ἡ καθόλου ὀρθόδοξος τοῦ Χριστοῦ Ἐκκλησία, τοῦτο παρέλαβεν παρ' αὐτῶν τῶν Ἀποστόλων καὶ Προφητῶν εἴτε ἐγγράφως εἴτε ἀγράφως, διὸ καὶ κατ' ἀνάγκην φέρει ἐν ἑαυτῷ τὴν σφραγίδα τοῦ ἀληθοῦς˙ "οὐ χρὴ", λέγει ὁ ἅγ. Εἰρηναῖος, "ζητεῖν παρ' ἄλλοις τὴν ἀλήθειαν, ἣν ῥάδιόν ἐστι παρὰ τῆς Ἐκκλησίας λαβεῖν˙ ἐπειδὴ οἱ Ἀπόστολοι ὡσεὶ εἰς πλουσίαν ἀποθήκην τὰ τῆς ἀληθείας ἅπαντα εἰς αὐτὴν κατατεθείκασαν, ἵνα πᾶς, ὅστις ἂν θέλῃ, λάβῃ ἐξ αὐτῆς πόμα ζωῆς˙ αὕτη γάρ ἡ τῆς ζωῆς εἴσοδος" (*κατὰ αἱρ.* III. δ΄. 1) ˙2.) ἡ ἀρχαιότης αὐτῆς˙ ἐκείνη δηλ.# ἡ παράδοσις εἶνε ἀληθῶς Ἀποστολική, ἥτις δύναται ν' ἀναχθῇ μέχρι τῶν Ἀποστολικῶν χρόνων˙ τοῦθ' ὅπερ καὶ ὁ ἅγ. Εἰρηναῖος ἤδη δηλοῖ λέγων "εἴ τισι περὶ μετρίου τινὸς ζητήματος εἴη ἡ ἀμφισβήτησις, οὐκ ἆρ' ἔδει πρὸς τὰς ἀχαιοτάτας ἀποδραμεῖν Ἐκκλησίας, ἐν αἷς οἱ Ἀπόστολοι ἀνεστράφησαν καὶ αὐτῶν περὶ τῆς προκειμένης ζητήσεως λαβεῖν τὸ ἀσφαλὲς καὶ τῷ ὄντι ἐναργές;" (*κατὰ αἱρ.* III. δ΄. 1 πρβλ. III. γ΄. 1). 3.) ἡ ὁμοφωνία περὶ αὐτῆς˙ ἐκείνη δηλ.# ἡ παράδοσις εἶνε ἀληθῶς Ἀποστολικής, περὶ ἧς συμφωνοῦσιν, ἂν οὐχὶ πάντως, τοὐλάχιστον οἱ πλεῖστοι τῶν Πατέρων καὶ διδασκάλων τῆς Ἐκκλησίας τῶν πρώτων πέντε αἰώνων˙ διότι ἡ τοιαύτη αὐτῶν ὁμόθυμος συμφωνία εἶνε, οὕτως }εἰπεῖν, ἡ λυδία λίθος τῶν ἀληθῶς Ἀποστολικῶν }11 παραδόσεων˙ τοῦθ᾽ὅπερ καὶ ὁ Τερτυλλιανὸς λέγων "*Quod apud multos unum invenitur, non est erratum, sed traditum*" (*de praescripit.* c. LXXXII.), ἤτοι "ὅ, τι παρὰ πολλοῖς τὸ αὐτὸ εὑρίσκεται, τοῦτο οὐκ ἐπενοήθη, ἀλλὰ παρεδόθη" (πρβλ. Μακαρίου *Εἰσαγαγ. εἰς τὴν ὀρθ. θεολ.* Παπιστ. ἐλέγχ. μέρος Α΄. § 12. καὶ Bergier *λεξικὸν τῆς θεολ.* ἐν λέξει "Tradition ").

δ΄.

Τούτων οὕτως ἐχόντων ὑπολείπεται νῦν ἡμῖν νὰ ὑποδείξωμεν καὶ τὴν πλουσίαν ἐκείνην ἀποθήκην, ἐν ᾗ οἱ Ἀπόστολοι κατὰ τὸν ἅγιον Εἰρηναῖον "τὰ τῆς ἀληθείας ἅπαντα κατατεθείκασι"˙ ἄλλαις λέξεσι μένει νὰ ἐξετάσωμεν ποία ἐκ τῶν δύο ἤδη ἀσυμφώνων καὶ διῃρημένων Ἐκκλησιῶν, τῆς Ἀνατολικῆς λέγω καὶ τῆς Δυτικῆς, εἶνε τὸ ἀληθὲς ταμεῖον καὶ ἀσφαλὲς φυλακτήριον τῶν ἱερῶν Παραδόσεων. Ἡ Παπικὴ Ἐκκλησία τῆς μιᾶς, ἁγίας, καθολικῆς καὶ Ἀποστολικῆς τοῦ Χριστοῦ ὀρθοδόξου Ἐκκλησίας, κρίμασιν, οἷς οἶδε Κύριος, ἀποσχισθεῖσα διϊσχυρίζεται, ὅτι ἀληθὲς τῶν ἀληθῶς Ἀποστολικῶν Παραδόσεων ταμεῖον εἶνε ἡ Ἀποστολικὴ τῆς Ῥώμης Ἐκκλησία, πιστὸς δὲ φύλαξ αὐτῶν εἶνε ὁ ἀλάθητος τοῦ Χριστοῦ ἐπὶ τῆς γῆς ἀντιπρόσωπος, ὁ κλειδοκράτωρ Πάπας! (ὅρα Klee *ἱστ. τῶν Δογμ.* περὶ παραδ. § 2)˙ ἀλλ᾽ἐάν τις ἀνοίξῃ τὴν ἀδέκαστον τῆς Ἐκκλησίας ἱστορίαν παρατηρεῖ ὅτι ἡ μέχρι τοῦ ἐννάτου περίπου αἰῶνος σεμνῶς καὶ ἀδιασείστως μετὰ τῆς Ἀνατολικῆς Ἐκκλησίας συμβαδίζουσα Δυτικὴ Ἐκκλησία, ἥτις μάλιστα, κατὰ τὴν μαρτυρίαν τοῦ Σωζομένου, "καθαρῶς διὰ τῶν Πατρίων ἰθυνομένη δογμάτων, ἔριδός τε καὶ τῆς περὶ ταῦτα τερθρείας ἀπήλλακτο" (*ἱστ. Ἐκκλ. γ΄.* 12), ἔκτοτε, ὡς μήποτ᾽ὤφειλε, τύφῳ τοῦ Ἑωσφόρου ἐπαρθεῖσα, ἅτε δὴ ὡς πρεσβυτέρα μεταξὺ ἴσων ἀδελφῶν θεωρουμένη, καὶ τῆς βασιλικῆς ὁδοῦ, ἣν μέχρι τότε ἐβάδιζε, παρεκνεύσασα ἔλαβε τὴν πρὸς τὰς καινοτομίας ἄγουσαν πᾶν θεμιτὸν καὶ ἀθέμιτον μέσον μεταχειριζομένη, ἵνα καὶ τὴν σώφρονα ἀδελφήν, τὴν Ἀνατολικὴν Ἐκκλησίαν, συμπαρασύρῃ μεθ᾽ἑαυτῆς εἰς τὸ βάραθρον τῶν κακοδοξιῶν, αἷς ἐμπέπτωκεν! Οὕτω δὲ ἀναλόγως τῶν φιλαρχικῶν αὐτῆς τάσεων ἀπὸ πλάνης εἰς πλάνην προβαίνουσα ἔν τε τοῖς πνευματικοῖς καὶ τοῖς κοσμικοῖς πράγμασιν οὐδὲν καταλέλοιπεν ἀπαρασάλευτον, οὐδὲν ἀκαινοτόμητον, οὐδὲν ἀπαράτρωτον, οὔτε δόγματα, οὔτε μυστήρια, οὔτε ἔθιμα, ἀλλὰ τὰ πάντα γραπτά τε καὶ ἄγραφα δεινῶς ἠλλοίωσέ τε καὶ παρεμόρφωσεν!

Ἐπιλείψειμε τῇ ἀληθείᾳ ὁ χρόνος καὶ ἁπλῶς ἀριθμοῦντα τὰς τῆς Παπικῆς Ἐκκλησίας παντόλμους καινοτομίας, ἃς μετὰ φρίκης ἀναφέρει ἥ τε Ἐκκλησιαστικὴ καὶ ἡ πολιτικὴ ἱστορία˙ ἀλλ᾽ ἵνα μὴ φανῶ ὅτι ἀναπόδεικτα λέγω ἐπιτραπήτω μοι ἵνα σύντομόν }τινα ποιήσω σύγκρισιν τῆς σήμερον }12
Παπικῆς λεγομένης Ἐκκλησίας πρὸς τὴν ἡμετέραν Ὀρθόδοξον Ἐκκλησίαν ἢ μᾶλλον πρὸς ἑαυτὴν ὅτε κατὰ πάντα τῇ ἡμετέρᾳ Ἐκκλησίᾳ σύμφωνος οὖσα προσωνομάζετο ὀρθόδοξος τῆς Ῥώμης Ἐκκλησία˙ διότι οὐδεὶς ἀπαθέστερον καὶ ἀμεροληπτότερον τῆς ἱστορίας δύναται νὰ καταδείξῃ ἡμῖν ποία ἐκ τῶν δύο ῥηθεισῶν Ἐκκλησιῶν εἶνε ὁ πιστὸς καὶ ἀληθὴς τῶν ἱερῶν Παραδόσεων φύλαξ. Καὶ ἐν πρώτοις μελετῶντες τὴν ἱστορίαν τῆς Ἐκκλησιαστικῆς ἱεραρχίας βλέπομεν, ὅτι ἐνῷ ἡ ἀρχαία Ῥωμικὴ Ἐκκλησία ἐθεώρει τὸν Ἐπίσκοπον τῆς Ῥώμης ὡς ἁπλοῦν πνευματικὸν τῆς Δυτικῆς καὶ μόνης διοικήσεως ἀρχηγόν, ἡ Παπικὴ Ἐκκλησία θεωρεῖ αὐτὸν ὡς ἀπόλυτον πνευματικόν τε καὶ κοσμικὸν ἀρχηγὸν ἁπάσης τῆς χριστιανωσύνης ἐναντίον τῆς τε Γραφῆς (Ματθ. κ΄. 26 Λουκ. κβ΄. 26) καὶ τῆς Παραδόσεως (Α΄. Οἰκ. Συν. καν. στ΄.)˙ ἐνῷ ἡ ἀρχαία Ῥωμ. Ἐκκλησία ἐθεώρει τὸν ἱεράρχην τῆς Ῥώμης ὡς *primus inter pares* (= πρῶτον μεταξὺ ἴσων) καὶ ὡς ὑποκείμενον τοῖς ἀποφάσεσι τῶν Οἰκουμενικῶν Συνόδων, εἰς ἃς καὶ αὐτὸς ὁ Ἀπ. Πέτρος ὑπέκυψε (Γαλατ. β΄. 11), ἡ Παπικὴ Ἐκκλησία θεωρεῖ αὐτὸν ὡς *summus Pontifex* (= ἄκρον Ἀρχιερέα) καὶ τιθεῖσα αὐτὸν ὑπεράνω τῶν Συνόδων τιμᾷ καὶ γεραίρει ὡς τὸν ἀλάθητον (ὢ τῆς μωρίας!) τοῦ Θεοῦ ἐπὶ τῆς γῆς ἀντιπρόσωπον (!) ἐναντίον τῆς τε Γραφῆς (Ματθ. κ΄. 26, 27 Ἐφες. β΄. 20) καὶ τῆς Παραδόσεως (Ἀποστ. καν. λδ΄. τῆς Α΄. Οἰκ. Συν. καν. στ΄. τῆς Β΄. Οἰκ. β΄. τῆς Δ΄. η΄. τῆς ΣΤ΄. λστ΄. κτλ.)˙ (Πρβλ. Φ. Βαφείδου *Ἐκκλ. ἱστ.* τόμ. β΄. § 189). Ἀλλ᾽ ἀνοίξωμεν δεύτερον καὶ τὴν τῶν θείων δογμάτων καὶ μυστηρίων ἱστορίαν καὶ ἴδωμεν εἴ γε ἐσεβάσθη αὐτὰ ἡ Παπικὴ Ἐκκλησία˙ ἀλλ᾽οἴμοι! καὶ ταῦτα ὁ Παπισμὸς ἀνέτρεψε˙ διότι ἐνῷ ἡ Ὀρθόδοξος Ῥωμαϊκὸς Ἐκκλησία ἐδίδασκεν ὅτι τὸ Πνεῦμα τὸ Ἅγιον ἐκ τοῦ Πατρὸς ἐκπορεύεται ἀναθεματίζουσα πᾶσαν προσθήκην ἢ ἀφαίρεσιν ἐν τῷ Συμβόλῳ τῆς πίστεως, ἡ Παπικὴ Ἐκκλησία οὐ μόνον διδάσκει τὸ *Filioque* (= καὶ ἐκ τοῦ υἱοῦ), ἀλλὰ καὶ προστίθησει αὐτὸ ἐν τῷ Συμβόλῳ τῆς πίστεως (ὅρα Φ. Βαφείδου *Ἐκκλ. ἱστ.* τόμ. β΄. § 130) ἐναντίον τῆς τε Γραφῆς (Ἰωάν. νε΄. 26) καὶ τῆς Παραδόσεως (ὅλων τῶν Οἰκ. Συνόδων καὶ πάντων τῶν μέχρι τοῦ θ΄. αἰῶνος Πατέρων τῆς τε Δυτικῆς καὶ τῆς Ἀνατολικῆς Ἐκκλησίας)˙ ἐνῷ ἡ ὀρθ. Ῥωμ. Ἐκκλησία ἐτέλει τὸ Βάπτισμα διὰ τρισῆς καταδύσεως, ἡ Παπικὴ ἀντεισήγαγε τὴν ἐπίχυσιν καὶ τὸν ῥαντισμὸν ἐναντίον τῆς τε

Γραφῆς (Μάρ. α΄. 10 Πραξ. η΄. 36–39. Ῥωμ. στ΄. 4. Κολ. β΄. 12) καὶ τῆς Παραδόσεως (Ἀποστ. καν. ν΄. τῆς Β΄. Οἰκ. Συν. ζ΄. τῆς ΣΤ΄. 45 παραδόξως δὲ πρβλ. καὶ Klee *Dogmatik* ἔκδ. γ΄. τόμ. γ΄. σελ. 129)˙ ἐνῷ ἡ ὀρθ. Ῥωμ. Ἐκκλησία εὐθὺς μετὰ τὸ ἅγιον Βάπτισμα ἐτέλει τὸ μυστήριον τοῦ Χρίσματος, ἡ Παπικὴ τελεῖ αὐτὸ οὐ μόνον διὰ τοῦ Ἐπισκόπου καὶ μόνον,
ἀλλὰ καὶ ἀφοῦ }φθάσῃ τὸ παιδίον εἰς ἡλικίαν 7 – 12 ἐτῶν, ὀνομάζουσα }13
αὐτὸ *Confirmatio* (= βεβαίωσιν), ἐναντίον τῆς τε Γραφῆς (Πράξ. η΄. 14–17. ιθ΄. 2–6) καὶ τῆς Παραδόσεως (τῆς ἐν Λαοδ. Συν. καν. μη΄. Δυονυσ. Ἀρεοπ. *Ἐκκλ. ἱερ.* ζ΄. Κυριλ. *Κατηχ.* ιη΄. 33)˙ ἐνῷ ἡ ὀρθ. Ῥωμ. Ἐκκλησία ἐτέλει τὴν θείαν Εὐχαριστίαν δι᾽ ἐνζύμου ἄρτου, ἡ Παπικὴ τελεῖ αὐτὴν δι᾽ ἀζύμου ἐναντίον τῆς τε Γραφῆς (Ματθ. κστ΄. 26. Μάρ. ιδ΄. 22. Λουκ. κδ΄. 30–35. Ἰωάν. στ΄. 35. 41. 48. 51. 58. Πράξ. β΄. 42. 46. κ΄. 7. Α΄ Κορ. ι΄. 16. ια΄. 20.) καὶ τῆς Παραδόσεως (Ἰουστίν. *ἀπολογ. α΄*. 66. Εἰρην. *κατὰ αἱρ.* δ΄. 18. Κυρίλ. *μυσταγ.* δ΄. 1–6. Ἀμβροσ. *de sacr.* IV. 4.), ἐνῷ ἡ ὀρθ. Ῥωμ. Ἐκκλ. ἐπεκαλεῖτο τὸν θεὸν ὅπως ἁγιάσῃ τὰ προκείμενα δῶρα εὐλογοῦσα αὐτὰ μετὰ τοῦ σημείου τοῦ Σταυροῦ, ἡ Παπικὴ ἀναφέρει ἁπλῶς καὶ ἱστορικῶς τὰς λέξεις τῆς συστάσεως ("τοῦτο ἐστι τὸ σῶμα μου" καὶ "τοῦτο ἐστι τὸ αἷμα μου") δοξάζουσα ὅτι δι᾽ αὐτῶν καὶ μόνον δεικνυόμενα τὰ ἅγια δῶρα ἁγιάζονται καὶ μετουσιοῦνται, ἐναντὶον τῆς καθαρῶς Ἀποστολικῆς καὶ θείας Παραδόσεως (ὅρα λειτουργίαν Ἀπ. Ἰακώβου καὶ πάσας ἐν γένει τὰς ἀρχαίας λειτουργίας ὀρθοδόξων τε καὶ μή. Πρβλ. καὶ Εἰρην. *κατὰ αἱρ.* δ΄. 24 Ὠριγ. *κατὰ Κέλ.* η΄. Κυρίλ. *μυσταγ.* α΄. 7. γ΄. 3. ε΄. 7. Βασιλ. *περὶ Ἁγ. Πν.* κζ΄. Αὐγ. *de Trinit.* III. 4. κτλ.), ἐνῷ τέλος ἡ ὀρθ. Ῥωμ. Ἐκκλ. παρεῖχε τὸ φρικτὸν τοῦτο μυστήριον πᾶσιν ἀνεξαιρέτως τοῖς πιστοῖς καὶ ὑπ᾽ ἀμφότερα τὰ εἴδη, ἡ Παπικὴ οὐ μόνον ἀπεστέρησεν αὐτοῦ τὰ μικρὰ παιδιὰ ἐναντίον τῆς Ἀποστολικῆς Παραδόσεως (Ἀποστ. Διαταγ. η΄. 13 Διονυσ. Ἀρεοπ. *Ἐκκλ. ἱερ.* ζ΄. 11. Κυπρ. *testim.* III. 25. Αὐγ. *de peccat. merit.* I. 20 καὶ ἄλλους), ἀλλὰ καὶ ἐτόλμησε ν᾽ ἀποκλείσῃ διὰ παντὸς τοὺς λαϊκοὺς ἀπὸ τῆς κοινωνίας τοῦ τιμίου αἵματος τοῦ Χριστοῦ ἐναντίον τῆς τε Γραφῆς (ῥητῶς διατασσούσης "πίετε ἐξ αὐτοῦ πάντες" Ματθ. κζ΄. 27 Μάρ. ιδ΄. 23) καὶ τῆς Παραδόσεως (ὅλων τῶν 7 Οἰκ. Συνόδων καὶ τῶν ἀρχαίων τῆς Ἐκκλ. Πατέρων)˙ ἐνῷ ἡ ὀρθ. Ῥωμ. Ἐκκλησία ἐθεώρει τὰ ἐν τῷ μυστηρίῳ τῆς μετανοίας ἐπιβαλλόμενα ἐπιτίμια ὡς ἔχοντα ἁπλῆν ἐπανορθωτικὴν τοῦ μετανοοῦντος δύναμιν, ἡ Παπικὴ παρεννοήσασα τὴν ἀληθῆ τοῦ μυστηρίου τούτου ἔννοιαν οὐ μόνον ὑποδιῄρεσεν αὐτὸ εἰς τρία, ἤτοι εἰς *contritionem* (= συντριβήν), *confessionem* (= ἐξομολόγησιν) καὶ *satisfactionem*

(= ἱκανοποίησιν), ἀλλὰ καὶ θεωρεῖ τὰ ἐπιτίμια ὡς ἔχοντα δύναμιν ἱκανοποιητικὴν τῆς ἐκ τῆς ἁμαρτίας τοῦ μετανοοῦντος προσβαλλομένης θείας δικαιοσύνης˙ καὶ ὡσεὶ μὴ ἤρκει τοῦτο προσέθηκεν ἀφ᾽ἑνὸς μὲν ὅτι δυνάμει τῆς Θεόθεν δοθείσης αὐτῇ ἐξουσίας τοῦ δεσμεῖν καὶ λύειν δύναται ν᾽ ἀπαλλάττῃ ἀπὸ τῶν ἐπιτιμίων τούτων τοὺς μετανοοῦντας διὰ τῶν συγχωρητηρίων ἀφέσεων, ἃς ἀρύεται ἐκ τοῦ ὃν αὕτη διακατέχει ἀνεξαντλήτου θησαυροῦ τῶν ὑπερικάνων ἀξιομισθιῶν οὐ μόνον τοῦ Χριστοῦ, ἀλλὰ καὶ τῶν Ἁγίων (!!!), ἀφ᾽ἑτέρου δὲ ὅτι αἱ ἀφέσεις αὗται ἐνεργοῦσι }καὶ μετὰ θάνατον ἀπελευθεροῦσαι τὸν τυχὸν ὑπὸ τὸ βάρος }14
τῶν ἐπιτιμίων ἀποθανόντα ἀπὸ τῶν κολάσεων τοῦ καθαρτηρίου πυρός (!!!)˙ πάντα δὲ ταῦτα διδάσκει ἡ Παπικὴ Ἐκκλησία ἐναντίον τῆς τε Γραφῆς (Λουκ. ιε΄. 18, 19. ιη΄. 13. Β΄. Κορ. ζ΄. 10. Α΄. Πέτρ. δ΄. 8. Πράξ. ι΄. 43. δ΄. 12. Ἑβρ. ζ΄. 25) καὶ τῆς Παραδόσεως (Κυπρ. *de lapis.* XXX. Βασιλ. *εἰς Ἠσαΐ.* 15. Χρυσοστ. *εἰς Β΄. Τιμ. ὁμιλ. ζ΄.* 3)˙ ἀλλὰ προχωρήσωμεν˙ ἐνῷ ἡ ὀρθ. Ῥωμ. Ἐκκλησία ὥρισε τὴν ἀγαμίαν ὡς ὑποχρεωτικὴν μόνοις τοῖς Ἐπισκόποις (κατὰ τὸν ιβ΄. καν. τῆς ἐν Τρούλλῳ Οἰκ. Συνόδου), ἡ Παπικὴ ἐπιβάλλει αὐτὴν πᾶσιν ἐν γένει τοῖς κληρικοῖς μεγάλοις τε καὶ μικροῖς ἐναντίον τῆς τε Γραφῆς (Ἐφεσ. ε΄. 31–32. Α΄. Τιμ. δ΄. 3) καὶ τῆς Παραδόσεως (Ἀποστ. καν. ε΄. τῆς ΣΤ΄. Οἰκ. καν. ιγ΄. καὶ μη΄. τῆς ἐν Καρθαγ. δ΄. καὶ λγ΄. τῆς ἐν Γαγγ. α΄. δ΄. καὶ ιδ΄.)˙ ἐνῷ ἡ ὀρθ. Ῥωμ. Ἐκκλησία ἐπέτρεπε τὴν διάλυσιν τοῦ γάμου ἐν περιπτώσει συζυγικῆς ἀπιστίας, ἡ Παπικὴ Θεωρεῖ αὐτὸν ὡς ὅλως ἀδιάλυτον ἐναντίον τῆς Γραφῆς (Ματθ. ε΄. 32) καὶ τῆς Παραδόσεως (τῆς ἐν Νεοκαισ. καν. η΄. τῆς ἐν Καρθαγ. καν. ριε΄. Βασιλ. καν. θ΄. κα΄. λθ΄. καὶ μη΄. τῆς ΣΤ΄. καν. πζ΄.)˙ ἐνῷ τέλος ἡ ὀρθόδ. Ῥωμ. Ἐκκλησία ἐτέλει τὸ Εὐχέλαιον καὶ διὰ τῶν ἱερέων καὶ ὑπέρ οἱοσδήποτε ἀσθενοῦς, ἡ Παπικὴ τέλει αὐτὸ μόνον διὰ τοῦ Ἐπισκόπου καὶ μόνον ὑπὲρ τοῦ ψυχορραγοῦντος ὡς τελευταῖον χρίσμα (= *extrema unctio*) ἐναντίον τῆς τε Γραφῆς (Ἰακώβ. ε΄. 14, 15) καὶ τῆς Παραδόσεως (Χρυσοστ. *περὶ ἱερωσ.* γ΄. 6. Κυρίλ. Ἀλεξ. *εἰς Μάρ.* στ΄. 13)˙ ἐν γένει περὶ τῶν καινοτομιῶν τούτων τῆς Παπικῆς Ἐκκλησίας ἐν τοῖς Μυστηρίοις ὅρα Φ. Βαφείδου *Ἐκκλ. ἱστ.* τόμ. β΄. § 192 καὶ §194˙ Δ.Ν. Βερναρδάκη *ἱερὰν Κατήχ.* περὶ Μυστηρίων˙ καὶ *Φωνὴ τῆς ὀρθοδοξίας* ὑπὸ Γρηγ. Μητροπολίτου Χίου τοῦ Βυζαντίου. Ἀλλ᾽ἀφοῦ τέλος αὐτὰ τὰ δόγματα καὶ τὰ μυστήρια τοσαύτην ὑπέστηκαν μεταβολὴν καὶ ἀλλοίωσιν ἐν τῇ Παπικῇ Ἐκκλησίᾳ, τί ὑποληπτέον περὶ τῶν ἄλλων Ἀποστολικῶν καὶ Ἐκκλησιαστικῶν ἐθίμων; ἆρά γε ἀφῆκεν αὐτὰ ὁ Παπισμὸς ἀνενόχλητα; πολλοῦ γε καὶ δεῖ˙ διότι ἐνῷ ἡ ὀρθ. τῆς Ῥώμης Ἐκκλησία ἀπηγόρευε τὸ

ἐν Σαββάτῳ νηστεύειν ἢ γονυπετεῖν, τὸ καταλύειν Τετάρτην ἢ Παρασκευήν, τὸ ἐσθίειν αἷμα ἢ πηκτὸν ἢ ἄλλο τε ἀκάθαρτον, τὸ χρῆσθαι οἱῳδήποτε μουσικῷ ὀργάνῳ ἐν ταῖς Ἐκκλησίαις, τὸ προσκυνεῖν ἀγάλματα ἢ εἰκόνας ἀγράφους, τὸ χειρτονεῖν πλείονας τοῦ ἑνὸς ἱερεῖς ἐν μιᾷ καὶ τῇ αὐτῇ λειτουργίᾳ, τὸ προσφέρειν καθ᾽ ἑκάστην πλείονας τῆς μιᾶς θυσίας ἐπὶ τοῦ αὐτοῦ θυσιαστηρίου, τὸ ξυρίζειν τὴν κόμην ἢ τὸν πώγανα, πολλῷ δὲ μᾶλλον τὸν μύστακα, ἐνῷ, λέγω, πάντα ταῦτα καὶ πολλὰ ἄλλα τοιαῦτα δι᾽ εὐταξίαν καὶ σεμνοπρέπειαν ἀπηγόρευεν ἡ ἀρχαία ὀρθόδοξος τῆς Ῥώμης Ἐκκλησία, ὡς ἀπαραλλάκτως πράττει μέχρι τῆς σήμερον ἡ ὀρθόδοξος Ἀνατολικὴ Ἐκκλησία, τουναντίον ἡ Παπικὴ Ἐκκλησία πάντα ταῦτα οὐ μόνον ἁπλῶς ἐπιτρέπει, }ἀλλὰ καὶ πολλὰ αὐτῶν αὐστηρῶς }15
ἐπιβάλλει ἐναντίον ὅλως τῆς καθαρῶς Ἀποστολικῆς καὶ Ἐκκλησιαστικῆς Παραδόσεως τῆς διατασσούσης "τὰ ἀρχαῖα ἔθη κρατείτω" (τῆς Α΄. Οἰκ. Συν. καν. στ΄.) - ἐν γένει περὶ τῶν τοιούτων τῆς Παπικῆς Ἐκκλησίας καινοτομιῶν ὅρα Εὐγεν. τοῦ Βουλγ. *Ἐπστολ. στηλιτευτ. κατὰ Λατίνων.* καὶ *Φωνὴν τῆς ὀρθοδ.* ὑπὸ Γρηγ. Μητρ. Χίου τοῦ Βυζαντίου˙ καὶ *Πηδάλιον Ἐκκλησιαστικόν*. Ταῦτα λοιπὸν καὶ τὰ τοιαῦτα τοῦ Παπισμοῦ διδάσκοντα εἰπάτω ἡμῖν πᾶς ἀμερόληπτος ποία ἐκ τῶν δύο ῥηθεῖσων Ἐκκλησιῶν εἶνε τὸ ἀληθὲς τῶν ἱερῶν Παραδόσεων ταμεῖον καὶ φυλακτήριον ἢ κατ᾽ Εἰρηναίου εἰπεῖν "ἡ πλουσία ἀποθήκη, εἰς ἣν οἱ Ἀπόστολοι τὰ τῆς ἀληθείας ἅπαντα κατατεθείκασι"; ἡ Παπικὴ Ἐκκλησία ἡ τοσαῦτα καὶ τηλικαῦτα ἀπὸ τοῦ 1054 μέχρι σήμερον καινοτομήσασα, ἢ ἡ Ὀρθόδοξος Ἀνατολικὴ Ἐκκλησία ἡ οὐδὲ κατὰ ἰῶτα ἓν ἢ μίαν κεραίαν ἀπὸ τῶν Ἀποστολικῶν χρόνων μέχρι τῆς σήμερον τὴν παραδοθεῖσαν αὐτῇ θείαν παρακαταθείκην ἀλλοιώσασα ἢ μειώσασα ἢ αὐξήσασα;

Β΄.

> Προσέχετε οὖν ἑαυτοῖς καὶ παντὶ τῷ ποιμνίῳ . . . ἐγὼ γὰρ οἶδα τοῦτο, ὅτι εἰσελεύσονται μετὰ τὴν ἄφιξίν μου λύκοι βαρεῖς εἰς ὑμᾶς μὴ φειδόμενοι τοῦ ποιμνίου˙ καὶ ἐξ ὑμῶν αὐτῶν ἀναστήσονται ἄνδρες λαλοῦντες διεσταμμένα, τοῦ ἀποσπᾷν τοὺς μαθητὰς ὀπίσω αὐτῶν. (Πράξ. κ΄. 28 – 30)

Ἑνῷ οἱ μεγάλοι τῆς Ῥώμης Ποντίφικες ὑπὸ τῆς ψυχοφθόρου φιλαρχίας οἰστρηλατούμενοι Θεῖά τε καὶ ἀνθρώπινα δόγματα ἀνέτρεπον καὶ οὕτω τῆς βασιλικῆς ὁδοῦ ἐκτρεπόμενοι ἀθρόως συμπαρέσυρον μεθ᾽ ἑαυτῶν ἐν τῷ ἐρεβώδει τοῦ Μεσαίωνος σκότει πάντας τοὺς λαοὺς τῆς Δύσεως

εἰς τὸ φρικαλέον τῶν ἀσεβεστάτων καινοτομιῶν βάραθρον, αἴφνης τινὲς ὡς ἐκ τοῦ ἤδη κατὰ τὸν ιε΄ον# αἰῶνα ὑποφάνσαντος[1] ἐν τῇ Δύσει φωτὸς τῆς τῶν Γραμμάτων ἀναγεννήσεως διαυγασθέντες μετὰ φόβου ἅμα καὶ τρόμου παρετήρησαν ὅτι κατὰ κρημνοῦ φέρονται˙ διὸ καὶ εὐθέως τὴν ὀλεθροφόρον αὐτῶν πορείαν διακόψαντες ἀπεφάσισαν ἵνα, εἰ δυνατόν, πασσυδεὶ μετὰ τῶν ἀποπλανησάντων αὐτοὺς ἀρχηγῶν ἐπανέλθωσιν εἰς τὴν βασιλικὴν ἐκείνην ὁδόν, ἐξ ἧς παρεξέκλιναν˙ ἀλλ᾽οἱ ἀταρτηροὶ αὐτῶν ὁδηγοί, οἱ ὑψαύχενες τῆς Ῥώμης Ποντίφικες, τύφῳ πολλῷ μεθυσθέντες δὲν ἠδύναντο πλέον ἐκ τοῦ ληθάργου αὐτῶν ν᾽ἀνανήψωσεν, ἀλλὰ νέας καθ᾽ἑκάστην ἀτραποὺς κατασκευάζοντες νέας ἐδημιούργουν ἀξιώσεις, ἃς ἐξ ἀρχαίων δῆθεν παραδόσεων λαβόντες εἶχον, καὶ οὕτως ἐπέτεινον ἡμέρᾳ }τῇ ἡμέρᾳ τὴν ἀρχὴν τοῦ Δεσποτισμοῦ καὶ τῆς τυραννίας }16
ἐπιταχύνοντες τὴν πρὸς τὸ βάραθρον τῆς ψυχικῆς ἀπωλείας πορείαν αὐτῶν˙ ἐντεῦθεν οἱ δύστηνοι ἐκεῖνοι τῶν ἀναγεννωμένων Γραμμάτων θεράποντες ἰδόντες τέλος ὅτι οὕτω κατὰ τῶν ὑπεράντλων Παπικῶν ἀξιώσεων διαμαρτυρόμενοι ἀνεμώλια κράζουσιν ἀπετίναξαν τὸν βαρὸν τῆς Παπικῆς τυραννίας ζυγὸν καὶ οὕτως ἀπεφάσισαν, ἵνα ἐπανέλθωσι μόνοι εἰς τὴν ἀρχαίαν ἐκείνην βασιλικὴν ὁδὸν˙ ἀλλ᾽ οἱ νήπιοι! ἀντὶ συνελθόντες εἰς ἑαυτοὺς νὰ ζητήσουσι τὴν ἀπλανῶς εἰς τὴν βασιλικὴν ὁδὸν ἄγουσαν, τοὐναντίον τὴν ὅλως ἀντίθετον τοῦ πνευματικοῦ τῆς Ῥώμης Δεσποτισμοῦ ὁδὸν λαβόντες κατήντησαν εἰς τὸ ἕτερον ἄκρον τῆς πνευματικῆς ἀναρχίας καὶ θρησκευτικῆς ὀχλαγωγίας˙ ἐντεῦθεν οἱ Διαμαρτυρόμενοι οὗτοι πᾶσαν παράδοσιν καὶ Ἐκκλησιαστικὴν διάταξιν ἀπορρίψαντες ὑπέλαβον τὴν Γραφὴν ὡς τὴν μόνην τῆς Χριστιανικῆς πίστεως πηγήν, ἣν ὅμως ἕκαστος αὐτῶν αὐτογνωμόνως ἄνευ τῆς ἱερᾶς Παραδόσεως ἑρμηνεύων Θεμελιοῖ τὴν θρησκευτικὴν αὐτοῦ πεποίθησιν ἐπὶ τῆς ἀτομικῆς αὐτοῦ συνειδήσεως.(1) Οὕτω δὲ πᾶσαν ἐν τῇ πίστει ἑνότητα ἀπολέσαντες ὑπερηκόντισαν τοὺς Παπιστὰς προλαβόντες αὐτοὺς εἰς τὸ Βάραθρον τῆς ψυχικῆς ἀπωλείας! Καὶ εἶνε μὲν ἀληθὲς ὅτι ἐν τῇ ὀρθοδόξῳ Ἀνατολικῇ Ἐκκλησίᾳ πρώτη καὶ κατ᾽οὐσίαν πλήρης τῆς ἐξ Ἀποκαλύψεως Χριστιανικῆς θρησκείας πηγὴ θεωρεῖται ἡ ἁγία Γραφή, διὸ καὶ οὐ μόνον ἐπικρατεῖ παρ᾽ αὐτῇ ἡ τάσις τοῦ στηρίζειν ὁτιδήποτε πίστεως ζήτημα πρώτιστα καὶ μάλιστα ἐπὶ τῆς ἁγίας Γραφῆς, ἀλλὰ καὶ φρονεῖ ὅτι οὐδὲν δόγμα ἔγκυρον, ὅπερ δὲν περιέχεται ἐν τῇ Γραφῇ εἴτε

(1) Ἐξ ὅλων τῶν Διαμαρτυρομένων μόνη ἡ Ἀγγλικανὴ Ἐκκησία διέσωσε μέρος τῆς ὀρθοδοξίας ὡς παραδεχομένη τὴν τῶν πέντε πρώτων αἰώνων Παράδοσιν, τὰς τέσσαρας δηλ.# πρώτας Οἰκ. Συνόδους.

κατὰ γράμμα εἴτε κατὰ πνεῦμα (ὅρ. Κυριλ. *Κατηχ.* ιστ΄. 2), ἐν τούτοις ὅμως δὲν θεωρεῖται ὑπ᾽αὐτῆς ἡ ἁγία Γραφὴ ὡς ἡ μόνη καὶ ἐπαρκὴς τῆς Χριστιανικῆς θρησκείας πηγή, ἀλλ᾽ ἀπαιτεῖ πρὸς συμπλήρωσιν αὐτῆς καὶ διασάφησιν τὴν τὸ αὐτὸ κῦρος ἔχουσαν ἱερὰν Παράδοσιν (ὅρ. Χρυσοστ. *ὁμιλ. δ΄. εἰς Β΄. θεσ.* β΄. 15. καὶ Βασιλ. *περὶ Ἁγ. Πν.* κζ΄. 2). Ἀλλ᾽ ἡμεῖς δείξαντες ἤδη τὴν ἀληθῆ τῆς ἱερᾶς Παραδόσεως ἔννοιαν ἀπέναντι τῶν κακοβούλως αὐτὴν διαστρεφόντων Παπιστῶν, δείξωμεν νῦν καὶ τὸ μέγα αὐτῆς ἀξίωμα ἀπέναντι τῶν ἀπορριπτόντων αὐτὴν Προτεσταντῶν, ἤτοι Διαμαρτυρομένων, ἀποδεικνύοντες αὐτὸ α΄.) Εἰς τῆς ἱστορίας τῆς θείας Ἀποκαλύψεως καὶ τῶν σαφῶν τῆς ἁγίας Γραφῆς μαρτυριῶν. β΄.) Εἰς τῆς φωνῆς τῆς Οἰκουμενικῆς Ἐκκλησίας καὶ τῆς ὁμοφώνου πάντων τῶν ἀρχαίων αὐτῆς Πατέρων καὶ διδασκάλων μαρτυρίας, καὶ γ΄.) Εἰς }τῆς }17
ἀπαραιτήτου τῆς ἱερᾶς Παραδόσεως χρήσεως πρὸς ὀρθὴν διάγνωσιν τῆς γνησιότητος, κανονικότητος καὶ θεοπνευστίας τῶν ἱερῶν βιβλίων, πρὸς ἀληθῆ αὐτῶν κατάληψιν, ἀντίληψιν καὶ ἑρμηνείαν, καὶ τέλος πρὸς γνῶσιν ἀληθειῶν τινων μὴ περιεχομένων μὲν ἐν τῇ Γραφῇ, ἀναγκαιοτάτων ὅμως εἴς τε τὴν πίστιν καὶ τὸν Χριστιανικὸν βίον.

α΄.

Ἐὰν τις ἀνοίξῃ τὰς ἱερὰς τῆς ἁγίας Γραφῆς δέλτους θέλει ἴδει εὐθὺς ἐν ἀρχῇ ὅτι αὐτὴ ἡ θεόπνευστος Γραφὴ μαρτυρεῖ ὅτι ὁ πρῶτος, ὅστις ἤρξατο νὰ καταγράφῃ τὰς τοῦ θεοῦ πρὸς τὸν ἄνθρωπον Ἀποκαλύψεις εἶνε ὁ θεόπτης Μωϋσῆς (Δευτερ. λα΄. 9. 24.)˙ ἑπομένως ἀπὸ τοῦ Ἀδὰμ μέχρι τοῦ Μωϋσῆ, ἤτοι ἐν διαστήματι τεσσάρων περίπου χιλιάδων ἐτῶν (ἀπὸ τοῦ 5508 – 1609), οὐκ ἄλλως βεβαίως ἐτηρεῖτο ἡ ἀληθὴς εἰς τὸν θεὸν πίστις καὶ μετεδίδετο εἰμὴ προφορικῶς, τ.ἔ. κατὰ παράδοσιν˙ ἀλλὰ καὶ ἀφοῦ ἀπὸ τοῦ Μωϋσῆ καὶ ἐφεξῆς εἰσήχθη ὁ τρόπος τῆς διὰ γραφῆς μεταδόσεως τῶν θείων Ἀποκαλύψεων μήπως ἔπαυσε καὶ ὁ τρόπος τῆς διὰ ζώσης φωνῆς ἀπὸ πατρὸς εἰς υἱὸν μεταδόσεως; οὐδαμῶς˙ αὐτὸς ὁ Μωϋσῆς ὁ ἤδη γραφῇ τὸν νόμον τοῦ θεοῦ καταγράψας ἐγγὺς τοῦ θανάτου εὑρισκόμενος προτρέπει τοὺς Ἰσραηλίτας οὕτω "Μνήσθητε ἡμέρας αἰῶνος, σύνετε ἔτη γενεῶν γενεᾶς˙ ἐπερώτησον τὸν πατέρα σου καὶ ἀναγγελεῖ σοι, τοὺς πρεσβυτέρους σου ἐροῦσί σοι" (Δευτερ. λβ΄. 7)˙ καὶ οὐχὶ "Ἀναγινώσκετε τὸν ὑπ᾽ ἐμοῦ γραφέντα νόμον καὶ μόνον" διότι ὁ Μωϋσῆς ἐγίνωσκεν ὅτι ἄνευ τῆς τῶν πατέρων αὐτῶν σαφοῦς καὶ λεπτομεροῦς παραδόσεως δὲν θὰ ἠδύναντο οἱ Ἰσραηλῖται νὰ κατανοήσωσι

τὰ ὑπ᾽αὐτοῦ γραφέντα ἁπλᾶ ὑπομνήματα (ἴδε αὐτόθι στ΄. 20, 21). Ἀλλ᾽
ἐὰν προχωρήσωμεν μέχρι καὶ αὐτῆς τῆς βασιλικῆς καὶ τῶν Προφητῶν
ἐποχῆς, πάλιν πρὸς τῇ γραφῇ εὑρίσκομεν καὶ τὴν παράδοσιν˙ οὕτως ὁ μὲν
προφήτης καὶ βασιλεὺς Δαβὶδ λέγει "Ἀνοίξω ἐν παραβολαῖς τὸ στόμα
μου, φθέγγομαι προβλήματα ἀπ᾽ ἀρχῆς, ὅσα ἠκούσαμεν καὶ ἔγνωμεν
αὐτὰ καὶ οἱ πατέρες ἡμῶν διηγήσαντο ἡμῖν . . . ὅπως ἄν γνῷ γενεὰ ἑτέρα,
υἱοὶ οἱ τεχθησόμενοι καὶ ἀναστήσονται καὶ ἀναγγελοῦσιν αὐτὰ τοῖς υἱοῖς
αὐτῶν" (Ψαλ. οζ΄. 2, 3, 6.)˙ ὁ δὲ προφήτης Ἰωὴλ λέγει τοῖς πρεσβυτέροις
τῶν Ἰσραηλιτῶν "ὑπὲρ τούτων τοῖς τέκνοις ὑμῶν διηγήσασθε, καὶ τὰ
τέκνα ὑμῶν τοῖς τέκνοις αὐτῶν, καὶ τὰ τέκνα αὐτῶν εἰς γενεὰν ἑτέραν"
(α΄. 3). Οὕτω λοιπὸν παραλλήλως πρὸς ἀλλήλους ἔβαινον οἱ δύο οὗτοι
τῆς μεταδόσεως τῆς θείας Ἀποκαλύψεως τρόποι, ὁ τῆς παραδόσεως δηλ#:
καὶ ὁ τῆς γραφῆς, καθ᾽ ὅλην τὴν διάρκειαν τῆς Ἰουδικῆς βασιλείας μέχρι
τῆς ἐλεύσεως }τοῦ Κυρίου καὶ θεοῦ καὶ Σωτῆρος ἡμῶν Ἰ. Χριστοῦ. Ἀλλὰ }18
πρὶν ἢ ἀφῶμεν τὴν Συναγωγὴν καὶ ἔλθωμεν εἰς τὴν Ἐκκλησίαν, ἴδωμεν τὶ
πρὸς τὰ ῥηθέντα ἀπαντῶσιν οἱ τὰς Παραδόσεις ἀθετοῦντες
Διαμαρτυρόμενοι˙ οὗτοι ἐνίστανται συνήθως ἐπάγοντες τὸ τοῦ (Δευτερ.
δ΄. 2) "οὐ προσθήσετε πρὸς τὸ ῥῆμα, ὃ ἐγὼ ἐντέλλομαι ὑμῖν"˙ ἡμεῖς ὅμως
ἀποκρινόμεθα αὐτοῖς μετὰ τοῦ ἱεροῦ Αὐγουστίνου (κεφ. 79 *εἰς τὸν Ἰωάν.*)
λέγοντες ὅτι ἐν τῷ χωρίῳ τούτῳ ὁ Μωϋσῆς ἀπαγορεύει τὴν προσθήκην
παντὸς ἐπιβλαβοῦς καὶ εἰς τὰ γεγραμμένα ἀπάδοντος, καὶ οὐχὶ τὴν
προσθήκην τῶν ἐπωφελῶν καὶ τοῖς γεγραμμένοις συνᾳδόντων˙ διότι
ἄλλως πῶς μετὰ τὸ Δευτερονόμιον προσετέθησαν οἱ Προφῆται; Ἀλλ᾽
ἔλθωμεν νῦν εἰς τὴν Χριστιανικὴν ἐποχὴν˙ ἡ ἱερὰ ἱστορία ἀψευδῶς
μαρτυρεῖ ὅτι ὁ ἀρχικὸς τρόπος τῆς μεταδόσεως τῆς Χριστιανικῆς πίστεως
ὑπῆρχε κυρίως καὶ κατ᾽ ἀρχὰς ἡ ζῶσα φωνὴ, τ.ἔ ἡ παράδοσις, δι᾽ἧς καὶ τὸ
πρῶτον διεμορφώθη ἡ Χριστιανικὴ συνείδησις καὶ οἱ εἰς τὸν θεῖον λόγον
πιστεύοντες ἀπετέλεσαν τὴν Χριστιανικὴν Ἐκκλησίαν. Αὐτὸς ὁ Κύριος
ἡμῶν Ἰ. Χριστός μόνον διὰ στόματος τὸ εὐαγγέλιον τῆς σωτηρίας κηρύξας
οὐδὲν ἔγραψεν οὔτε περὶ τοῦ βίου Αὐτοῦ οὔτε περὶ τῆς διδασκαλίας
Αὐτοῦ, ἀλλ᾽ ἐφρόντισε μόνον περὶ τῆς ἱδρύσεως τῆς ἁγίας Αὐτοῦ
Ἐκκλησίας διὰ ζώσης καὶ μόνον φωνῆς˙ καὶ πρὸς τοῦτο ἐν οἰκειοτάτῃ
μετὰ τῶν μαθητῶν Αὐτοῦ ζήσας σχέσει καὶ μυήσας αὐτοὺς τὰ περὶ τῆς
ἀποστολῆς Αὐτοῦ ἐξαπέστειλεν εἰς τὸ θεῖον κήρυγμα λέγων αὐτοῖς
"Πορευθέντες οὗν μαθητεύσατε πάντα τὰ ἔθνη . . . διδάσκοντες αὐτοὺς
τηρεῖν πάντα, ὅσα ἐνετειλάμην ὑμῖν" (Ματθ. κη΄. 19)˙ πρὸς πιστὴν δὲ καὶ
ἀκριβῆ τῆς θείας ταύτης διδασκαλίας μετάδοσιν ἐμπλήσας αὐτοὺς

Πνεύματος Ἁγίου κατὰ τὴν ἡμέραν τῆς Πεντικοστῆς[2] ὑπεσχέθη ὅτι καὶ αὐτὸς ἔσται μετ᾽αὐτῶν "πάσας τὰς ἡμέρας ἕως τῆς συντελείας τοῦ αἰῶνος" (Ματθ. κη΄. 20)˙ οἱ δὲ Ἀπόστολοι τῷ θείῳ τούτῳ ῥήματι ἑπόμενοι διεσπάρησαν πρὸς τὸ κήρυγμα τοῦ θείου λόγου εἰς ὅλα τὰ μέρη τὸν αὐτὸν κατ᾽ ἀρχὰς πάντες τῆς διδασκαλίας τρόπον ἀκολουθοῦντες, τ.ἔ. τὸν διὰ ζώσης φωνῆς˙ ἀλλ᾽ εἶτά τινες ἐξ αὐτῶν καὶ τῶν μαθητῶν αὐτῶν, οὐτὼ μόνον τὸν ἀριθμὸν, ἐκ διαφόρων κινούμενοι λόγων ἔγραψαν σύντομά τινα ὑπομνήματα τῆς λεπτομεροῦς αὐτῶν ἀπὸ στόματος διδασκαλίας. Οὕτως ὁ μὲν Ματθαῖος λ.χ. ἔγραψε τὸ Εὐαγγέλιον αὐτοῦ κατὰ τὴν παράκλησιν τῶν παρ᾽οἷς διέμενε κατ᾽ ἀρχὰς Παλαιστινῶν Χριστιανικῶν ἐπιθυμούντων ἵνα καὶ ἔγγραφον ἔχωσι τὴν διδασκαλίαν (Εὐσεβ. *Ἐκκλ. ἱστ.* γ΄. 24)˙ ὁ δὲ Λουκᾶς ἔγραψε τότε κατ᾽ αὐτὸν Ἐυαγγέλιον καὶ τὰς Πράξεις τῶν Ἀποστόλων χάριν τοῦ θεοφίλου (Λουκ. α΄. 4. Πράξ. α΄. 1)˙ ὁ δὲ Παῦλος ἔγραψε τὰς διαφόρους αὐτοῦ ἐπιστολὰς ἕνεκα διαφόρων ἑκάστοτε λόγων˙ καὶ οἱ ἄλλοι }τέλος ἱεροὶ συγγραφεῖς δι᾽ ἄλλας ἔγραψαν }19
περιστάσεις καὶ αἰτίας˙ διὸ καὶ δὲν ἐγένοντο αἱ ἱεραὶ αὐτῶν συγγραφαὶ ταχέως γνωσταὶ ἐν ἁπάσῃ τῇ Ἐκκλησίᾳ˙ ὅτι δὲ οἱ ἱεροὶ οὗτοι συγγραφεῖς δὲν κατέγραψαν πᾶν ὅ, τι διὰ ζώσης φωνῆς ἐδίδαξαν, τοῦτο δείκνυται, πρῶτον μὲν εἰς τούτον, ὅτε ὁ μὲν Ἀπ. Παῦλος ἐν τῇ πρὸς Ἑβραίους ἐπιστολῇ αὐτοῦ (στ΄. 1) ὑπισχνεῖται ἵνα αὐτὸς ἐλθὼν διατάξῃ τὰ τῆς Ἐκκλησίας καὶ διδάξῃ αὐτοὺς "περὶ μετανοίας ἀπὸ νεκρῶν ἔργων, πίστεως ἐπὶ θεόν, βαπτισμῶν διδαχῆς, ἐπιθέσεώς τε χειρῶν, ἀναστάσεώς τε νεκρῶν, καὶ κρίματος αἰωνίου", ἅτινα ὅμως ἐν οὐδεμιᾷ ἄλλῃ αὐτοῦ ἐπιστολῇ εὑρίσκομεν ἐκτεθειμένα˙ ταῦτα ἄρα ἐλθὼν ὁ ἴδιος ἐδίδαξεν αὐτοὺς διὰ ζώσης φωνῆς μόνον˙ ὁ δὲ Ἀπ. Ἰούδας ἀναφέρει παράδοσίν τινα περὶ τοῦ Ἀρχαγγέλου Μιχαὴλ, ὅτι δηλ#̣ οὗτος "τῷ διαβόλῳ διακρινόμενος διελέγετο περὶ τοῦ Μωϋσέως σώματος" (στ. 9), ἥτις ὅμως οὐδαμοῦ τῆς ἁγίας Γραφῆς ἀναφέρεται˙ ἀλλὰ καὶ ἐν ταῖς Πράξεσι (κ΄. 35) φέρονται τοῦ Κυρίου λόγοι "Μακάριόν ἐστι διδόναι μᾶλλον ἢ λαμβάνειν", οἵτινες ὅμως δὲν περιέχονται ἐν τοῖς Εὐαγγελίοις˙ δεύτερον δέ, τοῦτο δηλοῦσι ῥητῶς καὶ αὐτοὶ οὗτοι οἱ ἱεροὶ συγγραφεῖς˙ οὕτως ὁ Ἀπ. Παῦλος λέγει τοῖς Κορινθίοις (Α΄. ια΄. 34) "τὰ δὲ λοιπά, ὡς ἄν ἔλθω, διατάξομαι"˙ ἔτι δὲ σαφέστερα τοῦτο δηλοῖ ὁ Ἀπ. Ἰωάννης λέγων ἐν μὲν τῇ (β΄. 12) "πολλὰ ἔχων ὑμῖν γράφειν οὐκ ἐβουλήθην διὰ χάρτου καὶ μέλανος, ἀλλ᾽ ἐλπίζω ἐλθεῖν πρὸς ὑμᾶς καὶ στόμα πρὸς στόμα λαλῆσαι", ἐν δὲ τῇ (γ΄. 13) "πολλὰ εἶχον γράφειν˙ ἀλλ᾽ οὐ θέλω διὰ μέλανος καὶ καλάμου σοι γράψαι˙ ἐλπίζω δὲ εὐθέως ἰδεῖν σε καὶ στόμα πρὸς στόμα λαλήσομεν"

(πρβλ. καὶ Ἰωάν. κ΄. 31–32. κα΄. 25). Καὶ εἶνε μὲν ἀληθὲς ὅτι κατὰ θείαν ἀναμφιβόλως οἰκονομίαν παρεδοθῆσαι αἱ ἱεραὶ γραφαὶ τῇ Ἐκκλησίᾳ, διότι ἡ διὰ τοῦ προφορικοῦ κηρύγματος διαμορφωθεῖσα Χριστιανικὴ συνείδησις ἔπρεπε νὰ λάβῃ καὶ τινα ἐξωτερικὸν τύπον φυλάττοντα αὐτὴν ἀπὸ παντὸς ὀθνείου τὴν καθαρότητα αὐτῆς ἀπειλοῦντος, ἀλλ᾽ εἶνε ἐπίσης ἀληθὲς καὶ τὸ ὅτι οἱ Ἀπόστολοι δὲν εἶχον ἔργον νὰ συγγράφωσι˙ διὸ καὶ οἱ πλείους ἐξ αὐτῶν οὐδὲν οὐδενὶ ἔγραψαν˙ καὶ ὅμως καὶ αὐτοὶ οὐ μόνον ἐπιτυχῶς τὸν λόγον τοῦ θεοῦ πολλαχοῦ ἐκήρυξαν, ἀλλὰ καὶ Ἐκκλησίας ἵδρυσαν, ὧν πολλαὶ μέχρι τῶν ἀρχῶν τοῦ τρίτου καὶ πλέον αἰῶνος, ὡς ἡ ἀψευδὴς ἱστορία μαρτυρεῖ, ἐκτὸς τῆς ἱερᾶς Παραδόσεως οὐδὲν τῶν ἱερῶν βιβλίων ἐγνώριζον (ὅρα Εἰρη. *κατὰ αἱρ*. γ΄. 42.)˙ ἀλλὰ μήπως καὶ οἱ μετὰ τὸν γ΄ον # αἰῶνα ἐκχριστιανιζόμενοι διάφοροι λαοὶ ἐφ᾽ ὅσον δὲν εἶχον ἰδίαν τῆς ἁγίας Γραφῆς μετάφρασιν δὲν περιωρίζοντο εἰς μόνην τὴν ἱερὰν Παράδοσιν; ἀλλὰ καὶ ἀφοῦ ἐγένοντο αἱ μεταφράσεις μήπως ἡ Γραφὴ ἦν εἰς προσιτή; }πολλοῦ γε καὶ δεῖ˙ ἡ ἱστορία τῆς εὑρέσεως τῆς τυπογραφίας }20
μαρτυρεῖ ὅτι κατὰ τὸ διάστημα τῶν δέκα πέντε αἰώνων τὰ ἱερὰ βιβλία, ὡς καὶ πᾶν ἐν γένει τότε σύγγραμμα, ἦσαν τοσοῦτον πολύτιμα, ὥστε μόλις ὀλίγα τινὰ ἀντίγραφα ὑπῆρχον ἐν ἑκάστῃ Ἐκκλησίᾳ ἢ καὶ ἐν τοῖς οἴκοις φιλομούσων τινῶν πλουσίων˙ ἑπομένως πάντες οἱ λοιποὶ Χριστιανοὶ ἦσαν περιωρισμένοι εἰς τὴν διδασκαλίαν τῆς Ἐκκλησίας, παρ᾽ ἧς καὶ μόνης ἐδιδάσκοντο τὰ τῆς πίστεως δόγματα καὶ κηρύγματα˙ καὶ ἐν τούτοις τίς τολμᾷ νὰ διαμφισβητήσῃ εἰς τοσαῦτα Χριστιανῶν ἑκατομύρια τὴν ἀληθῆ πίστην καὶ σωτηρίαν; Ἀλλ᾽ἐκτὸς τῆς ἱστορίας καὶ αὐτὴ ἡ ἁγία Γραφὴ διὰ σαφεστάτων ῥημάτων μαρτυρεῖ τὴν τε ὕπαρξιν καὶ τὴν μεγάλην σημασίαν τῆς ἱερᾶς Παραδόσεως˙ οὕτως ὁ ἱερὸς Λουκᾶς φανερῶς ὁμολογεῖ ὅτι ἔγραψε τὸ κατ᾽αὐτὸν Εὐαγγέλιον κατὰ τὴν προφορικὴν τῶν Ἀποστόλων παράδοσιν. "Ἐπειδήπερ," λέγει, "πολλοὶ ἐπεχείρησαν ἀνατάξασθαι διήγησιν περὶ τῶν πεπληροφορημένων ἐν ἡμῖν πραγμάτων, καθὼς παρέδοσαν ἡμῖν οἱ ἀπ᾽ἀρχῆς αὐτόπται καὶ ὑπηρέται γενόμενοι τοῦ λόγου, ἔδοξε κἀμοὶ κτλ." (Λουκ. α΄. 1–2)˙ ὁ δὲ πλεῖον πάντων γράψας Ἀπ. Παῦλος ἐν μὲν τῇ πρώτῃ αὐτοῦ πρὸς τοὺς Κορινθίους ἐπιστολῇ (ια΄. 2) λέγει "ἐπαινῶ δὲ ὑμᾶς, ἀδελφοί, ὅτι πάντα μου μέμνησθε καὶ καθὼς παρέδωκα ὑμῖν τὰς παραδόσεις κατέχετε", ἐν ᾧ χωρίῳ σαφῶς ἐννοεῖ τὰς προφορικὰς παραδόσεις, διότι πρώτην ἤδη φορὰν γράφει πρὸς τοὺς Κορινθίους˙ ἐν δὲ τῇ δευτέρᾳ πρὸς τοὺς θεσσαλονικεῖς ἐπιστολῇ (β΄. 15) γράφει "Ἄρα οὖν, ἀδελφοί, οτήκετε καὶ κρατεῖτε τὰς παραδόσεις, ἃς ἐδιδάχθητε εἴτε διὰ λόγου εἴτε δι᾽ἐπστολῆς ἡμῶν"˙ ἐν τῷ χωρίῳ τούτῳ

ὑπάρχουσι δύο τινὰ ἀξιοσημείωτα 1.) μὲν ὅτι ὁ Παῦλος ἐντέλλεται τοῖς θεσσαλονικεῦσι τὴν τήρηση τῶν παραδόσεων, ἐνῷ ἤδη εἶχον οὗτοι ἀνὰ χεῖρα, τὰς δύο αὐτοῦ ἐπιστολὰς καὶ 2.) ὅτι σαφῶς ὁ Παῦλος ἀποδίδωσι τὴν αὐτὴν ἀξίαν καὶ σημασίαν εἴς τε τὴν ἁγίαν Γραφὴν καὶ τὴν ἱερὰν Παράδοσιν˙ τὸ δεύτερον δὲ τοῦτο ἔτι μᾶλλον ἀναδείκνυσιν ὁ Παῦλος παραγγέλλων ἀλλαχοῦ αὐτοῖς "ἐν ὀνόματι τοῦ Κυρίου ἡμῶν Ἰ. Χριστοῦ οτέλλεσθαι ἀπὸ παντὸς ἀδελφοῦ ἀτάκτως περιπατοῦντος καὶ μὴ κατὰ τὴν παράδοσιν, ἣν παρέλαβε παρ᾽ἡμῶν" (αὐτόθι γ΄. 6)˙ ὁ αὐτὸς πάλιν Ἀπόστολος γράφει πρὸς τὸν Τιμόθεον ἐν μὲν τῇ (Α΄. στ΄. 20) "Ὦ Τιμόθεε τὴν παρακαταθήκην (καὶ οὐχί: τὰς ἐπιστολὰς μου μόνον) φύλαξον, ἐκτρεπόμενος τὰς βεβήλους κενοφωνίας καὶ ἀντιθέσεις τῆς ψευδωνύμου γνώσεως", ἐν δὲ τῇ (Β΄. α΄. 13) "ὑποτύπωσιν ἔχε τῶν ὑγιαινόντων λόγων,
ὧν παρ᾽ἐμοῦ ἤκουσαν (καὶ οὐχέ: ἅ σοι ἔγραψα) ἐν }πίστει καὶ ἀγάπῃ τῇ }21
ἐν Χριστῷ Ἰησοῦ", καὶ (αὐτόθι β΄. 2) "καὶ ἃ ἤκουσας παρ᾽ἐμοῦ (καὶ οὐχί: ἃ σοι γράφω) διὰ πολλῶν μαρτύρων, ταῦτα παράθου πιστοῖς ἀνθρώποις, οἵτινες ἱκανοὶ ἔσονται καὶ ἑτέρους διδάξας". Τί τῶν θεοπνεύστων τούτων μαρτυρῶν σαφέστερον ἅμα καὶ ἀληθέστερον; καὶ ὅμως οἱ Διαματυρόμενοι πάντα λίθον κινοῦντες ἵνα τὸ κῦρος τῶν ἱερῶν Παραδόσεων προσβάλωσι ἐνίστανται ἐπάγοντες τὸ τοῦ Ἀπ. Παύλου λέγοντος "Ἀλλὰ καὶ ἐὰν ἡμεῖς ἢ ἄγγελος ἐξ οὐρανοῦ εὐαγγελίζηται ὑμῖν παρ᾽ὃ εὐηγγελισάμεθα ὑμῖν, ἀνάθεμα ἔστω˙ ὡς προειρήκαμεν καὶ ἄρτι πάλιν λέγω, εἴ τις ὑμᾶς εὐαγγελίζεται παρ᾽ ὃ παρελάβετε, ἀνάθεμα ἔστω" (Γαλ. α΄. 8–9)˙ ἀλλ᾽ἀγνοοῦσεν ὅτι ἡ ἔνστασις αὐτῶν αὕτη κατ᾽αὐτῶν στρέφεται˙ διότι ὁ Παῦλος ἐν τῷ χωρίῳ τούτῳ ἀποτρέπει τοὺς Γαλάτας ἀπὸ τῆς παραδοχῆς οὐχὶ τῶν ἀγράφων παραδόσεων, ἃς τοὐναντίον πολλαχοῦ τῶν ἐπιστολῶν αὐτοῦ θερμῶς συνίστησιν, ἀλλὰ τῶν ψευδοδισκαλιῶν ἀπατεώνων τινῶν "θελόντων μεταστρέψαι τὸ Εὐαγγέλιον τοῦ Χριστοῦ" (αὐτόθι α΄. 7), διὸ καὶ δὲν λέγει "εἴ τις ὑμᾶς εὐαγγελίζεται, παρ᾽ὃ γεγράφαμεν", ἀλλὰ "παρ᾽ὃ εὐηγγελισάμεθα" καὶ "παρ᾽ὃ παρελάβετε"˙ ἀλλ᾽ὁ μὲν Παῦλος διὰ ζώσης φωνῆς τὸν λόγον τοῦ θεοῦ τοῖς Γαλάταις εὐηγγελίσατο (διότι ἄλλην παρ᾽αὐτοῦ ἐπιστολὴν δὲν εἶχον), οἱ δὲ Γαλάται ἐκ τοῦ στόματος αὐτοῦ παρέλαβον τὸ εὐαγγέλιον τῆς σωτηρίας, τουθ᾽ὅπερ ἡμεῖς καλοῦμεν παράδοσιν. Ἀλλ᾽οἱ τῶν ἱερῶν Παραδόσεων κατήγοροι ἐνίστανται καὶ πάλιν ἐπάγοντες τὸ τῆς Ἀποκαλύψεως (κβ΄. 18) "Ἐάν τις ἐπιτεθῇ πρὸς ταῦτα . . . ἐπιθήσει ὁ θεὸς ἐπ᾽ αὐτὸν τὰς πληγὰς τὰς γεγραμμένας ἐν βιβλίῳ τούτῳ", ἀλλ᾽ἀμβλυωποῦσιν ὅτι ὁ ἱερὸς οὗτος Ἀπόστολος, ὅστις ἀντὶ τοῦ "διὰ μέλανος καὶ καλάμου γράφειν" προὐτίμα πάντοτε τὸ "στόμα

πρὸς στόμα λαλεὶν", ἀπαγορεύει διὰ τοῦ χωρίου τούτου οὐχὶ τὰς ἱερὰς Παραδόσεις, ἀλλὰ τὸ παρεμβάλλειν ἐν τῇ ἁγίᾳ Γραφῇ τὰ οἰκεῖα διδάγματα ὡς θεῖα ῥήματα, τοῦθ᾽ ὅπερ ἦν τότε ἴδιον πολλῶν ψευδοδισκάλων (οὐ μὴν ἀλλὰ καὶ πολλῶν σήμερον αἱρετικῶν, καθάπερ αἱ πολυσχιδεῖς τῶν Διαμαρτυρομένων αἱρίσεις πράττουσι!).

β΄.

Ἐκτὸς τῆς ἁγίας Γραφῆς τὸ μέγα τῆς ἱερᾶς Παραδόσεως ἀξίωμα τρανῶς διακηρύττει καὶ ἡ φωνὴ τῆς μιᾶς, ἁγίας, καθολικῆς καὶ Ἀποστολικῆς Ἐκκλησίας, ἥτις ὡς προερχομένη ἐκ τῶν ἁγίων Ἀποστόλων καὶ δι᾽αὐτῶν ἐξ αὐτοῦ τοῦ Κυρίου ἡμῶν Ἰ. Χριστοῦ, τῆς ἁγιωτάτης αὐτῆς Κεφαλῆς, δὲν
περιορίζεται ἐν χώρῳ ἢ χρόνῳ, ἀλλ᾽ ἐν μέσῳ τῶν αἰώνων }διαιωνιζομένη }22
χρησιμεύει ὡς εὐσταθὴς τῆς ἀληθείας μάρτυς˙ τὸ δὲ καθολικὸν αὐτῆς, τὸ θέοπνευστον ὡς καὶ τὸ ἀλάθητον στηρίζονται ἐπ᾽ αὐτῶν τῶν τοῦ Κυρίου ἀψευδῶν ῥημάτων˙ "οὗ γὰρ εἰσι, λέγει, δύο ἢ τρεῖς συνηγμένοι εἰς τὸ ἐμὸν ὄνομα, ἐκεῖ εἰμι ἐν μέσῳ αὐτῶν" (Ματθ. ιη΄. 20), καὶ "ἐγὼ μεθ᾽ ὑμῶν εἰμι πάσης τὰς ἡμέρας μέχρι τῆς συντελείας τοῦ αἰῶνος" (αὐτόθ. κη΄. 20), καὶ "ἐγὼ ἐρωτήσω τὸν πατέρα, καὶ ἄλλον παράκλητον δώσει ὑμῖν, ἵνα μένῃ μεθ᾽ ὑμῶν εἰς τὸν αἰῶνα, τὸ πνεῦμα τῆς ἀληθείας" (Ἰωάν. ιδ΄. 16), καὶ "ὅταν δὲ ἔλθῃ ἐκεῖνος τὸ πνεῦμα τῆς ἀληθείας, ὁδηγήσει ὑμᾶς εἰς πᾶσαν τὴν ἀλήθειαν" (Ἰωάν. ιστ΄. 13). Ταύτης λοιπὸν τῆς τοιαύτης Ἐκκλησίας ἡ φωνή, ἤτοι ἡ ὁμόφωνος συμφωνία πάντων τῶν ἔν τε ταῖς ἑπτὰ Οἰκουμενικαῖς καὶ ταῖς ἐννέα Τοπικαῖς Συνόδοις συναθροισθέντων ἁγίων Πατέρων, ἀριδήλως μαρτυρεῖ τὸ μέγα τῆς ἱερᾶς Παραδόσεως ἀξίωμα˙ διότι καὶ ἐν ταῖς Συνόδοις ταύταις, ὡς εἴδομεν, καθωρίζοντο τὰ ὀρθόδοξα δόγματα καὶ ἐξηλέγχοντο τὰ κακόδοξα ἐπὶ τῇ βάσει τῆς Παραδόσεως μᾶλλον ἢ τῆς Γραφῆς˙ ὅθεν οἱ Πατέρες τῆς Ζ΄. Οἰκουμενικῆς Συνόδου ἐν μὲν τῇ (ζ΄η# πράξει) αὐτῶν εἶπον "Φυλάττομεν ἀκαινοτομήτους τὰς ἐγγράφους ἢ ἀγράφους τεθεσπισμένας ἡμῖν παραδόσεις" (καλέσαντες τὴν χρῆσιν αὐτῶν Βασιλικὴν ὁδόν), ἐν δὲ τῷ α΄. αὐτῶν κανόνι λέγουσιν "'Ασπασίως τοὺς θείους κανόνας ἐνστερνιζόμεθα, καὶ ὁλόκληρον τὴν αὐτῶν διαταγὴν καὶ ἀσάλευτον κρατύνομεν, τῶν ἐκτεθέντων ὑπὸ τῶν σαλπίγγων τοῦ Πνεύματος πανευφήμων Ἀποστόλων, τῶν τε ἓξ ἁγίων καὶ Οἰκουμενικῶν Συνόδων καὶ τῶν τοπικῶς συναθροισθεισῶν ἐπὶ ἐκδόσει τοιούτων διαταγμάτων, καὶ τῶν ἁγίων Πατέρων ἡμῶν· Ἐξ ἑνὸς γὰρ ἅπαντες καὶ τοῦ αὐτοῦ Πνεύματος αὐγασθέντες, ὥρισαν τὰ

συμφέροντα". Ἐν τούτοις ὅμως καὶ μεθ' ὅλα ταῦτα οἱ ἐκτόπως κατὰ τῶν ἱερῶν Παραδόσεων μαινόμενοι Διαμαρτυρόμενοι τολμῶσι τὴν τοιαύτην Ἐκκλησίαν, ἥτις διέσωσεν ἡμῖν καθαρὰν καὶ ἀλώβητον τὴν θείαν παρακαταθήκην, νὰ κατηγορήσωσιν ὡς διαφθείρασαν τὴν ἀληθῆ Χριστιανικὴν πίστιν! ἀλλ' ἐὰν τοῦτο οὕτως εἶχε καὶ ἡ Ἐκκλησία τῷ ὄντι ἐξέπεσε τῆς ἀληθείας (ἄπαγε τῆς βλασφημίας!), ὡς οἱ τολμητίαι οὗτοι διατείνονται, τότε, ἐρωτῶμεν αὐτούς, ποῦ εἰσιν αἱ θεῖαι ἐκεῖναι τοῦ Σωτῆρος ἐπαγγελίαι, ὅτι ἔσται μετ' αὐτῆς "πάσας τὰς ἡμέρας μέχρι τῆς συντελείας τοῦ αἰῶνος" καὶ ὅτι "πέμψει αὐτῇ τὸ πνεῦμα τῆς ἀληθείας ἵνα ὁδηγῇ αὐτὴν εἰς πᾶσαν τὴν ἀλήθειαν" κτλ.; ὤ! τῆς μεγάλης τῶν ἀσυνέτων τούτων ἀνθρώπων τόλμης καὶ ἀνοίας!

Ἀλλ' ἐκτὸς τῆς φωνῆς τῆς Οἰκουμενικῆς Ἐκκλησίας τὸ μέγα τῆς
ἱερᾶς Παραδόσεως }κῦρος ἐπιβεβαιοῖ καὶ ἡ μαρτυρία πάντων τῶν ἁγίων }23
τῆς Ἐκκλησίας Πατέρων καὶ διδασκάλων καὶ ἄλλων Ἐκκλησιαστικῶν συγγραφέων, ὧν τὴν μεγάλην συμασίαν οὐ μόνον ἅπαντες οἱ Ὀρθόδοξοι καὶ οἱ Παπισταὶ ἀνακηρύττουσιν, ἀλλὰ καὶ αὐτῶν τῶν Διαμαρτυρομένων πολλοὶ αἰσθάνονται καὶ ὁμολογοῦσι. Καὶ ἐν πρώτοις ἴδωμεν τὰς μαρτυρίας τῶν ἐπιφανεστέρων Ἀποστολικῶν Πατέρων, οἵτινες ὡς ἄμεσοι τῶν Ἀποστόλων μαθηταὶ καὶ διάδοχοι παντὸς ἄλλου κάλλιον γινώσκουσι τὴν γνησίαν Ἀποστολικὴν διδασκαλίαν˙ οὕτως ὁ μὲν θεοφόρος Ἰγνάτιος, ὡς μαρτυρεῖ ὁ Καισαρείας Εὐσέβιος *(Ἐκκλ. ἱστ. γ'*. 36), "τὰς κατὰ πόλιν, αἷς ἐπεδήμει, παροικίας . . . παρῄνει, προὔτρεπέ τε ἀπρὶξ ἔχεσθαι τῆς τῶν Ἀποστόλων παραδόσεως, ἣν ὑπὲρ ἀσφαλείας καὶ ἐγγράφως ἤδη μαρτυρόμενος, διατυποῦσθαι ἀναγκαῖον ἡγεῖτο"˙ τὰ αὐτὰ προὔτρεπε καὶ ὁ ἱερομάρτυρος Πολύκαρπος, ὡς ὁ μαθητὴς αὐτοῦ Εἰρηναῖος μαρτυρεῖ λέγων, ὅτι "ἐπὶ Ἀνικήτου ἐπιδημήσας (ὁ Πολύκαρπος) τῇ Ῥώμῃ, πολλοὺς ἀπὸ τῶν προειρημένων αἱρετικῶν ἐπέστρεψεν εἰς τὴν Ἐκκλησίαν τοῦ θεοῦ, μίαν καὶ μόνην ταύτην ἀλήθειαν κηρύξας ὑπὸ τῶν Ἀποστόλων παρειληφέναι, τὴν ὑπὸ τῆς Ἐκκλησίας παραδεδομένην" (*κατὰ αἱρ. γ'*. 3)˙ ὁ δὲ Παπίας ὁμολογεῖ ὅτι πλὴν τῶν θείων Γραφῶν παρέλαβε καὶ τινας ἄλλας ἀληθεῖς διδασκαλίας παρὰ τῶν Ἀποστόλων˙ "οὐ γὰρ τὰ ἐκ τῶν βιβλίων," ἐπιλέγει, "τοσοῦτόν με ὠφελεῖν ὑπελάμβανον, ὅσον τὰ παρὰ ζώσης φωνῆς καὶ μενούσης" (Εὐσεβ. *Ἐκκλ. ἱστ. γ'*. 39)˙ τέλος ὁ ἅγιος Διονύσιος ὁ Ἀρεοπαγίτης λέγει "Δεχόμεθα τοίνυν ὡς ἁπλῶς ἀναγκαῖον εἰς τὴν τοῦ ἀνθρώπου σωτηρίαν τόν τε θεῖον νόμον καὶ τὰς προφητικὰς θεσμοθεσίας καὶ τὰς Εὐαγγελικὰς ἐντολὰς εἰς τὰς Ἀποστολικὰς διατάξεις καὶ τὰς ἱερὰς τῆς Ἐκκλησίας ἀγράφους παραδόσεις, ὧν οἱ παραβάται

αἱρετικοὶ ὀνομάζονται" (*περὶ Ἐκκλ. ἱεραρχ.* α΄.). Κατὰ δὲ τὸ β΄ου αἰῶνα ὁ Ἡγήσιππος, ὡς μαρτυρεῖ ὁ Εὐσέβιος (*Ἐκκλ. ἱστ.* δ΄. 22), πολλὰς περιελθὼν πόλεις καὶ ἐπαρχίας πανταχοῦ εὗρε τὴν αὐτὴν γνησίαν Ἀποστολικὴν διδασκαλίαν˙ "ἐν πέντε δὴ οὖν συγγράμμασιν οὗτος τὴν ἀπλανῆ παράδοσιν τοῦ ἀποστολικοῦ κηρύγματος ἁπλουστάτῃ συντάξει γραφῆς ὑπεμνηματίσατο" (Εὐσεβ. *Ἐκκλ. ἱστ.* δ΄. 8)˙ ὁ δὲ ἅγιος Εἰρηναῖος ἀποκρούων τοὺς αἱρετικοὺς διὰ τῆς παραδόσεως μᾶλλον ἢ διὰ τῆς Γραφῆς λέγει αὐτοῖς "τὴν Ἀποστολικὴν παράδοσιν τὴν γνωστὴν ἅπαντι τῷ κόσμῳ δύναται ἰδεῖν ἐν ἑκάστῃ Ἐκκλησίᾳ πᾶς ὁ θέλων ἰδεῖν τὴν ἀλήθειαν" (*κατὰ αἱρ.* γ΄. 3). Κατὰ τὸν γ΄ου αἰῶνα ὁ Τερτυλλιανὸς οὐ μόνον παρῄνει τῶν Ἀποστολικῶν ἔχεσθαι παραδόσεων, ἀλλὰ καὶ δι᾽ αὐτῶν κυρίως ἀνῄρει τὰς
τῶν Αἱρετικῶν }κακοδοξίας˙ ἰδοὺ τί λέγει "Apostolos Domini habemus }24
auctores, qui nec ipsi quidquam ex suo arbitrio, quod inducerent, elegerunt, sed acceptam a Christo disciplinam fideliter nationibus adsignaverunt" (*de praescript.* c. VI)˙ ὁ δὲ Κλήμης ὁ Ἀλεξανδρεὺς λέγει "Ἀλλ᾽ οἱ μὲν τὴν ἀληθῆ τῆς μακαρίας σῴζοντες διδασκαλίας παράδοσιν εὐθὺς ἀπὸ Πέτρου τε καὶ Ἰωάννου καὶ Ἰακώβου καὶ Παύλου τῶν ἁγίων Ἀποστόλων, παῖς παρὰ πατρὸς ἐκδεξάμενος, ὀλίγοι δὲ οἱ πατράσιν ὅμοιοι˙ ἧκον δὴ σὺν θεῷ καὶ εἰς ἡμᾶς τὰ προγονικὰ ἐκεῖνα καὶ ἀποστολικὰ καταθησόμενοι σπέρματα" (*Στρωμ.* κεφ. α΄. 1. §11. 12)˙ ὁ δὲ πατὴρ τῆς κριτικῆς Ὠριγένης λέγει "Τηρητέα οὖν ἡ Ἀποστολικὴ παράδοσις παρὰ τῶν Ἀποστόλων τῇ τάξει τῆς διαδοχῆς παραδοθεῖσα καὶ μέχρις ἡμῶν ἐν ταῖς Ἐκκλησίαις ὑπάρχουσα˙ μόνη δ᾽ αὕτη ἡ ἀλήθεια πιστευτέα ἡ μηδὲν διαφέρουσα τῆς Ἐκκλησιαστικῆς καὶ Ἀποστολικῆς παραδόσεως" (*περὶ Ἄρχων* βιβλ. α΄. κεφ. β΄.)˙ ὁ δὲ ἅγιος Κυπριανὸς λέγει "Ῥᾴδιον ψυχαῖς εὐσεβέσι καὶ ἁπλαῖς, καὶ πλάνας ἀποφεύγειν καὶ τὴν ἀλήθειαν εὑρίσκειν˙ ἅμα γὰρ εἰς τὴν πηγὴν τῆς θείας τραπῶμεν παραδόσεως ἀπόλλυται ἡ πλάνη" (*ἐπιστ.* ξγ΄.). Κατὰ τὸν δ΄ου τέλος αἰωνα, καθ᾽ ὃν ἤκμασαν οἱ μέγιστοι καὶ ἐπιφανέστεροι τῆς Ἐκκλησίας Πατέρες καὶ διδάσκαλοι, ἱκανὸν ἡγοῦμαι πρὸς ἀποστόμωσιν τῶν τῆς ἱερᾶς Παραδόσεως ἐχθρῶν ἵνα ἀναφέρωμεν τὰς περὶ αὐτῆς μαρτυρίας τριῶν μόνον Πατέρων, οὕσπερ ὅμως ἅπαντες οἱ αἰῶνες θεωροῦσιν ὡς τρεῖς μεγίστους τοῦ Χριστιανικοῦ στερεώματος φωστῆρας, Βασίλειον λέγω τὸν Μέγαν, Γρηγόριον τὸν Θεολόγον καὶ Ἰωάννην τὸν Χρυσόστομον. Καὶ ὁ μὲν Μέγας Βασίλειος τάδε λέγει "Τῶν ἐν τῇ Ἐκκλησίᾳ πεφυλαγμένων δογμάτων καὶ κηρυγμάτων, τὰ μὲν ἐκ τῆς ἐγγράφου διδασκαλίας ἔχομεν, τὰ δὲ ἐκ τῆς τῶν Ἀποστόλων παραδόσεως διασωθέντα ἡμῖν ἐν μυστηρίῳ παρεδεξάμεθα, ἅπερ ἀμφότερα τὴν αὐτὴν

ἰσχὺν ἔχει πρὸς τὴν εὐσέβειαν˙ καὶ τούτοις οὐδεὶς ἀντερεῖ, οὐκοῦν ὅστις γε κἂν κατὰ μικρὸν γοῦν θεσμῶν ἐκκλησιαστικῶν πεπείραται˙ εἰ γὰρ ἐπιχειρήσαιμεν τὰ ἄγραφα τῶν ἐθῶν, ὡς μὴ μεγάλην ἔχοντα τὴν δύναμιν, παραιτεῖσθαι, λάθοιμεν ἂν εἰς αὐτὰ τὰ καίρια ζημιοῦντες τὸ Εὐαγγέλιον, μᾶλλον δὲ εἰς ὄνομα ψιλὸν περιϊστῶντες τὸ κήρυγμα˙ οἷον (ἵνα τοῦ πρώτου καὶ κοινοτάτου πρῶτον μνησθῶ) τὸ τῷ τύπῳ τοῦ Σταυροῦ τοὺς εἰς τὸ ὄνομα τοῦ Κυρίου ἡμῶν Ἰησοῦ Χριστοῦ ἠλπικότας κατασημαίνεσθαι, τίς ὁ διὰ γράμματος διδάξας; Τὸ πρὸς ἀνατολὰς τετράφθαι κατὰ τὴν προσευχήν, ποῖον ἡμᾶς ἐδίδαξεν γράμμα; Τὰ τῆς Ἐπικλήσεως ῥήματα ἐπὶ τῇ ἀναδείξει τοῦ ἄρτου τῆς εὐχαριστίας καὶ τοῦ ποτηρίου τῆς εὐλογίας, τίς τῶν ἁγίων ἐγγράφως ἡμῖν καταλέλοιπεν; οὐ γὰρ δὴ τούτοις ἀρκούμεθα, ὧν ὁ ἀπόστολος ἢ τὸ Εὐαγγέλιον ἐπεμνήσθη, ἀλλὰ καὶ προλέγομεν καὶ ἐπιλέγομεν ἕτερα ὡς μεγάλην ἔχοντα πρὸς τὸ μυστήριον τὴν ἰσχύν, ἐκ τῆς ἀγράφου διδασκαλίας παραλαβόντες˙ εὐλογοῦμεν δὲ τό τε ὕδωρ τοῦ Βαπτίσματος, καὶ τὸ ἔλαιον τῆς χρίσεως, καὶ προσέτι αὐτὸν τὸν βαπτιζόμενον, ἀπὸ ποίων ἐγγράφων; οὐκ ἀπὸ τῆς σιωπωμένης καὶ μυστικῆς παραδόσεως; τί δέ; αὐτὴν τοῦ ἐλαίου τὴν χρῖσιν, τίς λόγος γεγραμμένος ἐδίδαξε; τὸ δὲ τρὶς βαπτίζεσθαι τὸν ἄνθρωπον, πόθεν; ἄλλα δέ, ὅσα περὶ τὸ βάπτισμα, ἀποτάσσεσθαι τῷ Σατανᾷ καὶ τοῖς ἀγγέλοις αὐτοῦ, ἐκ ποίας ἐστὶ γραφῆς; οὐκ ἐκ τῆς ἀδημοσιεύτου ταύτης καὶ ἀποῤῥήτου διδασκαλίας, ἣν ἐν ἀπολυπραγμονήτῳ καὶ ἀπεριεργάστῳ σιγῇ οἱ Πατέρες ἡμῶν ἐφύλαξαν; . . ." (*περὶ ἁγ. Πν.* κεφ κζ΄.)˙ ὁ δὲ Θεολόγος Γρηγόριος λέγει "Ὁρῶν (ὁ Ἰουλιανός) τὸν ἡμέτερον λόγον μέγαν μὲν ὄντα τοῖς δόγμασι καὶ ταῖς ἄνωθεν μαρτυρίαις . . . ἔτι δὲ μείζω καὶ γνωριμώτερον τοῖς παραδεδομένοις καὶ εἰς τόδε τετηρημένοις τύποις τῆς Ἐκκλησίας, ἵνα μηδὲ τοῦτο ἀκακούργητον μένῃ, τί μηχανᾶται καὶ τί ποιεῖ;" (*κατὰ Ἰουλ. στηλιτ. Α΄.),* καὶ ἀλλαχοῦ "φυλάσσοντες τὴν καλὴν παρακαταθήκην, ἣν παρὰ τῶν πατέρων εἰλήφαμεν προσκυνοῦντες Πατέρα καὶ Υἱὸν καὶ Ἅγιον Πνεῦμα, ἐν Υἱῷ τὸν Πατέρα, ἐν Πνεύματι τὸν Υἱὸν γινώσκοντες, εἰς ἃ βεβαπτίσμεθα, εἰς ἃ πεπιστεύκαμεν, οἷς συντετάγμεθα" (*Εἰρηνικά.* α΄)˙ τέλος ὁ ἱερός Χρυσόστομος ἑρμηνεύων τὸ τῆς (Β΄. θεσ. β΄. 15) χωρίου λέγει "Ἐντεῦθεν δῆλον, ὅτι οὐ πάντα δι᾽ἐπιστολῆς παραδίδοσαν (οἱ Ἀπόστολοι), ἀλλὰ πολλὰ καὶ ἀγράφως ὁμοίως δὲ κἀκεῖνα καὶ ταῦτά ἐστιν ἀξιόπιστα˙ ὥστε καὶ τὴν παράδοσιν τῆς Ἐκκλησίας ἀξιόπιστα ἡγούμεθα˙ παράδοσίς ἐστι, μηδὲν πλέον ζήτει" (*ὁμιλ. δ΄. εἰς τὴν Β΄. Θεσσαλ.*).

Μεθ'ὅλην ὅμως τὴν σαφῆ ταύτην καὶ λαμπροτάτην περὶ τῆς ἱερᾶς Παραδόσεως μαρτυρίαν τῶν ἀρχαιοτάτων τῆς Ἐκκλησίας Πατέρων καὶ διδασκάλων οἱ Διαμαρτυρόμενοι ἐκ μέσου τὰς Παραδόσεις ἆραι πειρώμενοι ἀντιτάσσουσιν ἡμῖν τὰς μαρτυρίας Πατέρων τινῶν δῆθεν τὰς ἱερὰς Παραδόσεις ἀπορρεπτόντων˙ ὁ Εἰρηναῖος ἐν πρώτοις, λέγουσι, πολεμῶν τοὺς Γνωστικοὺς καὶ ἰδίᾳ τοὺς Μαρκιανίτας ἀπορρίπτει τὰς παραδόσεις δι' ὧν λέγει αὐτοῖς "Legite diligentius id quod ab apostolis est Evangelium nobis datum, et legite diligentius prophetas, et invenietis . . . omnem }doctrinam Domini nostri praedictam in ipsis" (*κατὰ Αἱρ.* IV. 36 }26
§1), ἤτοι "Ἀνάγνωτε ἐπιμελῶς τό τε παρὰ τῶν Ἀποστόλων δοθὲν ἡμῖν Εὐαγγέλιον καὶ τοὺς Προφήτας, καὶ εὑρήσετε ἐν αὐτοῖς . . . ἅπασαν τὴν τοῦ Κυρίου ἡμῶν διδασκαλίαν προειρημένην"˙ ἀλλὰ πόσα ἀδίκως ὁ Πατὴρ οὗτος διαβάλλεται! διότι ἐν τῷ χωρίῳ τούτῳ ὁ Εἰρηναῖος οὐ μόνον δὲν ἀπορρίπτει τὰς ἱερὰς Παραδόσεις, ἀλλὰ καὶ τοὐναντίον ὑπερασπίζει αὐτὰς καὶ περιθριγκοῖ ἀπέναντι τῶν ψευδῶν τῆς ψευδωνύμου Γνώσεως παραδόσεων˙ προτρέπει δὲ τοὺς Μαρκιωνίτας εἰς τὴν ἀνάγωνσιν τῶν Εὐαγγελίων καὶ Προφητῶν οὐχὶ ὅτι δὲν παραδέχεται καὶ τὴν ἱερὰν Παράδοσιν (ἣν τοὐναντίον, ὡς εἴδομεν, παραδέχεταί τε καὶ τοῖς ἄλλοις συνίστησι), ἀλλὰ διότι θέλει νὰ καταδείξῃ εἰς τοὺς ῥηθέντας αἱρετικοὺς ὅτι ἥ τε Π.Δ. καὶ ἡ Κ.Δ. εἶνε ἔργον ἑνὸς καὶ τοῦ αὐτοῦ θεοῦ, τοῦθ' ὅπερ ἠρνοῦντο οἱ αἱρετικοὶ οὗτοι˙ διὸ καὶ λέγει αὐτοῖς μετὰ προσοχῆς ν'ἀναγνῶσι τά τε Εὐαγγέλια καὶ τοὺς Προφήτας ἵνα πεισθῶσι περὶ τῆς πλήρους ἀμφοτέρων τῶν Διαθήκων συμφωνίας˙ ὅτι δὲ ὁ Εἰρηναῖος ἐν τῷ ἀνωτέρῳ χωρίῳ ἀπορρίπτει οὐχὶ τὰς ἱερὰς Παραδόσεις, ἀλλὰ τὰς ψευδεῖς ἐκείνας καὶ κακοδόξους διδασκαλίας, ἃς οἱ Μαρκιωνῖται διετείνοντο ὅτι παρέδωκεν αὐτὸς ὁ Κύριος κρυφίας εἰς ὡρισμένους τινὰς μαθητὰς ἵνα οὗτοι ἀποκαλύψωσιν αὐτὰς μόνοις τοῖς ἱκανοῖς ἐννοῆσαι αὐτὰς καὶ διατηρῆσαι, τοῦτο δείκνυσιν ὁ αὐτὸς ἐν οἷς ὀλίγῳ ἀνωτέρω λέγει "καὶ γὰρ εἴ τινα ἀπόκρυφα μυστήρια ᾔδεισαν οἱ Ἀπόστολοι, ἃ ἰδίᾳ καὶ λάθρα τῶν λοιπῶν ἐδίδασκον τοὺς τελείους, τούτοις ἂν οὐχ ἥκιστα παρέδοσαν, οἷς καὶ αὐτὰς τὰς Ἐκκλησίας παρετιθοῦντο" (*κατὰ αἱρ.* III. γ΄. 1)˙ δικαίως ἑπομένως πολεμῶν τοὺς Μαρκιωνίτας ὁ ἅγιος Εἰρηναῖος ἀπορρίπτει τὰς ψευδεῖς αὐτῶν παραδόσεις τὰς ὅλας ἐναντίας εἴς τε τὴν ἁγίαν Γραφὴν καὶ τὴν ἱερὰν Παράδοσιν. Ἀλλὰ καὶ ὁ Ἱερώνυμος, λέγουσιν, ἐν τῷ κατὰ Ἑλβιδίου συγγράμματι αὐτοῦ (τόμ. II. § 19) ἀπορρίπτει πᾶσαν παράδοσιν λέγων "Sed ut haec quae scripta sunt, non negamus, ita ea quae non sunt scripta, renuimus", ἤτοι "ὥσπερ τὰ γεγραμμένα οὐκ ἀπαρνούμεθα, οὕτω

τὰ μὴ γεγραμμένα οὐκ ἀποδεχόμεθα", καὶ ἀλλαχοῦ (*εἰς τὸν Ματθ.* κγ΄. 35-36) λέγει "Hoc quia de scripturis non habet auctoritatem, eadem facilitate comtemnitur, qua probatur", ἤτοι "τὸ ἐκ τῶν Γραφῶν μὴ ἐπιμαρτυρόμενον ῥᾳδίως καταφρονεῖται, οἷα δὴ καὶ κατασκευάζεται"· ἀλλὰ πόσον κακοβούλως καὶ ὁ Πατὴρ οὗτος συκοφαντεῖται! διότι ταῦτα λέγων ὁ Ἱερώνυμος ἐννοεῖ οὐχὶ τὰς ἱερὰς }Παραδόσεις, ὧν τὴν τήρησιν }27
πολλαχοῦ τῶν συγγραμμάτων αὐτοῦ συνίστησιν, ἀλλὰ τὰς ψευδεῖς καὶ ἀνυποστάτους τῶν Ἑλβιδίων τερθρείας, οἷον λ.χ. ὅτι ὁ Χριστὸς ἐξῆλθεν ἐκ τῆς παρθενικῆς νηδύος ῥυπώδης ὡς τὰ ἄλλα βρέφη, ὅτι Ζαχαρίας ὁ υἱὸς τοῦ Βαραχίου ἦν πατὴρ Ἰωάννου τοῦ Βαπτιστοῦ καὶ ἄλλα τοιαῦτα ψευδολογήματα. Ἀλλὰ καὶ ὁ Ἱεροσολύμων Κύριλλος, λέγουσιν, ὁμιλῶν περὶ τοῦ Ἁγ. Πνεύματος ἐκσυρίττει τὴν ἱερὰν Παράδοσιν συνιστὰς μόνον τὴν ἁγίαν Γραφήν· τὸ χωρίον ἔχει οὕτω· "Μηδὲ ἐμοὶ τῷ ταῦτά σοι λέγοντι ἁπλῶς πιστεύσῃς, ἐὰν τὴν ἀπόδειξιν τῶν καταγγελλομένων ἀπὸ τῶν θείων μὴ λάβῃς Γραφῶν" (*Κατηχ.* δ΄. 17). Ἀλλὰ τὶς ἐχέφρων ἀνὴρ ἀναγινώσκων τὸ χωριὸν τοῦτο, ἔστω καὶ οὕτως ἀπομεμονωμένον, θέλει συναγάγει τὸ ἀτοπώτατον συμπέρασμα ὅτι ὁ ἅγιος Κύριλλος ἀπορρίπτει τὰς ἱερὰς Παραδόσεις; διότι ἐκτὸς τοῦ ὅτι αἱ ἱεραὶ Παραδόσεις κατὰ πάντα συνᾴδουσι πρὸς τὰς ἁγίας Γραφάς, καὶ ὁ ἱερὸς Κύριλλος εἶπε τὸ χωρίον τοῦτο ἔχων ἐνώπιον αὐτοῦ ἀκροατὰς κατὰ πάντα εἰς τοὺς λόγους αὐτοῦ εὐπειθεῖς, καὶ ἑπομένως οὐδόλως ἐφοβεῖτο μήπως οὗτοι διαμφισβητήσωσιν αὐτῷ τὴν ὀρθότητα τῆς ὑπ᾽ αὐτοῦ ἀποδιδομένης εἰς τὰ διάφορα Γραφικὰ χωρία ἑρμηνείας· ἐνῷ ἐὰν εἶχεν ἄλλους ἀκροατάς, Ἀρειανοὺς φέρ᾽ εἰπεῖν ἢ Πνευματομάχους, οἵτινες βεβαίως θὰ διημφισβήτουν αὐτῷ τὴν ἔννοιαν ὅλων τῶν Γραφικῶν χωρίων ἢ θὰ ἀντέτασσον αὐτῷ ἕτερα χωρία, τότε πῶς ἄλλως θὰ ἠδύνατο ὁ ἅγιος Κύριλλος ν᾽ἀποδείξῃ εἰς αὐτοὶς ἀληθῆ ἔννοιαν τῶν ὑπ᾽ αὐτῶν παρερμηνευομένων Γραφικῶν χωρίων εἰμὴ διὰ τῆς παραδόσεως; ἀλλὰ μήπως καὶ πολλαχοῦ ἀλλαχοῦ τῶν κατηχήσεων αὐτοῦ ὁ ἱερὸς Κύριλλος δὲν συνίστησι τὰς ἱερὰς Παραδόσεις; (ὅρ. *Κατηχ.* δ΄. 35).

Τούτους καὶ ἄλλους ἀρχαίους τῆς Ἐκκλησίας Πατέρας καὶ διδασκάλους ἀδίκως ὅλως καὶ κακοβούλως οἱ Διαμαρτυρόμενοι συκοφαντοῦντες ζητοῦσιν, ἵνα ἀθετήσωσι τὸ κῦρος τῶν ἱερῶν Παραδόσεων ὡς δῆθεν ἀνθρωπίνων ἐνταλμάτων καὶ οὐδὲν πλέον! Ἀλλ᾽ ἐνταῦθα ὀφείλομεν ἵνα χάριν τῆς ἀληθείας παρατηρήσωμεν ὅτι οὐχὶ πάντες οἱ Διαμαρτυρόμενοι πάσας τὰς ἱερὰς Παραδόσεις ἀπαρρίπτουσιν, ἀλλ᾽ ἄλλοι μὲν ὅλας ἐν γένει τὰς ἱερὰς Παραδόσεις ἀπορρίπτοντες ὅλως ἀσυστόλως κατὰ τῶν ἁγίων

ὑμῶν Πατέρων ἐπιτίθενται, ἄλλοι δὲ μετριοπαθέστερόν πως φερόμενοι διατείνονται ὅτι μόνον αἱ τῶν τεσσάρων πρώτων αἰώνων παραδόσεις εἶνε ἀληθεῖς Ἀποστολικαὶ παραδόσεις. Καὶ οἱ μὲν πρῶτοι δικαιολογοῦσι τὴν παράλογον αὐτῶν κατὰ τῶν ἁγίων Πατέρων κα-}ταφορὰν λέγοντες ὅτι οἱ }28
ἀρχαῖοι ἐκεῖνοι τῆς Ἐκκλησίας Πατέρες ὄντες ἄνθρωποι εὔπιστοι, εὐαπάτητοι καὶ ὅλως τῆς κριτικῆς ἐπιστήμης ἄμοιροι, πρὸς δὲ καὶ τῇ Πλατωνικῇ φιλοσοφίᾳ λίαν ὄντες προσκείμενοι, ἣν ἐζήτουν νὰ συμβιβάσωσι μετὰ τοῦ Χριστιανισμοῦ ἐν πολλοῖς παρεξέκλιναν τῆς ὀρθῆς Χριστιανικῆς διδασκαλίας εἴτε πολλὰς ὑπόπτους γραφὰς ὡς γνωσίας παραδεχθέντες εἴτε εἰς ἄλλας πλάνας καὶ ἀπάτας περιπεσόντες, οἷον λ.χ. ὅτι ὁ θεὸς καὶ οἱ Ἄγγελοι εἶνε ἐνσώματοι, ὅτι ὁ Χριστὸς ἔζησεν ἐπὶ τῆς γῆς πλέον ἢ τεσσαράκοντα ἔτη, ὅτι μέλλει ὁ Χριστὸς νὰ βασιλεύσῃ ἐπὶ τῆς γῆς πρὸ τῆς δευτέρας παρουσίας χίλια ἔτη, ὅτι ἑορταστεὸν τὸ Πάσχα τὴν 14ην Νισὰν καὶ τὰ τοιαῦτα˙ ἐντεῦθεν, λέγουσιν, ἡ παράδοσις διαφθαρεῖσα ἐγένετο πηγὴ νέων δογμάτων καὶ διδαγμάτων μηδόλως ἐν τῇ Γραφῇ περιεχομένων. Πρὸς ταῦτα ὅμως ἡμεῖς ἀπαντῶντες παρατηροῦμεν 1.) ὅτι ἐὰν τῷ ὄντι οἱ Πατέρες ἐκεῖνοι ἦσαν τόσον ἀμαθεῖς καὶ εὐαπάτητοι, ὥστε διέφθειραν τὴν ἀληθῆ Χριστιανικὴν πίστιν, τότε πταίουσιν αὐτοὶ οἱ Ἀπόστολοι, οἵτινες τοιούτους διαδόχους κατέστησαν ἐν τῇ Ἐκκλησίᾳ! τότε αἱ τοῦ Κυρίου ἐπαγγελίαι ὅτι ἔσται μετὰ τῆς Ἐκκλησίας "πάσας τὰς ἡμέρας" καὶ ὅτι αὐτὸ τὸ Πνεῦμα τὸ Ἅγιον "ὁδηγήσει αὐτὴν εἰς πᾶσαν τὴν ἀλήθειαν" ἔμειναν ἀνεκτέλεστοι! τότε τέλος καὶ αὐτὴ ἡ σωτηρία ἡμῶν εἶνε ἀμφίβολος! 2.) ἐὰν τῷ ὄντι οἱ Πατέρες ἐκεῖνοι ἐξ ἐλλείψεως κριτικῆς γνώσεως παρεδέχθησαν γραφάς τινας ὑπόπτους ὡς γνησίας, τότε, ἐρωτῶμεν, πόθεν δυνάμεθα νὰ βεβαιωθῶμεν περὶ τῆς γνησιότητος τῶν Γραφῶν, ἃς ἔχομεν σήμερον; ἀλλ᾽ ἐὰν 3.) πράγματι οἱ Πατέρες ἐκεῖνοι περιέπεσαι εἴς τινας πεπλανημένας ἰδέας, ποία, ἐρωτῶμεν, τοιαύτη οἱουδήποτε Πατρὸς πεπλανημένη γνώμη θεωρεῖται ἐν τῇ Ἐκκλησίᾳ ὡς Ἀποστολικὴ παράδοσις; μήπως δὲν κατεδικάσθησαν οἱ Χιλιασταί, οἱ Τεσσαρεσκαιδεκατῖται καὶ πᾶσαι ἐν γένει αἱ κακόδοξοι καὶ εἴτε τῇ ἁγίᾳ Γραφῇ εἴτε τῇ ἱερᾷ Παραδόσει ἀντιβαίνουσαι ἐκεῖναι γνῶμαι; ὅτι οἱ Πατέρες ἠδύναντο νὰ πλανηθῶσι, τοῦτο οὐδ᾽ ἡμεῖς ἀρνούμεθα˙ ἀλλὰ τὸ ζήτημα εἶνε ἐὰν τοιαῦταί τινες πεπλανημέναι ἰδέαι ἐγένοντό ωστε ἐν τῇ Ἐκκλησίᾳ παραδεκταὶ ὡς Ἀποστολικαὶ παραδόσεις, καὶ ἐὰν ἑπομένως ἡ γνησία Ἀποστολικὴ διδασκαλία ἐνοθεύθη κατά τε ὑπὸ τῶν Πατέρων ἢ διεφθάρη˙ ἡμεῖς διατεινόμεθα ὅτι οἱ Πατέρες οὐ μόνον δὲν ἐνόθευσαν τὴν Ἀποστολικὴν

διδασκαλίαν ἢ διέφθειραν, ἀλλ᾽ οὐδ᾽ ἠδύναντο νὰ νοθεύσωσιν αὐτὴν ἢ
διαστρέψωσι 1.) διότι οἱ Πατέρες ἐκεῖνοι καὶ Ποιμένες τῆς Ἐκκλησίας
δημοσίᾳ τὰ τῆς πίστεως δόγματα διδάσκοντες καὶ δὴ καὶ ἐν συνάξεσι
Χριστιανῶν παιδιόθεν τὴν Χριστιανικὴν πίστιν }διδαχθέντων ἢ καὶ }29
αὐτῶν τῶν Ἀποστόλων ἢ διαδόχων αὐτῶν ἀκουσάντων οὐ μόνον δὲν
ἠδύναντο νὰ διαστρέψωσι τὴν Ἀποστολικὴν διδασκαλίαν, ἀλλ᾽ οὐδ᾽
ἀκουσίως ἀπ᾽ αὐτῆς νὰ παρεκκλίνωσι˙ διότι ἐὰν καὶ ἐτόλμησέ τίς ποτε νὰ
εἰσαγάγῃ τι ξένον ἐν τῇ διδασκαλίᾳ τῶν Ἀποστόλων, ὁ τοιοῦτος μετὰ
πρώτην καὶ δευτέραν νουθεσίαν ὡς ἐθνικὸς ὑπὸ τῆς Ἐκκλησίας ἐθεωρεῖτο
καὶ ἐκτὸς τοῦ περιβόλου αὐτῆς ἐξωθεῖτο˙ εἶνε γνωστὴ ἡ τύχη Παύλου τοῦ
Σαμοσατέως, Σαβελλίου, Ἀρείου, Νεστορίου, Εὐτυχοῦς καὶ Διοσκόρου
καὶ τῶν λοιπῶν Αἱρεσιαρχῶν˙ πόσον δὲ ἦν ἡ Ἐκκλησία ἀμερόληπτος ἐν
τῇ ὑπερασπίσει τῆς θείας παρακαταθήκης, ἧς θεόθεν φύλαξ καὶ ὑπέρμαχος
ἐτάχθη, δείκνυσιν ἡ ὑπ᾽αὐτῆς καταδίκη ἀνδρῶν ἄλλως ἐπισήμων καὶ
μεγαλοφυῶν, οἷοι Θεόδωρος ὁ Μοψουεστίας, Ἀπολλινάριος ὁ
Λαοδικείας, καὶ ὁ πάντων θαυμασιώτατος Ὠριγένης ὁ Ἀδαμάντιος˙ 2.) δὲ
δὲν ἠδύναντο, λέγομεν, οἱ Πατέρες νὰ διαστρέψωσι τὴν Ἀποστολικὴν
διδασκαλίαν, διότι πολεμοῦντες πρὸς Αἱρετικοὺς κακοβούλως τὴν ἁγίαν
Γραφὴν παρεξηγοῦντας καὶ διαστρέφοντας ἐπεκαλοῦντο εἰς μαρτύριον
τοῦ ἀληθοῦς τῆς Γραφῆς νοήματος τὴν Ἀποστολικὴν παράδοσιν, ἣν μὴ
δυνάμενοι οἱ Αἱρετικοί, ὡς τὴν Γραφήν, νὰ διαστρέφωσι καὶ
παρερμηνεύωσι κατέφευγον εἰς διάφορα σοφίσματα καὶ φιλοσοφικὰ
ἐπιχειρήματα κατηγοροῦντες ὁτὲ μὲν τῶν Ἀποστόλων ἐπὶ ἀμαθείᾳ, ὁτὲ δὲ
τῶν Πατέρων ἐπὶ κακῇ τῆς Ἀποστολικῆς διδασκαλίας ἀντιλήψει! πῶς
λοιπὸν ἐν μέσῳ τοιούτων φοβερῶν ἐχθρῶν ἠδύναντο οἱ ἅγιοι ἐκεῖνοι
Πατέρες καὶ διδάσκαλοι νὰ διαστρέψωσιν ἔστω καὶ ἓν μόνον τῆς
Χριστιανικῆς πίστεως δόγμα; Ἐντεῦθεν πολλοὶ τῶν Διαμαρτυρομένων τὸ
ἀναντίρρητον κῦρος τῶν ἱερῶν Παραδόσεων κατανοοῦντες ἀποφαίνονται
ὅτι εἶνε μὲν ἀναγκαία ἡ Παράδοσις, ἀλλ᾽ἀσφαλῶς δυνάμεθα
ν᾽ἀκολουθήσωμεν μόνον τὴν τῶν τριῶν ἢ τεσσάρων πρώτων αἰώνων
παράδοσιν˙ διότι λέγουσι, κατὰ τοὺς τέσσαρας πρώτους τοῦ Χριστιανισμοῦ
αἰῶνας τὰ πάντα ἦσαν πρόσφατα, μηδεμιᾶς ἔτι διαφθορᾶς ἐν τῇ Ἐκκλησίᾳ
εἰσελθούσης, ἡ δὲ Χριστιανικὴ πίστις ἦν ἔτι περιωρισμένη ἐν ὀλίγοις
δόγμασι, τοῦθ᾽ὅπερ δὲν διετηρήθη καὶ κατὰ τοὺς μετέπειτα χρόνους,
καθ᾽οὓς ἡ μὲν καθαρὰ Ἀποστολικὴ παράδοσις ἠλλοιώθη, τὰ δὲ δόγματα
ἐπολλαπλασιάσθησαν. Ἀλλ᾽ἀπαντῶντες πρὸς τοὺς τὰ τοιαῦτα
διατεινομένους Διαμαρτυρομένους εὐθὺς ἐξ ἀρχῆς ἐρωτῶμεν αὐτοὺς

ποῖα εἶνε τὰ νέα ταῦτα δόγματα, ἅτινα λέγουσιν ὅτι μετὰ τὸν δ΄ον αἰῶνα
ἐδημιουγήθησαν; μήπως τὴν ἐν σχέσει πρὸς τὰ ἑκάστοτε ἀναφυόμενα
θεολογικὰ ζητήματα ἀνάπτυξιν τοῦ περιεχομένου τῆς θείας Ἀποκαλύψεως
καὶ διατύπωσιν θεωροῦσιν ὡς δημιουγίαν νέων δογμάτων; }- ἀλλὰ τότε }30
πολὺ ἀπατῶνται συγχέοντες τὸ οὐσιῶδες μετὰ τοῦ ἐπουσιώδους καὶ τὸ
σταθερὸν καὶ ἀεὶ ὡσαύτως ἔχον μετὰ τοῦ συμβεβηκότος καὶ ἑκάστοτε
μεταβλητοῦ˙ ἡμεῖς ὅμως μηδαμῶς τὸ ἀναπτύσσειν μετὰ τοῦ δημιουργεῖν
συγχέοντες διατεινόμεθα ὅτι ἡ Ἐκκλησία κηρύττουσα εἰς πάντα τὰ ἔθνη
πάντων τῶν αἰώνων τὸ Εὐαγγέλιον τῆς σωτηρίας δύναται τὴν οὐσίαν καὶ
τὸ πνεῦμα τῆς Ἀποστολικῆς διδασκαλίας διατηροῦσα νὰ ἐκτιθῇ τὰς
Χριστιανικᾶς ἀληθείας καὶ διαμορφοῖ ἀναλόγως πρὸς τὰς ἀνάγκας τῶν
διαφόρων ἐποχῶν˙ καὶ τοῦτο εἶνε λίαν φυσικὸν καὶ λογικόν˙ διότι τί
ὤφειλεν ἆρά γε ἡ Ἐκκλησία νὰ πράξῃ, ὅτε ἔνθεν μὲν Νεστόριοι καὶ
Διόσκοροι ἐξεγείροντο συγχέοντες τὰ ἀσύγχυτα καὶ χωρίζοντες τὰ
ἀχώριστα, ἔνθεν δὲ οἱ πιστοὶ πτοούμενοι ἀπέναντι τῆς μιαρᾶς ταύτης τῶν
αἱρετικῶν διδασκαλίας ἐσαλεύοντο ἐν τῇ πίστει καὶ ἐκλονοῦντο; ἔπρεπεν
ἆρά γε ν᾽ἀφήσῃ τοὺς αἱρετικοὺς τούτους ἐλευθέρως νὰ διασπείρωσι
μεταξὺ τῶν πιστῶν τὰ ζιζάνια τῆς ψυχοφθόρου αὐτῶν διδασκαλίας, ἤ
ἔπρεπεν ἀμέσως ἐκριζώσασα τὰ ζιζάνια νὰ καθαρίσῃ ἀκριβέστερα καὶ
διατυπώσῃ σαφέστερον τὴν Χριστιανικὴν διδασκαλίαν; ἡ Ἐκκλησία
ἔπραξε τὸ δεύτερον˙ ἀλλὰ τοῦτο πράξασα ἐθέσπεσέ τι νέον ἤ πρὸς τὴν
ἱερὰν παράδοσιν τῶν τεσσάρων πρώτων αἰώνων ἀντιβαῖνον; καθαρίσασα
λ.χ. τὸ ὁμοούσιον τοῦ Υἱοῦ καὶ τὸ θεάνθρωπον Αὐτοῦ ἐν γένει εἰσήγαγε
νέα δόγματα; ἄπαγε! ᾿Αλλ᾽ἔλθωμεν ἤδη καὶ εἰς τὸ δεύτερον τῆς ἐνστάσεως
μέρος, ὅτι δηλ# ἡ ἀληθὴς Ἀποστολικὴ παράδοσις ἠλλοιώθη μετὰ τὸν δ΄ον
αἰῶνα καὶ διεφθάρη˙ ἀλλ᾽ ἵνα ἀφῶμεν ἀφ᾽ἑνὸς μὲν τὸν ἔνθερμον τῶν τῆς
Ἐκκλησίας Πατέρων ζῆλον ὑπὲρ τῶν Ἀποστολικῶν παραδόσεων,
ἀφ᾽ἑτέρου δὲ τὴν μεγάλην εἰς αὐτὰς ἀφοσίωσιν τῶν πιστῶν˙ τοῦτο μόνον
τοὺς ἀντιπάλους ἡμῶν ἐρωτῶμεν, πῶς δηλ# ἠδύνατο ἡ "ἅπαντι τῷ κόσμῳ
γνωστὴ Ἀποστολικὴ παράδοσις" (Εἰρην.) ν᾽ἀλλοιωθῇ καὶ διαφθαρῇ ἐν
πάσαις καθόλου ταῖς ἐπὶ μέρους Ἐκκλησίαις, ὧν πολλὰς ἵδρυσαν καὶ διὰ
τοῦ αἵματος αὐτῶν ἐπεσφράγισαν αὐτοὶ οἱ Ἀπόστολοι; οὐδὲ κἄν μία ἐξ
αὐτῶν Ἐκκλησία ἠδυνήθη νὰ ἐμμείνῃ πιστὴ ἐν τῇ Ἀποστολικῇ διδασκαλίᾳ;
ἀλλὰ τότε δυοῖν θἄτερον κατ᾽ἀνάγκην ὡς ἀληθὲς παραδεκτέον, ἤ ὅτι ἡ
ἀληθὴς τοῦ Χριστοῦ Ἐκκλησία ἐπὶ πολλοὺς αἰῶνας ἐξέλιπεν, ὡς
διατείνονται οἱ ἀναμορφωταὶ Διαμαρτυρόμενοι, τοὺθ᾽ὅπερ ὅμως εἶνε
ὅλως ἄτοπον καὶ ταῖς θείαις τοῦ Σωτῆρος ἐπαγγελίαις (Ματθ. κη΄. 20.

Ἰωάν. ιστ΄. 13.) ἐναντίον, ἤ ὅτι οὐδέποτ᾽ἐξέλιπεν ἡ Ἐκκλησία τοῦ Χριστοῦ, καὶ τότε ψεύδονται οἱ Διαμαρυρόμενοι διϊσχυριζόμενοι ὅτι ἐπανῆλθον εἰς τὴν γνησίαν Ἀποστολικὴν διδασκαλίαν }(Προβλ. }31
Θεολοικὸν Εὐγ. τοῦ Βουλγ. “περὶ παραδόσεως”. Κ. Κοντογόνης, *Πατρολογίαν* ἐν ταῖς διδασκαλίαις τῶν Πατέρων περὶ παραδόσεως. Bergier, *Λεξικὸν τῆς θεολ.* ἐν λέξει “Tradition” καὶ ἄλλους).

γ΄.

Εἰ καὶ τὰ μέχρι τοῦδε εἰρημένα τρανότατα ἀποδεικνύουσιν οὐ μόνον τὸ μέγα τῆς ἱερᾶς Παραδόσεως ἀξίωμα, ἀλλὰ καὶ τὸ πρὸς τὴν ἁγίαν Γραφὴν ἰσότιμον αὐτῆς καὶ ἰσοδύναμον, ἐν τούτοις ὅμως ὑπολείπεται ἡμῖν ἤδη ἵνα διὰ βραχέων καταδείξωμεν καὶ τὸ ὅτι ἡ ἱερὰ Παράδοσις εἶνε τοσοῦτον ἀναγκαία, καὶ ἑπομένως ἡ αξία αὐτῆς εἶνε τοσοῦτον μεγάλη, ὥστε ἄνευ αὐτῆς ἡ ἁγία Γραφὴ μόνη δὲν δύναται ν᾽ἀποδώσῃ τὸ πλῆρες καὶ ἀληθὲς τοῦ Χριστιανισμοῦ πνεῦμα˙ ἄλλαις λέξεσι τὸ ἀναντίρρητον τῆς ἱερᾶς Παραδόσεως κῦρος ἀποδείκνυται τέλος εἰς τῆς ἀπολύτου αὐτῆς ἀνάγκης πρῶτον μὲν πρὸς τὴν ὀρθὴν λύσιν διαφόρων ἀποριῶν τὴν γνησιότητα καὶ θεοπνευστίαν τῶν ἱερῶν τῆς Γραφῆς βιβλίων ἀφορωσῶν, δεύτερον δὲ πρὸς τὴν ἀληθῆ τῆς ἁγίας Γραφῆς ἑρμηνείαν καὶ κατάληψην καὶ τρίτον πρὸς τὴν γνῶσιν ἀληθειῶν τινων ἐν τῇ Γραφῇ μὲν μὴ περιεχομένων, ἀναγκαίων ὅμως εἴς τε τὴν πίστιν καὶ τὸν Χριστιανικὸν βίον.

Καὶ πρῶτον μὲν τὴν ἀπόλυτον τῆς ἱερᾶς Παραδόσεως ἀνάγκην πρὸς τὴν ἀκριβῆ διάκρισιν τῶν γνησίων καὶ θεοπνεύστων τῆς ἁγίας Γραφῆς βιβλίων ἀπὸ τῶν ψευδεπιγράφων καὶ ἀποκρύφων μαρτυρεῖ ἡ ἀδέκαστος τῆς Ἐκκλησίας ἱστορία ἀπ᾽αὐτῶν τῶν Ἀποστολικῶν χρόνων μέχρι τῆς σήμερον˙ ἤδη ὁ κριτικώτατος Ὠριγένης, ὡς ἱστορεῖ ὁ Εὐσέβιος (*Ἐκκλ. ἱστ.* στ΄. 25), ὁμιλῶν περὶ τῶν ἱερῶν τῆς Κ.Δ. βιβλίων λέγει “ὡς ἐν παραδόσει μαθὼν περὶ τῶν τεσσάρων Εὐαγγελίων, ἃ καὶ μόνα ἀναντίρρητά ἐστιν ἐν τῇ Ἐκκλησίᾳ τοῦ θεοῦ τῇ ὑπ᾽οὐρανόν”. Ἀλλὰ καὶ ὁ Εὐσέβιος αὐτὸς λέγει ὅτι διέκρινε τὰς ἐνδιαθήκους τῶν ἱερῶν βιβλίων ἀπὸ τῶν ὁμολογουμένων χρώμενος κανόνι τῇ αρχαίᾳ παραδόσει (*Ἐκκλ. ἱστ. γ΄.* 25.). Ἐν τούτοις οἱ τῆς ἱερᾶς Παραδόσεως πολέμιοι νομίζουσιν ὅτι λύεται τοῦτο τὸ ζήτημα τῆς τῶν ἱερῶν βιβλίων γηνσιότητος καὶ θεοπνευστίας ἐὰν λάβωμεν ὡς ὁδηγὸν κατά τινας μὲν ἐξ αὐτῶν τὸν ὀρθὸν λόγον, κατ᾽ ἄλλους δὲ αὐτὴν τὴν ἁγίαν Γραφήν. Ἀλλ᾽ἑκάτεροι δεινῶς ἀπατῶνται˙ διότι ἐὰν μὲν πρὸς στιγμὴν παραδεχθῶμεν ὡς ὁδηγὸν μόνον τὸν ὀρθὸν λόγον, τότε οὐδέποτε

θὰ ἠδυνάμεθα νὰ ἔχομεν πλήρη βεβαιότητα εἴτε περὶ τῆς γνησιότητος εἴτε περὶ τῆς θεοπνευστίας τῶν ἱερῶν τῆς Γραφῆς βιβλίων˙ διότι προκειμένου μὲν περὶ τῆς γνησιότητος αὐτῶν, }ἐπειδὴ οἱ ἀρχαῖοι τῶν ἱερῶν βιβλίων }32
κατάλογοι εἶνε, ὡς γνωστόν, λίαν περίπλουσι, διὰ τοῦτο δὲν δύναται ὁ λόγος ἐπὶ τούτων μόνον στηριζόμενος ν᾽ἀποφανθῇ μετ᾽ανενδοιάστου βεβαιότητος ὅτι ταῦτα μὲν τὰ βιβλία εἶνε γνήσια, ἐκεῖνα δὲ ἀπόκρυφα˙ προκειμένου δὲ περὶ τῆς θεοπνευστίας αὐτῶν, ἐπίσης οὐδὲν δύναται ὁ λόγος βέβαιον ν᾽ἀποδείξῃ εἰμὴ τὸ πολὺ τὸ ἔξοχον τῆς Γραφικῆς διδασκαλίας, ἀλλὰ καὶ τοῦτο πάλιν μετὰ πιθανότητος μόνον˙ πρόσθες δὲ καὶ τὸ ὅτι ὁ ἀνθρώπινος λόγος εἰς ἑαυτὸν ἀφιέμενος ἄγει ἡμᾶς εἰς πολλὰ ἄτοπα˙ διότι τότε ἕκαστος κατὰ τὸ δοκοῦν ἐξετάζων τὰ ἱερὰ τῆς Γραφῆς βιβλία δύναται τὰ μὲν συνᾴδοντα πρὸς τὸν σκοπὸν αὐτοῦ νὰ παραδεχθῇ ὡς γνήσια καὶ θεόπνευστα, τὰ δὲ ἀπᾴδοντα ν᾽ἀπορρίψῃ ὡς ἀπόκρυφα˙ κάλλιστον τοῦτον παράδειγμα παρουσιάζει ἡμῖν ἡ ἱστορία αὐτὸν τὸν ἀρχηγὸν τῆς Διαμαρτυρομένης αἱρέσεως, τὸν Λούθηρον, ὅστις ἐτόλμησε πολλὰ τῆς ἁγίας Γραφῆς βιβλία ν᾽ἀπορρίψῃ ὡς δῆθεν ἀπόκρυφα˙ οὕτως ἐκ μόνης τῆς Κ.Δ. ἀπέβαλεν ὁ τολμητίας ἕξ βιβλία, ἤτοι τὴν ἐπιστολὴν τοῦ Ἰακώβου, τὴν Β΄αν τοῦ Πέτρου, τὴν Β΄αν καὶ Γ΄ην τοῦ Ἰωάννου, τὴν πρὸς Ἑβραίους τοῦ Παύλου καὶ τὴν Ἀποκάλυψιν Ἰωάννου! (ὅρα *Symbolique* par Moehler t. II. chap. 5 § 41)˙ τὶ δὲ νὰ εἴπωμεν περὶ τῶν ὀρθολογιστῶν, οἵτινες τὸν ὀρθὸν λόγον μόνον ὡς ὁδηγὸν ἔχοντες οὐδὲν βιβλίον τῆς ἁγίας Γραφῆς ἐγκατέλιπον ἀπρόσβλητον; (ὅρ. *Δοκίμιον Ἐκκλ. ἱστ.* ὑπὸ Α. Δ. Κυριακοῦ σελ. 402). Ἀλλ᾽ἐὰν δεύτερον παραδεχθῶμεν ὡς ὁδηγὸν πρὸς γνῶσιν τῆς τῶν ἱερῶν βιβλίων γνησιότητός τε καὶ θεοπνευστίας αὐτὴν τὴν Γραφὴν, πάλιν δὲν ἐπιτυγχάνομεν τοῦ ζητουμένου˙ διότι περὶ μὲν τοῦ Κανόνος καὶ τῆς γνησιότητος τῶν ἀποτελούντων αὐτὸν βιβλίων οὐδεμίαν εὑρίσκομεν ἐν τῇ ἁγίᾳ Γραφῇ μαρτυρίαν˙ περὶ δὲ τῆς θεοπνευστίας ὑπάρχουσι μὲν χωρία τινά, οἷα τὰ (Β΄. Τιμ. γ΄. 16 καὶ Β΄. Πέτρ. α΄. 20), ἀλλὰ ταῦτα ἀναφέρονται ἢ μόνον εἰς τὴν Π.Δ., ἢ εἴς τινα ἐξ αὐτῆς βιβλία ἢ καὶ εἴς τινα μόνον χωρία˙ ἀλλὰ καὶ ἐπὶ τῇ ὑποθέσει ὅτι ὑπάρχουσί τινα εἰς ὅλην τὴν Γραφὴν ἀναφερόμενα, ταῦτα ὅμως ὡς μαρτυρίαι τῆς Γραφῆς περὶ ἑαυτῆς οὐδεμίαν παρέχουσιν ἡμῖν βεβαίαν καὶ ἀναντίρρητον ἀπόδειξεν˙ ἐκτὸς δὲ τούτου πόσαι ἀμφιβολίαι δὲν ἐγείρονται, ἀφιεμένης τῆς Γραφῆς εἰς ἑαυτήν; οὕτως ἡ ἀνακρίβεια πολλῶν ἀντιγράφων, ἡ λήθη τῶν ἀρχικῶν γλωσσῶν, ἡ ποικιλία τῶν μεταφράσεων, ἡ μεταβολὴ τῶν ἠθῶν καὶ ἐθίμων, αἱ γραμματικαὶ λεπτότητες καὶ ἄλλα πολλὰ μόνον ὑποψίας παρέχουσιν ἡμῖν καὶ ἀμφιβολίας περὶ τῆς γνησιότητος

καὶ θεοπνευστίας τῆς ἁγίας Γραφῆς˙ ἐνῷ ἐὰν λάβωμεν ὡς ὁδηγὸν τὴν γνησίαν Ἀποστολικὴν }Παράδοσιν πᾶσαι αἱ δυσκολίαι αὗται εὐκόλως }33 λύονται. Ἐντεῦθεν δὲ καὶ πολλοὶ τῶν Διαμαρτυρομένων κατανοήσαντες τὰ ἄτοπα ταῦτα, εἰς ἃ ἄγουσιν αἱ δύο ῥηθεῖσαι ἀρχαί, ἠναγκάσθησαν νὰ ὁμολογήσωσιν ὅτι δὲν δύναται ἄλλως νὰ λυθῇ τὸ ζήτημα τῆς τῶν ἱερῶν βιβλίων γνησιότητός τε καὶ θεοπνευστίαι εἰμὴ διὰ τῆς μαρτυρίας τῶν ἀρχαίων τῆς Ἐκκλησίας Πατέρων˙ διότι, λέγουσιν, οἱ Πατέρες ἐκεῖνοι πάντοτε παρέβαλλον τὰ διάφορα τῆς ἁγίας Γραφῆς ἀντίγραφα πρὸς τὰ δημοσίως ἐν τῇ Ἐκκλησίᾳ ἀναγινωσκόμενα χειρόγραφα καὶ οὕτως ἔκρινον περὶ τῆς γνησιότητος αὐτῶν ἤ μή. Ἀλλ᾽ ἀφοῦ οἱ Πατέρες ἐκεὶνοι εἶνε ἀξιόπιστοι προκειμένου περὶ τῆς γνησιότητος καὶ θεοπνευστίας τῶν ἱερῶν τῆς Γραφῆς βιβλίων, διατί, ἐρωτῶμεν, νὰ μὴν εἶνε ἀξιόπιστοι προκειμένου καὶ περὶ τῶν ἱερῶν Παραδόσεων, αἵτινες καὶ αὗται δημοσίᾳ ἐκηρύσσοντο καὶ ἐτελοῦντο; πῶς, λέγομεν, προκειμένου μὲν περὶ τοῦ γραπτοῦ τοῦ θεοῦ λόγου δύνανται οἱ ἅγιοι τῆς Ἐκκλησίας Πατέρες νὰ χρησιμεύσωσιν ἡμῖν ὡς ἀξιόπιστοι μαρτύρες, προκειμένου δὲ περὶ τοῦ ἀγράφου τοῦ θεοῦ λόγου δὲν εἶνε άξιόπιστοι; τοῦτο δὲν εἶνε παράλογον καὶ ὅλως ἄτοπον;

Δεύτερον δὲ τὴν ἀπόλυτον τῆς ἱερᾶς Παραδόσεως ἀνάγκην πρὸς ἀλάθητον τῆς ἁγίας Γραφῆς ἑρμηνείαν καὶ κατάληψιν σαφῶς δείκνυσι 1.) μὲν ἡ ἱερὰ ἱστορία διδάσκουσα ὅτι οὐ μόνον ὁ Κύριος "διηρμήνευε τοῖς μαθηταῖς αὐτοῦ ἐν πάσαις ταῖς Γραφαῖς τὰ περὶ αὐτοῦ" (Λουκ. κδ΄. 27), ἀλλὰ καὶ αὐτοὶ οἱ Ἀπόστολοι πολλάκις ἡρμήνευον τοῖς πιστοῖς τὰ βιβλία τῆς Π.Δ. (Πράξ. β΄. 25 καὶ ἑξῆς. η΄. 30–35) ἐντελλάμενοι αὐτοῖς ἔχεσθαι τόσα τῶν ἁγίων Γραφῶν, ὅσον καὶ τῶν ἱερῶν Παραδόσεων (Β΄. Θεσ. β΄. 15)˙ διὸ καὶ ἡ ἁγία τοῦ Χριστοῦ Ἐκκλησία ἀπ᾽αὐτῶν τῶν Ἀποστολικῶν χρόνων μέχρι τῆς σήμερον ἀπρὶξ ἐχομένη τῶν ἱερῶν Παραδόσεων στεντορείᾳ τῇ φωνῇ διακηρύττει ὅτι "ἀναγκαία ἐστὶ ἡ Παράδοσις πρὸς χειραγωγίαν εἰς τὴν ὀρθὴν τῆς ἁγίας Γραφῆς κατάληψιν, εἰς τὴν ὀρθὴν τῶν μυστηρίων διάπραξιν καὶ τῶν ἱερῶν τελετῶν τήρησιν ἐν τῇ ἁγνότητι τῆς πρώτης αὐτῶν διατάξεως" (*Ἐκτεταμ. Χρ. Κατηχ. τῆς ὀρθ. Ἐκκλ.* ἄρθρ. περὶ ἱερᾶς Παραδόσεως καὶ τῆς ἁγ. Γραφῆς). 2.) δὲ τὴν πρὸς ὀρθὴν τῆς ἁγίας Γραφῆς ἑρμηνείαν ἀπόλυτον τῆς ἱερᾶς Παραδόσεως ἀνάγκην δείκνυσι καὶ αὐτὴ ἡ Γραφή˙ ἐν αὐτῇ δηλ.:# ὑπάρχουσι πολλὰ μὲν τὰ μυστηριώδη καὶ τῷ ἀνθρωπίνῳ νῷ ἀκατάληπτα, οἷα τὰ ὑπερφυᾶ μυστήρια τῆς ἁγίας Τριάδος, τῆς θείας Ἐνσαρκώσεως κτλ., πολλὰ δὲ τὰ ἀσαφῆ καὶ δυσνόητα, οἷα καὶ αὐτὸς ὁ Ἀπ. Πέτρος εὗρεν ἀναγνοὺς τὰς ἐπιστολὴς τοῦ Ἀποστόλου

}Παύλου (Β΄. Πέτρ. γ΄. 16), καὶ ἄλλα τέλος λίαν συντόμως ἐκτεθειμένα }34
ἢ ἐν εἴδει νύξεων μόνον ἀναφερόμενα ἢ ἐν ἄλλαις περιεχόμενα ἀληθείαις, ἐξ ὧν μόνον διὰ συλλογισμῶν δύνανται νὰ ἐξαχθῶσιν, οἷα τὰ περὶ τῆς Ἀειπαρθενίας τῆς Θεοτόκου, τῆς ἐπικλήσεως τῶν Ἁγίων καὶ τῶν Ἀγγέλων, τῆς μετὰ θάνατον καταστάσεως τῶν ψυχῶν, τοῦ νηπιοβαπτισμοῦ καὶ ἄλλα πολλά˙ ταῦτα λοιπὰ πάντα πῶς δυνάμεθα ὀρθῶς νὰ κατανοήσωμεν καὶ ὀρθοδόξως νὰ ἐξηγήσωμεν, ἐὰν δὲν ἐπικαλεσθῶμεν εἰς βοήθειαν ἡμῶν τὴν θεῖον κῦρος ἔχουσαν ἱερὰν Παράδοσιν; διὰ τοῦτο λίαν ὀρθῶς ὁ ἱερὸς ἀποφαίνεται Ἐπιφάνιος λέγων “Δεῖ δὲ καὶ παραδόσει κεχρῆσθαι˙ οὐ γὰρ πάντα ἀπὸ τῆς θείας Γραφῆς δύναται λαμβάνεσθαι˙ διὸ τὰ μὲν ἐν γραφαῖς, τὰ δὲ ἐν παραδόσει παρέδωκαν οἱ ἅγιοι Ἀπόστολοι” (*κατὰ αἱρ.* ξα΄. 6). Καὶ ὅμως οἱ ἡμέτεροι ἀντίπαλοι ἀντὶ τοῦ θεοπαραδότου τούτου ἐν τῇ ἑρμηνείᾳ τῆς ἁγίας Γραφῆς ὁδηγοῦ ἄλλοι ἄλλον προτείνουσιν˙ οὕτως οἱ μὲν θέλουσι τὸν λόγον μόνον ὡς ὁδηγόν, οἱ δὲ αὐτὴν τὴν ἁγίαν Γραφήν, καὶ ἄλλοι τέλος ἐσωτερικόν τινα θεῖον καταυγασμόν. Ἡμεῖς ὅμως λέγομεν ὅτι ἕκαστος τῶν τριῶν τούτων ὁδηγῶν οὕτως ἀπομεμονωμένος ἄνευ τῆς ἱερᾶς Παραδόσεως ἄγει ἡμᾶς εἰς ἐπισφαλῆ συμπεράσματα αὐτὴν τὴν σωτηρίαν ἡμῶν ἐπαπειλοῦντα˙ διότι α΄.) ὅσον ἀφορᾷ τὸν ἀνθρώπινον λόγον δὲν ἀρνούμεθα μὲν ὅτι οὗτος δύναται καὶ ὀφείλει νὰ λαμβάνῃ μέρος ἐν τῇ ἑρμηνείᾳ τῆς ἁγίας Γραφῆς, ἐπὶ τῇ συνθήκῃ ὅμως νὰ ὑποτάσσηται πάντοτε εἰς τὸν θεῖον λόγον, ὅτε καὶ ἀποβαίνει ἡμῖν οὐ μόνον χρήσιμος, ἀλλὰ πολλάκις καὶ ἀπαραίτητος˙ δὲν ἀποδεχόμεθα ὅμως αὐτὸν ὡς τὸν μόνον ὁδηγόν˙ πρῶτον μὲν διότι ὁ ἀνθρ# λόγος ἐπειδὴ ὑπόκειται εἰς πολλὰς μεταβολὰς οὕτως, ὥστε πολλάκις πᾶν ὅ, τι σήμερον νομίζει ἀληθές, τοῦτο τὴν ἐπιοῦσαν θεωρεῖ ψευδές, διὰ τοῦτο λαμβανόμενος ὡς ὁδηγὸς ἐν τῇ τῶν ἁγίων Γραφῶν ἑρμηνείᾳ ἄγει εἰς πολλὰς ἀλλήλαις ἀντιφασκούσας ἑρμηνείας˙ δεύτερον δὲ καὶ ὡς πεπερασμένος ὁ ἀνθρ# λόγος δὲν δύναται μετὰ βεβαιότητος νὰ ἑρμηνεύῃ εἰμὴ τὰς προσιτὰς αὐτῷ ἐν τῇ Γραφῇ ἀληθείας, ἐνῷ τὰς ὑπερφυεῖς καὶ μυστηριώδεις ἀληθείας ἢ κατὰ τὸ δοκοῦν θὰ ἑρμηνεύσῃ ἢ ὡς ἀκαταλήπτους θ᾽ἀπορρίψῃ˙ μαρτυροῦσι μοι τὸν λόγον οἱ ἐκ κόλπων τοῦ Προτεσταντισμοῦ ἐξελθόντες Σωκινιανοί, οἵτινες ἔχοντες ὡς ὁδηγὸν μόνον τὸν ὀρθὸν λόγον διημφισβήτησαν τὴν ἀλήθειαν παντὸς τῷ λόγῳ ἀπροσίτου δόγματος, ἐκ οὗ τέλος ἀπέρριψαν τὰ μὲν θαύματα ὡς
ἀδύνατα, τὰ δὲ μυστήρια ὡς ἀκατανόητα! εἶτα δ᾽ἐλθόντες }οἱ Κουάκεροι }35
ἀπεφάνθησαν, ὅτι ἀρκετοῦ ὄντος ἡμῖν τοῦ λόγου δὲν ἔχομεν ἀνάγκην τῆς θείας Ἀποκαλύψεως! (ὅρ. *Δοκίμιον Ἐκκλ. ἱστ.* ὑπὸ Α. Δ. Κυριακοῦ σελ. 395 καὶ 396–7)˙ β΄.) ὅσα ἀφορᾷ τοὺς λέγοντας ὅτι δεῖ ἑρμηνεύειν

τὴν Γραφὴν διὰ τῆς Γραφῆς, ἀποκρινόμεθα πρὸς αὐτοὺς ὅτι ναὶ μὲν τὸ ἑρμηνεύειν τὰ ἀσαφῆ τῆς Γραφῆς χωρία διὰ τῶν σαφεστέρων εἶνε μάλιστα καὶ ἀπαραίτητος τῆς ἱερᾶς ἑρμηνευτικῆς κανών, ἀλλὰ δὲν εἶνε καὶ ὁ μόνος ἐν τῇ ἑρμηνείᾳ τῆς Γραφῆς ὁδηγός˙ διότι ἡ Γραφὴ ὡς γραφὴ δὲν δύναται βεβαίως νὰ ἐπανορθοῖ ἡμᾶς τοιαύτην ἢ τοιαύτην ἔννοιαν διδόντας εἰς τὰ διάφορα αὐτῆς χωρία˙ ἀλλ᾽ἀπεναντίας, καὶ μάρτυς ἡ ἱστορία, βλέπομεν ὅτι οἱ πάντες, ὀρθόδοξοί τε καὶ ἑτερόδοξοι, διϊσχυρίζονται ὅτι εὑρίσκουσιν ἐν αὐτῇ ἕκαστοι τὴν ἰδίαν αὐτῶν διδασκαλίαν˙ τίς λοιπὸν μεταξὺ τοσούτων ἀλλήλαις ἀντιφασκουσῶν τῆς ἁγίας Γραφῆς ἑρμηνειῶν δύναται μετὰ βεβαιότητος ν᾽ἀποφανθῇ ὅτι αὕτη ἢ ἐκείνη ἡ ἑρμηνεία εἶνε ἡ ὀρθή; καθ᾽ἡμᾶς εἷς ἐστιν ὁ τῆς Ἀριάδνης μίτος ὁ χειργωγῶν ἡμᾶς ἀσφαλῶς ἐν τῷ λαβυρίνθῳ τῶν πολυειδῶν τούτων τῆς ἁγίας Γραφῆς ἑρμηνειῶν, ἡ ἄνωθεν ἄχρις ἡμῶν κατιοῦσα ἱερὰ Παράδοσις. γ΄.) τέλος ὅσα ἀφορᾷ τοὺς προτείνοντας τὸν ἐσωτερικὸν καταυγασμὸν ὡς τὸν μόνον ὁδηγὸν ἐν τῇ ὀρθῇ τῆς ἁγίας Γραφῆς ἑρμηνείᾳ βεβαιοῦμεν καὶ τούτους ὅτι δὲν ἀρνοῦμεθα μὲν ὅτι καθὼς ἐν τῇ πράξει παντὸς ἀγαθοῦ, οὕτω καὶ ἐν τῇ ἑρμηνείᾳ τῆς ἁγίας Γραφῆς χρῄζομεν τοῦ ἄνωθεν φωτισμοῦ (Ἰακώβ. α΄. 17. Β΄. Ἰωάν. β΄. 27 καὶ ὁ ἱερὸς Χρυσόστομος λέγει "τοῖς ἐρευνῶσι χρεία τῆς ἄνωθεν αἴγλης, ἵνα καὶ εὕρωσι τὸ ζητούμενον, καὶ φυλάξωσι τὸ θηρώμενον" *εἰς ψαλ. ριθ΄.*), δὲν παραδεχόμεθα ὅμως ὅτι ὁ ἐσωτερικὸς οὗτος καταυγασμὸς εἶνε ἐπαρκὴς καὶ πάντοτε ἀσφαλὴς ἐν τῇ ἑρμηνείᾳ τῆς ἁγίας Γραφῆς ὁδηγός˙ διότι τῆς ἐσωτερικῆς ταύτης ἐλλάμψεως μυστηριώδους οὔσης καὶ ἀκαταλήπτου δύναται πᾶς φαντασιόπληκτος κατὰ τὰς ὑποκειμενικὰς αὐτοῦ ἰδέας τὴν Γραφὴν ἑρμηνεύων νὰ διαδιδῷ τὰ ἴδια ληρήματα ὡς θεῖα ῥήματα ἢ καὶ νὰ καταντήσῃ ἐπὶ τέλους εἰς τὴν ἐντελῆ τῶν ἁγίων Γραφῶν ἀποβολήν˙ μάρτυς ἡ ἱστορία, ἥτις παρουσιάζει ἡμῶν τοὺς Σβεδενβουργιανούς, οἵτινες διϊσχυριζόμενοι ὅτι Θείας λαμβάνουσιν ἐλλάμψεις καὶ ἐσωτερικὰς ἀποκαλύψεις συνεπέραναν ὅτι τοῦ Ἁγίου Πνεύματος ἀμέσως ἡμᾶς φωτίζοντος δὲν ἔχομεν ἀνάγκην τῆς ἁγίας Γραφῆς! (ὅρ. *Δοκίμ. Ἐκκλ. ἱστ.* ὑπὸ Α. Δ. Κυριακοῦ σελ. 398). Ἀλλὰ καὶ μεθ᾽ ὅλα τὰ ἄτοπα ταῦτα οἱ Διαμαρτυρόμενοι οἱονεὶ μυωπάζοντες ὑπὸ τῆς ἀχλύος τῆς ἑαυτῶν αἱρέσεως καὶ μὴ δυνάμενοι }νὰ βλέπωσι τὸ λαμπρὸν φῶς τῆς }36
ἀληθείας ἐνίστανται ἐπάγοντες τὸ τοῦ Ἀπ. Παύλου λέγοντος "ἑκάστῳ δὲ δίδοται ἡ φανέρωσις τοῦ Πνεύματος πρὸς τὸ συμφέρον" (Α΄. Κορ. ιβ΄. 7)˙ ἀλλ᾽ὁποία τῶν Γραφικῶν χωρίων διαστροφὴ καὶ παρερμηνεία! διότι ἐν τῷ χωρίῳ τούτῳ ὁ Παῦλος ὁμιλεῖ περὶ τῶν διαφόρων χαρισμάτων τοῦ Ἁγ. Πνεύματος, ἅτινα πολλά τε καὶ ποικίλα ὄντα δὲν χορηγοῦνται πάντα τε

καὶ πᾶσιν, ἀλλ' "ᾧ μὲν διὰ τοῦ Πνεύματος δίδοται λόγος σοφίας, ἄλλῳ δὲ λόγος γνώσεως κατὰ τὸ αὐτὸ Πνεῦμα· ἑτέρῳ δὲ πίστις κτλ." (αὐτόθι ιβ΄. 8–11)· οὕτω δὲ καὶ τὸ πρὸς κατάληψιν τῆς ἁγίας Γραφῆς καὶ ἑρμηνείαν χάρισμα δὲν χορηγεῖ τὸ Πνεῦμα πᾶσιν, ἀλλ'οἷς βούλεται· ἠβουλήθη δὲ χορηγῆσαι αὐτὸ τοῖς θεοφόροις Πατράσι, παρ'ὧν ἡμεῖς ἄνωθεν κατὰ παράδοσιν ἀποδεχόμεθα τὸν ἀληθῆ νοῦν τῶν ἁγίων Γραφῶν.

Τρίτον τέλος τὸ μέγα τῆς ἱερᾶς Παραδόσεως ἀξίωμα δείκνυσι καὶ ἡ ἀπόλυτος αὐτῆς ἀνάγκη πρὸς γνῶσιν ἀληθειῶν τινων, αἵτινες δὲν περιέχονται μὲν ἐν τῇ ἁγίᾳ Γραφῇ, εἶνε ὅμως ἀπαραίτητοι εἴς τε τὴν πίστιν καὶ τὸν Χριστιανικὸν βίον· αἱ τοιαῦται ἀλήθειαι εἶνε ἱστορικαί τε καὶ τελετουργικαὶ ἀφορῶσαι τὰς νηστείας, τὰς ἑορτὰς, τὴν τῶν ναῶν οἰκοδομήν, τὴν χρῆσιν τῶν ἱερῶν ἀμφίων καὶ ἄλλων τινῶν ἀντικειμένων, ἅτινα πάντα ἀποτελοῦσιν ἰδιαίτερα τῆς θεολογίας μαθήματα, τὴν λειτουργικὴν δηλ#., τὴν Ἐκκλησιαστικὴν Ἀρχαιολογίαν καὶ τὸ Κανονικὸν Δίκαιον, ὁπόθεν δείκνυται καὶ ἡ μεγάλη αὐτῶν σημασία ἐν τῇ ἡμετέρᾳ Ἐκκλησίᾳ. Ἀλλ'οἱ Διαμαρτυρόμενοι ἔχοντες ὡς ἀξίωμα τὸ "Πᾶν τὸ μὴ ἐν τῇ Γραφῇ ἀναφερόμενον εἶνε ἔνταλμα ἀνθρώπινον" ἀπορρίπτουσι τὰς ῥηθείσας ἀληθείας ὡς ἁπλᾶ δῆθεν τῶν θείων Πατέρων ἐπινοήματα· ἀλλ'οἷα ἡ τῶν Διαμαρτυρομένων τούτων ἀχαριστία πρὸς τοὺς ἁγίους ἡμῶν Πατέρας! ἐνῷ ἀφ'ἑνὸς κατηγοροῦσιν αὐτοὺς ὡς νέων δογμάτων καὶ διδαγμάτων εἰσηγήτορας, ἀφ'ἑτέρου ὅμως ἑρμηνεύουσι τὴν Γραφὴν φωτίζοντες τοὺς ἐκ τῆς αἱρετικῆς ἀχλύος μυωπάζοντας αὐτῶν ὀφθαλμοὺς διὰ τοῦ φωτὸς τῶν θείων αὐτῶν συγγραμμάτων· ἀλλ'ἡ ἀφροσύνη τῶν Διαμαρτυρομένων προβαίνει δυστυχῶς καὶ περαιτέρω· ἐνῷ ἀφ'ἑνὸς ἀθετοῦσι τὰς ἱερὰς Παραδόσεις τῶν Ἀποστόλων ὡς δῆθεν ἐντάλματα ἀνθρώπων, ἀφ'ἑτέρου τίθενται ὑπὸ τὸν ζυγὸν ἀληθῶς ἀνθρωπίνων παραδόσεων, ἃς τυφλοῖς ὄμμασιν ὡς θεῖα ἐντάλματα ἀκολουθοῦσι! διότι ἕκαστος Διαμαρτυρόμενος, εἴτε Λουθηρανὸς εἶνε εἴτε Καλβινιστὴς εἴτε ἄλλης Προτεσταντικῆς αἱρέσεως ὀπαδός, λαμβάνων ἀνὰ χεῖρας τὴν ἁγίαν Γραφὴν εὑρίσκει ἐν αὐτῇ αὐτὴν ἐκείνην ἀκριβῶς τὴν διδασκαλίαν, ἣν παιδιόθεν }παρά τε τῶν γονέων αὐτοῦ ἤκουσε, καὶ ὑπὸ τῶν διδασκάλων }37
αὐτοῦ ἐδιδάχθει, καὶ ἐκ τῆς αἱρέσεως, ἐν ᾗ ἐγεννήθη καὶ ἀνετράφη, ἐποτίσθη· ἐντεῦθεν ἑκάστη Προτεσταντικὴ αἵρεσις ἔχει καὶ τὰ ἴδια αὐτῆς συμβολικὰ βιβλία, ἤτοι τὰς δογματικὰς αὐτῆς παραδόσεις, ἃς ὁ ἀρχηγὸς αὐτῆς ἐδημιούγησε καὶ διετύπωσε, καὶ ἃς ἕκαστον τῶν μελῶν αὐτῶν ὑποχρεοῦται νὰ φυλάττῃ ὥσπερ τινὰ θεόσδοτον παρακαταθήκην, καθ'ἣν ὀφείλει καὶ τὴν ἁγίαν Γραφὴν νὰ ἑρμηνεύῃ καὶ τὸν βιὸν αὐτοῦ

ὅλον νὰ ῥυθμίζῃ! Τί ἔπραξαν λοιπὸν οἱ Διαμαρτυρόμενοι διατεινόμενοι ὅτι ἀνεμόρφωσαν τὴν Ἐκκλησίαν; τὰς ἱερὰς Ἀποστόλων Παραδόσεις λακπατήσαντες κατηκολούθησαν παραδόσεις ἀνθρώπων, οἷοι οἱ Λούθηροι, οἱ Ζβίγγλιοι καὶ ἄλλοι, ἀνθρώπων, οἵτινες κατὰ τὴν μαρτυρίαν ἐπισήμων ἱστορικῶν (Fleury. *Hist. Eccles.* τομ. κε΄. σελ. 476. ἐκδ. Παρισίων 1724) οὐχὶ ἐξ εὐσεβοῦς ζήλου, ἀλλ᾽ἕνεκα ἰδίων παθῶν ἐκήρυξαν ἑαυτοὺς ἀποστόλους ἀναμορφωτέων Ἐκκλησιῶν! ἀλλ᾽ἐν τίνι ἐξουσίᾳ ἐπεχείρησαν οὗτοι τὴν ἀναμόρφωσιν τῆς Ἐκκλησίας; ἡ θεία διδασκαλία ἀπαιτεῖ θείαν ἀποστολήν· "πῶς δὲ κηρύξουσιν ἐὰν μὴ ἀποσταλῶσι;" (Ῥωμ. α΄. 15)· ποῖα λοιπὸν εἶνε τὰ γνωρίσματα τῆς θείας αὐτῶν ἀποστολῆς; ἀπείθεια εἰς τοὺς ὑπ᾽αὐτοῦ τοῦ Χριστοῦ διὰ τῶν Ἀποστόλων Αὐτοῦ καταστάντας ἐν τῇ Ἐκκλησίᾳ ποιμένας καὶ διδασκάλους (Ἑβρ. ιγ΄. 7, 17. Λουκ. ι΄. 16), περιφρόνησις τῆς ὑπ᾽αὐτοῦ τοῦ Χριστοῦ διὰ τῶν Ἀποστόλων Αὐτοῦ ἱδρυθείσης ἐπὶ τῆς γῆς Ἐκκλησίας (Ματθ. ιη΄. 17), ἀθέτησις τοῦ ἀγράφου λόγου τοῦ Θεοῦ, ἤτοι τῆς ἱερᾶς Παραδόσεως (Β΄. Θεσ. β΄. 15) καὶ ἄλλα χείρονα κατορθώματα, ἰδοὺ τὰ ἀληθῆ γνωρίσματα, μᾶλλον δ᾽εἰπεῖν στυγερὰ στίγματα, τῶν ψευδαποστόλων τούτων! Ἐντεῦθεν δ᾽οἱ Διαμαρτυρόμενοι εἰς μόνην τὴν Γραφήν, μᾶλλον δ᾽εἰπεῖν εἰς τὸ γράμμα αὐτῆς προσκεκολλημένοι ὄντες φωνασκοῦσιν ἐν τῇ δοκησισοφίᾳ αὐτῶν καὶ λέγουσι: Ποῦ διατάσσει ἡ Γραφὴ τὸ κατασημαίνεσθαι τῷ τύπῳ τοῦ Σταυροῦ, τὸ προσεύχεσθαι κατ᾽Ἀνατολάς, τὸ εὐλογεῖν τό τε ὕδωρ τοῦ Βαπτίματος καὶ τὸ ἔλαιον τοῦ Χρίσματος καὶ τὰς λοιπὰς ἐν γένει Ἐκκλησιαστικὰς διατάξεις καὶ τελετάς; Ἀλλ᾽ἐπιτραπήτω ἡμῖν ἵνα καὶ ἡμεῖς ἐρωτήσωμεν τοὺς δοκησισόφους τούτους, οἵτινες "φάσκοντες εἶναι σοφοὶ ἐμωράνθησαν" (Ῥωμ. α΄. 22): Ποῦ ἀπαγορεύει ἡ Γραφὴ τὸ σημεῖον τοῦ Σταυροῦ, τὴν κατ᾽Ἀνατολὰς προσευχὴν, τὴν εὐλογίαν τοῦ τε ὕδατος τοῦ Βαπτίσματος καὶ τοῦ ἐλαίου τοῦ Χρίσματος καὶ ὅλας ἐν γένει τὰς λοιπὰς ἐν τῇ Ἐκκλησίᾳ τηρουμένας παραδόσεις; Ἀλλ᾽ὦ ψευδοδιδάσκαλοι καὶ "ἐνώπιον ἑαυτῶν ἐπιστήμονες" (Ἡσαϊ. ε΄. 21), }εἴπατε ἡμῖν: πῶς ἐνῷ ἀφ᾽ἑνὸς ἀπορρίπτετε τὰς ἱερὰς Παραδόσεις διὰ τὸν }38
λόγον, ὅτι δὲν ὑπάρχουσιν ἐν τῇ Γραφῇ, ἀφ᾽ἑτέρου ὅμως παραδέχεσθε καὶ τηρεῖτε ἄλλας καίπερ ἐν τῇ Γραφῇ μὴ περιεχομένας, οἷον τὴν τήρησιν τῆς Κυριακῆς, τὴν ἑορτὴν τοῦ Πάσχα, τὸν νηπιοβαπτισμὸν καὶ ἄλλα τοιαῦτα; (προβλ. καθόλου Μακαρίου *Εἰσαγαγωγ. εἰς τὴν ὀρθ. θεολ.* μέρος β΄. περὶ Παραδόσεως. Εὐγενίου τοῦ βουλγ. *Θεολογικὸν* "περὶ παραδόσεως" καὶ Bergier, *Λεξικὸν τῆς θεολ.* ἐν λέξει "Tradition" καὶ ἄλλους.).

Ἀλλ᾽ἵνα μὴ μακρηγορήσωμεν ἐπὶ πλεῖον μετὰ τῶν λογομάχων τούτων ἀνθρώπων, οἵτινες "ἐξετράπησαν εἰς ματαιολογίαν, θέλοντες

εἶναι νομοδιδάσκαλοι, μὴ νοοῦντες μήτε ἃ λέγουσι, μήτε περὶ τίνων διαβεβαιοῦνται" (Α΄. Τιμ. α΄. 7), ἐπιφραγίζομεν τὴν ἡμετέραν ταύτην θεολογικὴν θέσιν διὰ τῆς ἀληθεστάτης ἅμα καὶ λαμπροτάτης τῆς ἁγίας ἡμῶν Ἐκκλησίας μαρτυρίας περὶ τῆς ἀληθοῦς τῆς ἱερᾶς Παραδόσεως ἐννοίας καὶ τῆς μεγάλης καὶ ἀναντιλέκτου αὐτῆς ἀξίας˙ "Πᾶσα[3] αἱρετικῶν βδελυρία δέχεται μὲν τὴν θείαν Γραφὴν, παρεξηγεῖται δ᾽αὐτὴν μεταφοραῖς καὶ ὁμωνυμίαις καὶ σοφίσμασι σοφίας ἀνθρωπίνης χρωμένη συγχέουσα τὰ ἀσύγχυτα καὶ παίζουσα ἐν οὐ παικτοῖς˙ ἄλλως γὰρ ἄν, ἄλλου ἄλλην ὁσημέραι περὶ αὐτῆς γνώμην ἐσχηκότος, οὐκ ἂν εἴη ἡ Καθολικὴ Ἐκκλησία Χριστοῦ χάριτι ἕως τῆς σήμερον Ἐκκλησία, μίαν γνώμην ἔχουσα περὶ πίστεως καὶ ἀεὶ ὡσαύτως καὶ ἀπαραλλάκτως[4] πιστεύουσα, ἀλλ᾽ἐσχίσθη ἄν εἰς μυρία,[5] καὶ αἱρέσεσιν ὑπέκειτο, καὶ μηδ᾽ἦν ἡ Ἐκκλησία Ἁγία, στύλη καὶ ἑδραίωμα τῆς ἀληθείας, ἄσπιλός τε καὶ ῥυτίδος χωρίς, ἀλλ᾽ἡ Ἐκκλησία πονηρευσμένων, ὡς φαίνεται γεγονυῖα ἀναμφιβόλως ἡ τῶν Αἱρετικῶν,[6] οἵ οὐκ αἰσχύνονται παρὰ τῆς Ἐκκλησίας μανθάνειν, ἔπειτα ταύτην πονηρῶς ἀποκρούεσθαι˙ ὅθεν καὶ τὴν τῆς Καθολικῆς Ἐκκλησίας μαρτυρίαν οὐχ ἧττον τῆς, ἣν κέκτηται ἡ θεία Γραφή, εἶναι πιστεύομεν˙ ἑνὸς γὰρ καὶ τοῦ Ἁγίου αὐτοῦ[7] Πνεύματος ὄντος ἀμφοτέρων δημιουργοῦ˙ ἶσόν ἐστι πάντως ὑπὸ τῆς Γραφῆς καὶ ὑπὸ τῆς Καθολικῆς Ἐκκλησίας διδάσκεσθαι˙ ἔπειτα ἄνθρωπον μὲν ὅντινα οὖν λαλοῦντα ἀφ᾽ἑαυτοῦ ἐνδέχεται ἁμαρτῆσαι καὶ ἀπατῆσαι καὶ ἀπατηθῆναι, τὴν δὲ Καθολικὴν Ἐκκλησίαν ὡς μηδέποτε λαλήσασαν ἤ λαλοῦσαν ἀφ᾽ἑαυτῆς, ἀλλ᾽ἐκ τοῦ Πνεύματος τοῦ θεοῦ (ὃ καὶ διδάσκαλον ἀδιαλείπτως πλουτεῖ εἰς τὸν αἰῶνα),[8] ἀδύνατον πάντῃ ἁμαρτῆσαι ἤ ὅλως ἀπατῆσαι καὶ ἀπατηθῆναι˙ ἀλλ᾽ἔστιν ὡσαύτως τῇ θείᾳ
Γραφῇ ἀδιάπτωτος καὶ ἀένναον τὸ[9] }κῦρος ἔχουσα" (ὅρα *Ἐπιστολὴν τῶν* }39
τεσσάρων Πατριαρχῶν τῆς Ἀνατολῆς ὅρ. β΄.).

Τέλος.

Ἔγραφον ἐν τῇ κατὰ Χάλκην
Θεολογ. Σχολῇ

Τῇ
1η# Μαΐου
1886

Ῥαφαὴλ Μ. ἱεροδιάκονος
ἐκ Δαμασκοῦ

NOTES

1. ὑποφαίνοντος.
2. Πεντηκοστῆς.
3. This differs from the standard text, which adds “γὰρ”.
4. This differs from the standard text, which reads “ἀπαρασαλεύτως”.
5. This differs from the standard text, which reads “μύρια”.
6. This text is missing “καὶ μάλιστα τῶν ἀπὸ Καλουΐνου”.
7. This differs from the standard text, which reads “τοῦ αὐτοῦ Ἁγίου”.
8. The standard text lacks parentheses.
9. This differs from the standard text, which lacks the definite article “τό”.

APPENDIX 3

Regulations of the Theological School (1874)

IN CONSTANTINOPLE FROM THE
PATRIARCHAL PRINTING PRESS
1874

Regulations of the Theological School in Halki of the Great Church of Christ

CHAPTER 1

Concerning the School in General.

1. The sacred seminary organized in the patriarchal stauropegial Monastery of the Holy Trinity in Halki in the year 1844, and bearing the name "Theological School of the Great Church of Christ," has in view as a purpose the education and formation proper to clergymen of the Most High.

2. The School is maintained by annual subscriptions of the Ecumenical Patriarch and the holy hierarchs of the Ecumenical Throne, and by gifts and offerings by enlightened Christians.

3. The School is dependent immediately upon the Patriarch and the Sacred Synod around him, who manage its affairs through a committee of hierarchs, which bears the name of trustee board (ἐφορία), and is under the direction of a headmaster (σχολάρχης).

4. The School has its own seal, which bears the image of the Holy Trinity with an inscription, "Theological School of the Great Church of Christ," and which is divided into four parts: the Ecumenical Patriarch controls one; the trustee board, two; and the headmaster, the fourth.

CHAPTER 2

5. The trustee board is composed of four members with equal votes, elected by the Patriarch and the Sacred Synod from hierarchs of the

Synod, which has its own four-member seal with the inscription "Trustee Board of the Theological School in Halki," 1865. One of the members undertakes also the management of the treasury of the School.

6. The trustee board (1) attends to everything related in general to the maintenance, makeup, and improvement of the School (on this account also its members consecutively and at intervals visit the School in person and receive direct information concerning its internal condition); (2) recruits the necessary and competent professors, examining their qualifications, in accordance with the present regulations; (3) attends to the annual admittance of students, examines their credentials and securities according to the requirements of the regulations, and, after a prior examination by the faculty committee and the physician of the School, offers them entrance; (4) likewise attends also to the remaining persons necessary to the School, as is prescribed in the chapters concerning them; and (5) accepts whatever donations are made to the School and attends to their registration in the volume of offerings and the fulfillment of the intention of donors.

7. The trustee board corresponds with the headmaster, to whom it also conveys every regulation concerning the School.

8. The trustee board, which holds regular meetings in its offices, located in those of the Patriarchate, considers everything that concerns the improvement of the building.

9. The trustee board has its own secretary who at the same time is the undersecretary of the Sacred Synod and who maintains in order the correspondence and books of its office. These are: (1) book of the official correspondence of the trustee board; (2) book of minutes of the meetings of the trustee board; (3) treasury of the revenues and expenses of the School; (4) volume of donations; and (5) duplicate book of reception of certificates and a similar duplicate book of admittance.

10. The overseer who manages the treasury collects a proof of receipt for the annual subscriptions of the supporters of the School, as well as the exceptional contributions; maintains special correspondence with the steward, who provides the fixed allotments for the maintenance of the School; and conveys in a timely fashion the salaries of the professors and the others under salary.

11. The members of the trustee board are appointed for one year, but the same person may stay by a new nomination for a second year.

CHAPTER 3

Concerning the Personnel of the School.

12. The personnel of the School comprise the headmaster, the requisite professors, the prescribed number of students, a caretaker, a secretary, a librarian, a confessor, the chaplains, a physician, a steward, and the requisite servants necessary for various functions of the School and of the sacred temple in it—all of whom ought to be children of the Orthodox Church.

13. Outside of these, no one else can reside for any reason within the School.

CHAPTER 4

Concerning the Headmaster.

14. The headmaster—ordained, known for his virtue and most competent, and educated in profane and indeed sacred letters—is chosen and appointed by the Ecumenical Patriarch and the Sacred Synod.

15. All staff in the School is under the headmaster, inasmuch as all things in it are also immediately dependent on him.

16. The headmaster always remains in the School, supported by it and having his own servant; and during his brief absence from the School, he appoints a substitute from the ordained professors, announcing this also to the others.

17. The headmaster ought to be vigilant concerning the exact execution of the laws and regulations of the School and to enforce the prescribed penalties of the regulations for their violation; and he is also answerable for the teaching of theological and other classes.

18. The headmaster ought to know precisely the professors' teaching methods and the students' conduct of study, which he sees and hears, and which, if necessary, he adjusts for improvement.

19. If the headmaster might be informed that one of the professors is negligent in his obligations, he provides him a modest observation, and when this corrects nothing, refers him to the trustee board.

20. The headmaster, who corresponds with the trustee board, reports to it anything whatsoever that concerns the School, and when necessary, can refer the matter directly even to the Patriarch himself; and the same conveys also any request of the professors to the trustee board.

21. The headmaster can convene, whenever he might judge, the faculty committee for consideration of any subject whatsoever that affects the affairs of the School, and he chairs it. Decisions take place by majority vote, and in case of a tie, the headmaster's vote decides; and for this purpose minutes are kept, in which the opinions of those voting are reported precisely, and which all sign.

22. The headmaster ought to account for his actions as headmaster to the trustee board of the School and through it to the Ecumenical Patriarch and the Sacred Synod surrounding him.

CHAPTER 5

Concerning the Professors.

23. The staff of professors consists for the present, in addition to the headmaster, of ten professors.

24. The professors are recruited, after previous agreement with the headmaster, by the trustee board, and are appointed by the Patriarch and the Sacred Synod.

25. The professors ought to be clergymen, and if not, the professors of theology at least ought to be clergymen.

26. Every appointed professor, in addition to the good reputation of his character, ought to have an academic diploma or proof that demonstrates his personal study of the subjects that he is called upon to teach, except if his competency might be apparent from prior teaching success or from learned writings.

27. All professors are obedient to the headmaster, whom they ought to inform regarding the method of their teaching and the instructional writings used for class.

28. The professors ought to (1) precisely and unfailingly be prepared for the appointed days and hours in class, and if one might happen to be

sick, he ought to inform the headmaster concerning this; (2) maintain an accurate roll of student absence and attendance; and (3) lead a life consistent with the vocation of the School.

29. The professors reside within the School and are supported by it, dining with the headmaster and students at a common table, but taking supper in a special mess, which is served by one of the servants of the School. However, one or two of the professors by turns dine with the students at the common table.

30. The professors, when called by necessity, are able to receive permission from the headmaster for a brief absence.

31. A professor resigns only following the close of the school year, after submitting through the headmaster a written resignation to the trustee board at least one month before classes end.

32. A professor is discharged by them[1] and terminated on the recommendation of the headmaster, if he might prove incompetent or neglectful concerning the performance of his obligations, or otherwise run contrary to the mission of the School; and once expelled, he is henceforth inadmissible.

33. A professor who teaches for the entire school year and resigns receives also the vacation stipend, and upon his request, receives a voucher of his service from the trustee board alone.

34. A professor who teaches faithfully for twenty years at the School obtains the right to have a pension from the Great Church.

CHAPTER 6

Concerning the Students.

35. The number of students does not exceed sixty; nevertheless, it can be increased, in proportion to the material resources of the School.

36. Each of the hierarchs is entitled to have only one supported student under his personal patronage and can bring in even a second, if the rest of the hierarchs do not have such a one that they might bring into the School before reaching the prescribed number of students.

37. In order to be admitted into the School, the students ought (1) to be children of the Orthodox Church; (2) to be neither younger than eighteen years of age nor older than twenty-two, outside of those who have already completed gymnasium studies, who are accepted even up to twenty-five years of age; (3) not to be subject either to organic or to any chronic illness; (4) to hold a certificate that has been certified by the Hierarch concerning their honest character and good conduct; and (5) to know the following subjects: grammar, etymology, and the principles of syntax of the Greek language, with their application in writing, practical arithmetic, political geography, sacred history, and sacred catechism.

38. However, they also ought to provide a pledge to one of the hierarchs (1) that they will fulfill strictly all the obligations imposed on them by the regulations, and (2) that, upon reaching the age prescribed by the sacred canons, they will become clergy.

39. If the patron of any of the students might die before the completion of intention of the patronage stipulated in the above article, that student ought to arrange for another patron, who will undertake all of the obligations of the deceased one.

40. The School accepts students only before the commencement of the school year.

41. The entering student can be placed in a higher grade until the fourth year, if after being examined he might be shown to be versant without exception in the subjects of the higher grades.

42. The student is expelled (1) if he might be caught at fault concerning morals, and might be a violator of the laws and regulations of the School; and (2) if he might be shown to be negligent and incorrigible. And in such cases—as also if when one of the students changes his mind before he might complete the series of classes, either because he might wish to leave the School, or wish not to be a clergyman after reaching the age according to the canons—his patron is obligated to indemnify the School, paying twenty-five Turkish liras for each year of his residence at the School.

43. The funds that the patron ought to pay if the student might not be a clergyman after reaching the legal age remain as a deposit in the treasury of the School and are returned to the patron whenever the student might become a clergyman.

44. Those who contract contagious or organic illness, as well as those who are shown incapable of learning during the first year, are expelled without any indemnification.

CHAPTER 7

Concerning the Classes

45. The classes taught in the School are those of sacred theology with required humanities. The classes of sacred theology are presently the following: church history, sacred commentary and exegesis of Holy Scripture, dogmatic and moral theology, patrology and Hebrew archeology, pastoral theology, homiletics, catechesis, teleturgical and church law, and theological exercises. The humanities classes are sacred history, sacred catechesis, anthropology, psychology, logic, ethics and history of philosophy, Greek and Latin language and philology, rhetoric and composition, geometry, mathematics, arithmetic, algebra, mathematical geography, political history, chronology, Slavonic and Bulgarian language, Turkish and French, and theoretical and practical church music. The entire series of teaching in the School is covered in seven years, according to the following general program:

Classes of the First Year.

1.) Sacred history in detail, sacred geography and Hebrew archeology (three times weekly). 2.) Greek language (Chrysostom, Xenophon, Arrian, Plutarch) with syntax and composition exercises (nine). 3.) Theoretical arithmetic (three). 4.) French language (elementary classes, grammar) (three). 5.) Political geography (two). 6.) Church music (preparatory *octōēchos*[2]) (two).

Classes of the Second Year.

1.) Sacred catechism in detail (three). Greek language and syntax with composition exercises (Basil the Great, Gregory, Plato, Lysias, Demosthenes) (six). 3.) Latin language (elementary classes, Cornelius Nepos, Eutropius, grammar) (six). 4.) Geometry (six). 5.) French language (syntax) (six). 6.)

Political history (six). 7.) Composition, biography, chorography, moral characters (one). 8.) Church music (*stichērarikon*[3] and theory of music) (two).

Classes of the Third Year.

1.) Church history from the first until the ninth centuries (three). 2.) Greek philology (Herodotus, Thucydides) (three). 3.) Latin language (syntax, Caesar, Livy, Ambrose) (four). 4.) Algebra (3). 5.) Political history (three). 6.) Mathematical geography and chronology (two). 7.) Composition, letter-writing (one). 8.) Church music (*kalophōnikon*[4] and theory of music) (two).

Classes of the Fourth Year.

1.) Church history (up to the present) (three). 2.) Introduction to theology (one). 3.) Anthropology, namely, somatology and psychology, logic. 4.) Greek philology (Homer, Euripides, Theocritus, poems of Gregory) (four). 5.) Latin philology (Sallust, Ovid, Cicero, Tertullian) and composition exercises (three). 6.) Slavonic language (grammar) (6). 7.) Turkish language (three). 8.) Rhetoric (two). 9.) Composition (rhetorical preparatory exercises) (one).

Classes of the Fifth Year.

1.) Dogmatic theology (three). 2.) Sacred commentary (one). 3.) Practical philosophy (moral and physical law) (three). 4.) Greek philology (Sophocles, Aeschylus, Pindar) (three). 5.) Latin philology (Virgil, Horace, Augustine) (three). 6.) Slavonic language (syntax and composition exercises) (three). 7.) Turkish language (three). 8.) Theological exercises (historical dissertation).

Classes of the Sixth Year.

1.) Moral theology (three). 2.) Patrology (two). 3.) Exegesis of the Holy Scriptures (three). 4.) Homiletics (two). 5.) History of philosophy (three). 6.) Bulgarian language (six). 7.) Turkish language (three). 8.) Theological exercises (commentary of the Holy Scriptures and a festal sermon).

Classes of the Seventh Year.

1.) Pastoral, catechetical, and teleturgical theology (three). 2.) Church history (three). 3.) Theological thesis. 4.) Homiletic exercises.

46. The classes of the final year last until the end of February, and the remaining time is left to preparation for the examinations for the diploma.

47. On every Sunday a short moral homily by the headmaster and the professors of the School consecutively in turns takes place in the temple of the School for the students.

48. Each class lasts for one hour.

49. Each class ought to be taught complete within the appointed years of the program, namely, from beginning until end.

50. Immediately after examinations the headmaster and professors consult together to determine the hours and days for each class's lessons, which are fixed in a schedule that is signed by the headmaster.

51. All classes of the scholastic year without exception are obligatory for the students completing them.

52. Texts of Greek orators, poetry of Homer and Pindar, and texts of the Fathers of the Church that are assigned by choice of the professor are learned by heart by the students obligatorily.

53. The homiletic exercises of the seventh year take place from the pulpit of the sacred temple of the School within the hearing of all, professors and students.

CHAPTER 8

Concerning the Commencement of Classes.

54. The scholastic year begins on September 1 and ends on August 31. It is divided into a period of lessons that begin on September 1 and last until May 30, a period of review from June 1 until the 30th of the same month, and a period of examinations and recess from July 1 until the end of August.

55. The students ought to return to the School a few days before commencement, but the professors at least one week before. Within this week the new entering students are also present for examination.

56. The commencement of classes begins with a sacred celebration, after which a sermon that is preached by the headmaster follows.

CHAPTER 9

Concerning the Examinations in General.

57. The examinations are (1) daily, (2) annually, and (3) for a diploma.

58. In the daily examinations, the students are examined on each class by the professor teaching it, who notes in a special audit roll the grade of the answers and presents this on a monthly basis to the headmaster. In this roll the student absences by chance are also noted.

59. The annual examinations and those for a diploma take place in common.

60. The common examinations begin on July 1, when the Ecumenical Patriarch, at least two hierarchs of the Synod, and the members of the trustee board are present.

61. Before the commencement of the examinations, after a sacred celebration takes place, the headmaster reads a report of the material, moral, and intellectual state of the School in general, in which he also indicates its needs that must be attended to, and in addition an exact list of the donations offered to the School, and afterward either he or one of the professors with his permission delivers a short sermon on an ecclesiastical topic.

CHAPTER 10

Concerning the Annual Examinations.

62. The examination committee is composed only of professors of the School and is presided over by the headmaster. And each of the professors mainly examines his own students, but fellow professors can reciprocally propose questions for the examining professor, with the permission of the headmaster.

63. The students are examined by lot on all of the classes that they take throughout the year, in the following manner: for each class, except in the case of languages, during the daily lessons the professor gives propositions that relate to the yearly examinations, and one month before the examinations all these are set in order by the professor in questions,

the number relative to the extent of the class, that are all given to the students for review. However, in the case of languages, the students ought to prepare themselves for an examination on at least over a third of the texts given them, which are assigned by the professor one month before the examinations.

64. The order of the students being examined is assigned by a schedule, which the headmaster, who confers with the professors, sends out before the examinations.

65. The composition and exercise professors provide class compositions and exercises worked on throughout the year and read an exact list of them. The compositions and these exercises that are written clearly are bound and stored in the archives of the School. Likewise, even the final-year theses and homiletic exercises form a special codex.

66. After the end of examinations, the examination committee in a special meeting decides concerning the grade level of each examinee, taking into account especially the daily audit rolls. The grade levels are the following: "Fair," "Good," and "Excellent."

67. The grade level of the examinee is determined as follows. During the first year the professors who taught the examinee decide a grade of which each judges him worthy, especially for each of the classes taught by him. The headmaster's vote is added to them. And a "Fair" is reckoned as one, a "Good" as two, and an "Excellent" as three. These numbers are added, their total is also divided by the number of classes (which increases by unit), and the quotient determines the grade level of the examinee. If a balance might remain, if this is less than half of the divisor, it is not counted, but if it is greater than or equal to half, it indicates that the examinee is worthy of half the higher level. But if one might receive an "Excellent" in all the votes, this is indicated in the documentation by the adverb "unanimously." In the following years up to even the sixth, the voting takes place likewise, and each time the level of the immediately previous year is also added, as is noted in the documentation, which itself also has the force of a vote. The numbers that are gathered from these votes are divided by the addition of the examined classes, which was increased by two, and the quotient determines the level of the examinee.

68. Whoever of the examined might receive an "Excellent" or "Good" is advanced in order that he might attend more advanced classes, and receives a certificate from the headmaster.

69. The result of the examination committee's decision is announced in public.

70. Whoever might receive a "Fair" ought to show himself worthy of more advanced classes before the next commencement of classes through new examinations; otherwise, he repeats the classes of the previous year. If he might also receive a "Fair" even a second time, he is expelled from the School as negligent, subject to the obligations of article 42.

71. If one of the students might not wish to sit for an examination, he is expelled as negligent, according to article 42, unless he is ill, and this will be confirmed in writing by the physician, and then his examination is postponed to the time of the commencement of classes.

72. Any students who receive an "Excellent" for three consecutive years, or an "Excellent" unanimously for two consecutive years, receive a commensurate award from the School.

CHAPTER 11

Concerning the Examinations for a Diploma.

73. The examinations for a diploma precede the annual ones.

74. All who finish the entire series of the School's classes are subject without exception to examinations for a diploma.

75. The examination committee of examinees for a diploma is composed of the professors of theology, but if any of the other professors have a diploma of theology, they are also part of the examination committee.

76. The examinations for a diploma are written and oral, and the written ones take place fifteen days before the annual examinations, in the following manner. Each of the professors of theology prepares an equal number of file cards from each class for the students, each of which cards contains three questions, of which the student ought to answer one in writing, under the supervision of the headmaster and professor, within three hours, while not consulting either a book, copybook, or anyone of those present; each professor signs the answer and submits it to the headmaster. These written answers to various questions are submitted by the headmaster to the examination committee, and the

answers are taken under consideration, by voting concerning the level of the examinee, and set out during general examinations for reading by all.

77. The oral examinations take place during the first day of the annual examinations, as follows. Each of the professors addresses various questions on each of the theological classes to the examinee, in the form of a dialogue, and then, after the thesis of the examinee is read, the examinee answers the challenges counterargued by the professorial committee.

78. At least one month before the annual examinations, each of the undergraduates (τελειοδιδάκτων) ought to present to the headmaster a thesis on a theological subject that he chose with the approval of the headmaster, written in refined Greek language (καθαρεύουσαν Ἑλληνικὴν γλῶσσαν) and having at least the length of a folio (ἑνὸς τυπογραφικοῦ φύλλου). The headmaster makes it known particularly also to the remaining professors.

79. After the completion of examinations, the headmaster and professors of theological classes, who meet specially, take votes by secret ballot concerning the grade level in general of each of the examined students, taking into consideration also the levels of the annual examinations on theological classes. The dividend of the number of levels is divided by the number of professors, which is increased by two.

80. The levels are the same as the annual examinations and are determined according to article 67. And those who receive a "Good" or "Excellent" are deemed worthy of the diploma, which is signed by the headmaster and secretary, stamped with the School seal, and approved by the Ecumenical Patriarch. Those who receive a "Fair" can, after presenting themselves at the School during the time of examinations in the following year, submit themselves to a second testing. Those who are not clergy in the School receive the diploma when they become clergy.

81. One who is not judged worthy of the diploma, and who does not wish to be submitted a second time to examination, leaves without any document, and indemnifies the School, according to article 42. However, if, also after consenting to the second testing, he might fail, if he might be a clergyman, he is expelled without indemnification, receiving documentation of residence at the School, conduct, and attendance of

classes, which is signed by the headmaster and secretary, and has been approved by the Patriarch. However, if not, he is subject to the obligations of articles 42 and 45, namely, he gives surety to the School until his ordination.

82. The diplomas are conferred *gratis* from the School, and equally distributed, and when the diplomas have been approved by the headmaster and secretary, they are kept in a special codex.

83. The presentation of the diplomas takes place solemnly on the first Sunday after the conclusion of the examinations for a diploma, as follows. After a sacred celebration takes place, the headmaster makes a suitable public address, and then the secretary reads the approval given by the examination committee. One of the members of the trustee board reads aloud each of the diplomas. The headmaster, when he invites up each graduate and bestows the diploma, declares him a teacher of **Orthodox Christian theology**.

CHAPTER 12

Concerning the Recesses.

84. After the conclusion of annual examinations, a recess from classes, which lasts until September 1, takes place.

85. While recesses last, it is permitted for students to leave the School on prescribed days for Constantinople with written permission of the headmaster. But if one might wish to go outside of Constantinople, this occurs with the written permission of his patron.

86. The professors can likewise leave for wherever they wish after coming to an agreement with the headmaster.

87. The days on which recesses of classes also take place are the dominical and Marian feast days, Christmas and Epiphany eve, the Saturdays of Meatfare and Cheesefare, the Great and Renewal Weeks, October 26, November 8, December 6, January 7 and 30, the memorial day of St. Photios (which is celebrated on February 6 as a feast day of the sacred monastery), April 23, June 29 and 30, and the name day of the Ecumenical Patriarch at the time.

CHAPTER 13

Concerning the Religious Obligations.

88. The students chant the sacred services by turns in the temple of the monastery with every care, according to the order that the Orthodox Church received from the divine Fathers. The headmaster assigns the choirs of chanters and choristers at the beginning of the academic year through a special schedule. However, on important days the headmaster can change the schedule.

89. All professors and students at the School without exception regularly attend sacred services, unless prevented for a good reason, and listen with extreme piety and calm.

90. Before table and after table, the customary prayer takes place, but after evening table, compline is read immediately.

91. The students confess and partake of the hallowed mysteries at least four times annually: (1) the Nativity of Christ; (2) Holy Pascha; (3) the feast day of the Holy Apostles; and (4) the feast day of the Dormition of the Theotokos. Before sacred communion, holy unction is celebrated.

92. All those living at the School keep inviolably all the fasts established by the church, but if bodily sickness requires some allowance, only the headmaster can permit this on the advice of the physician.

CHAPTER 14

Concerning the Academic Obligations.

93. The beginning of each class is indicated by the bell designated for this. The students ought to be present in the classrooms before the arrival of the professor, and hours of class are from 8:00 a.m. until 12:00 p.m., and after 12:00 p.m. during the winter from 1:30 p.m. until 3:30 p.m., and during the spring from 2:00 p.m. until 4:00 p.m.

94. None of the students is permitted to be absent from classes, except for sickness, and this with the knowledge of the headmaster.

95. During class the students listen with extreme calm and attention, neither whispering nor asking each other puzzling questions, but above all they ask and reply becomingly to whatever they are asked by the professor.

96. If one of the students during class might deviate from prescribed obligations, the professor, in proportion to the misconduct (1) calls for correct conduct, (2) reprimands and removes him from class, and (3) brings charges against him to the headmaster.

97. None of the students is permitted to contradict or disobey because of a remark or reprimand that was addressed to him by the professor over a class, but if he might think himself wronged, he reports this only to the headmaster.

CHAPTER 15

Concerning the Attire and Apparel of the Students.

98. All the student of the School wear simple uniform clothing, namely, a black *skoufos*,[5] a black tunic reaching the feet, a black pelt from a lamb, slippers or winter shoes, and a coat of the same color. Each of the students also has two sets of clothing, one for workdays and the other cleaner for feast days.

99. Outside of the two sets of clothing in the preceding article, the student ought, when he is entering the School before the commencement of classes, to bring with him (1) four shirts, an equal number of pants, six pairs of socks, four waistcoats, two dark *skoufoi*, four handkerchiefs, two pairs of shoes or slippers; (2) a bed with what is required for all weather of the year, namely, an iron frame and a board, a mattress, a blanket for the winter, four sheets, a pillow with two ὀψιδίων,[6] four towels and a light quilt for the spring, one chair, and one table.

100. The students, outside of the books read specifically for teaching in the School, can have also others for personal reading, books that, however, are not contrary to piety, the policy of the state, and good morals. The latter such books' use is forbidden.

CHAPTER 16

Concerning Food and the Table.

101. The School provides without exception to all those living in it the same food: a breakfast, which consists of coffee and a piece of bread after the morning service; a lunch, which consists of juice and two plates of food and cheese or olive oil, and also fruits according to season, at 12:00 p.m.; and supper, which consists of three dishes, in addition to juice, at 8:00 p.m.

102. At table each one has the seat assigned to him, and eats with decorum and calm, all conversation with those sitting with him being forbidden.

103. No one can be absent or leave from the table without the permission of the headmaster, and only those who are sick receive the appropriate food separately.

104. No one at table is permitted to make observations on what is being served.

105. During mealtime each of the students in turn reads audibly from an ecclesiastical book, assigned by the headmaster.

CHAPTER 17

Concerning Entrance and Exit from the School.

106. The students, all together at the same time, go out for a walk twice daily: after the 12:00 p.m. meal on the porches of the School, and after the evening meal for an hour in the lower parts of the hill; and they walk by twos and threes in good order and calmly, within the boundaries that have been designated, while escorted and overseen by the caretakers.

107. No outsider is permitted to visit the School or the students without the permission of the headmaster, who sets the place and time of the appointment.

108. It is forbidden for all outsiders to remain overnight in the School.

109. None of the students is permitted to be absent from the School, except for a great need, which has been reported in writing to the headmaster; at the time when the student returns, he ought to present himself immediately to the headmaster.

CHAPTER 18

Concerning Disciplinary Duties.

110. The students ought to observe strictly every law of the present regulations that applies to them, and every specific order of the headmaster concerning them.

111. The students ought, wherever they might be, to give due respect to the supporters of the School, the headmaster, and the professors, when showing regard to those who approach them.

112. They ought to be sincere and truthful toward all, and especially toward the superiors of the School. Falsehood is punished.

113. They ought to present themselves to one another as brothers and conduct themselves with decency and modesty, avoiding all insolence, ridicule, or contempt, and any violent attack. Quarrels and abuse, factions and divisions, and secret meetings are forbidden completely, and those that occur are punished.

114. None of the students is permitted to take the law into his own hands even through a simple remark toward the least of the servants, and if he might think himself wronged by anyone, he ought to refer himself only to the headmaster.

115. The students, wherever they might be, ought to behave worthily of their calling, while avoiding both every dubious relationship and entering into places incompatible with the character befitting a sacred person.

116. Any request of the students to the headmaster and teachers ought to take place at the proper place and time.

117. Except by the porter or caretaker, books, clothes, letters, and such things are not brought into or out of the School.

118. The students are forbidden to stay in a cell belonging to another. However, visiting another cell is permitted only during the day for a short

time and reasonable excuse. In addition, eating secretly, consuming drink, and smoking are forbidden.

CHAPTER 19

Concerning Punishments.

119. If one of the student might not fulfill any of his duties, according to the circumstances, either he is admonished, or reprimanded privately or in public, or subject to appropriate obligation, or finally, expelled from the School. The headmaster applies the punishment of expulsion after prior agreement with the church through the trustee board. However, if one of the students might be shown to instigate a revolt for the overthrow of the School's established order, not only does he pay the School's expenses that ensued on his account, according to article 42, but also he is punished by church authority.

120. One who is expelled once from the School is henceforth inadmissible.

CHAPTER 20

Concerning the Secretary.

121. The secretary of the School is appointed by the trustee board, lives at the School, and is under the immediate supervision of the headmaster, and his work is (1) the editing of the acts of the School; (2) the editing of official documents and official correspondence of the headmaster; (3) their filing in suitable books; (4) the registry of the students in the matriculation book; and (5) the strict maintenance of documents sent to the headmaster, receipts, and various books of the office.

122. The following are the books of the School's office: (1) the matriculation book, in which the forename, surname, father, race (τὸ γένος),[7] age, patron, and the year of each student's entrance into the School are recorded; (2) the codex of proceedings, in which the annual reports of the headmaster, the approvals of the examinations for a diploma, and the annual programs

of studies and examinations, and any other action of the faculty committee, are entered; (3) the codex of diplomas, in which the copies of the diplomas and certificates that were conferred to the exiting students are preserved; (4) a record book, in which the official correspondence of the headmaster is entered; and (5) annual catalogues of classes.

123. The secretary serves on the faculty committee, although he does not have a vote. After the headmaster he signs the official documents of the School, and sits at table with the professors.

CHAPTER 21

Concerning the Library and Librarian.

124. The School has a public library for use by those who teach and are taught at the School, and all those outsiders who are learned and lovers of letters endeavoring to derive profit from it.

125. The library has its own seal, which bears the following inscription: "Library of the Theological School in Halki," which is kept by the headmaster.

126. In the building of the library are its reading room and office. The School's most ancient objects as well as scientific instruments are kept in it.

127. A quantity of money, proportionate to the means of the School, is dedicated each year to the acquirement of books and other things that have scientific value for enlargement of the library.

128. The headmaster safeguards the monetary bequests dedicated particularly to the School's library, and from their annual interest books are purchased based on the list given by the headmaster.

129. The custody of the library and the management of its office are assigned to a librarian, who is appointed by the headmaster and is directly under the headmaster.

130. The librarian ought to arrange the books in their proper places for easy access by anyone seeking them, while he attends to the sound preservation and cleanliness of the books, scientific instruments, and ancient objects under his responsibility, and he ought to have an accurate catalogue of all things with the numbered notation of their place.

131. All the books bear the seal of the library, and ones that were donated also bear the notation of the donor's name.

132. The hours during which the library is open are determined by the headmaster through a schedule, which is issued at commencement and posted on the door of the library.

133. The professors are able to visit the library without restriction, to stay in it, and to take books from it, with a receipt and for a specified time. However, only fourth-, fifth-, and sixth-year students are permitted, by a pass that the headmaster issues one time, to enter the reading room and to study in it when they are finished with classes, but never to take books from it for personal reading.

134. Those who study in the reading room read to themselves, without the least noise, while at the same time attending to the cleanliness of the book being read.

135. When reported to the headmaster, violators of the rules above are reprimanded by him; and when they do not correct themselves, they are barred from future entrance into the library.

136. Learned outside visitors are able to read during the appointed hours in the reading room, while maintaining silence, but they never borrow books from the library.

137. Whoever ruins a book is obligated to pay twice the value of the complete copy, or to replace the volume.

138. Manuscripts never leave the library.

139. Those who donate books to the School or any other donation worthy of mention receive an acknowledgment from the headmaster.

140. Books sent from wheresoever it may be for distribution to the students are deposited in the library and distributed by only the headmaster accordingly to those students who apply themselves and progress.

141. The competent professor alone takes out experimental instruments, spheres, maps, and other objects necessary in lessons, during the hour of the class.

CHAPTER 22

Concerning the Confessor and Chaplains.

142. The confessor and chaplains are appointed, on the recommendation of the headmaster, by the trustee board, with the knowledge and

permission of the Ecumenical Patriarch, and are under the direction of the headmaster.

143. The confessor, if he might not happen to live at the School, ought to come without delay to it as often as the headmaster calls upon him for celebration of the sacred mystery of confession.

144. The chaplains, who are always in residence at the School, celebrate with all required strictness the Divine Liturgy, and all the prescribed sacred prayers of the day and night services; every time when the headmaster presides, he is assisted by hierodeacon students whom the headmaster might chose.

145. During every sacred mystagogy, the chaplains ought to remember indispensably in the sacred *prothesis*,[8] along with the founders of the sacred monastery, the names of the founders, supporters, benefactors, trustees, professors, and students of this sacred Theological School, living and dead, which have been recorded in the sacred diptychs.

146. The headmaster assigns to one of the chaplains also the care of the vestry (τοῦ σκευοφυλακίου).

CHAPTER 23

Concerning the Physician

147. The School has a learned physician, who is appointed by the trustee board, and an infirmary.

148. Although the physician resides outside the School, nevertheless he visits it at least once each day, and is informed by the caretaker if one of those in it is ill, and visits him. He examines the new entering students, according to article 37, section 3. In addition, he examines by inspection the type and quality of the food prepared for those at the School, and the condition of chamber pots.

149. The infirmary is assigned to the immediate care and supervision of the physician.

150. The caretaker transports the sick student to the infirmary and provides to him the treatment prescribed by the physician through the nurse assigned for this purpose.

151. The School provides medications *gratis* to those needing them.

152. If one of the students contracts a chronic or contagious illness, the physician reports this in writing to the headmaster, who decides either concerning his temporary removal from the School, or concerning his complete expulsion, according to article 44.

CHAPTER 24

Concerning the Caretakers

153. The immediate supervision of the students' conduct is assigned to two caretakers, who are appointed by the trustee board and obedient directly to the headmaster.

154. Ordained men, of irreproachable conduct, prudent and vigilant concerning the performance of their duties, are appointed caretakers.

155. The work of the caretakers is to supervise the students everywhere while they are studying together and sleeping together, in church, at table, while walking, and in sickness; and to take care that not one of them might be deficient in his duties.

156. The caretaker ought to report to the headmaster any act of the students that is contrary to discipline, honesty concerning morals, and sacerdotal character; and in case of negligence or any other intemperance, the student is expelled immediately.

CHAPTER 25

Concerning the Steward

157. The steward is appointed by the trustee board but is immediately under the headmaster.

158. He ought to supply the provisions for each need and attend to the physical infrastructure of the School.

159. In addition, he sought to attend to the garden and general estates of the monastery.

160. He maintains a daily correspondence with the treasurer of the School, from whom he requests at the proper time what is required.

161. He ought to record in a special register exactly what he furnished on each occasion for the School and present the register to the headmaster in the evening. At the end of each month, he sends this to the treasurer after the headmaster has approved it.

162. He reports the servant who contravenes the steward's requests to the headmaster, who imposes on the servant the appropriate punishment or even expels him on his own authority; and in this case the steward ought to request without delay the restoration of the servant from the trustee board.

163. If the steward might appear to be neglecting some of his own duties, the headmaster first warns him, but when he does not correct the deficiency, refers the matter to the trustee board or takes the proper measures immediately.

CHAPTER 25

Concerning the Servants.

164. The servants are appointed by the trustee board and are subject to the immediate management of the steward; and their number is proportionate to the needs of the School.

165. The servants ought to be of good morals and without bodily defect or illness.

ADDITIONAL ARTICLES.

166. Any preceding legislation, contrary to the rules of the present regulation, remains invalid.

167. Each of those in the School receives from the headmaster one copy of the present regulation for his guidance.

In Constantinople, in the year of the Lord 1867, during the month of August.

† GRĒGORIOS OF CONSTANTINOPLE confirms.

† NIKODĒMOS OF KYZIKOS
† GERASIMOS OF CHALCEDON
† NEOPHYTOS OF DERKOI
† DIONYSIOS OF CRETE
† AGATHANGELOS OF DRAMA
† PAISIOS OF BITHYNIA
† GRĒGORIOS OF CHIOS
† NIKODĒMOS OF BODENA
† NEOPHYTOS OF KORYTSA

End.

NOTES

1. That is, by the members of the trustee board.
2. ἡ ὀκτώηχος is a liturgical book that contains the eight tones, or modes of singing church hymns, and that is used according to a moveable liturgical cycle based on the Pascha.
3. τὸ στιχηράριον was a liturgical book that contained the verses that accompany hymns and was replaced by another book, τὸ δοξαστάριον, in the early nineteenth century. As used here, the word *stichērarikon* (στιχηραρικόν) probably refers to the study of the verses.
4. καλοφωνία ("beautiful sound") is a form of embellished chanting. The use of the word *kalophōnikon* (καλοφωνικόν) most likely refers to its study.
5. The σκοῦφος is a short, cylinder-shaped cap mostly worn by monks and monastic clergy.
6. Unknown meaning.
7. During this period the term *race* (τὸ γένος) was used in a way similar to the modern usage of "national origin."
8. The word *prothesis* (πρόθεσις) refers to the preparation of bread and wine for the celebration of the Eucharist.

APPENDIX 4

A Contemporary Account of Life at Halki

A Page from My Studies

by Basileios Antōniadēs[1]

A radiograph that arrived from Berlin on December 5 announced that Vanuteli,[2] the senior cardinal in Rome, had celebrated his ninetieth birthday on that Sunday. The announcement called to my mind an entire page from my studies at Halki, and a sin. I suppose (I cannot swear) that it concerned the same Vanuteli, who, at least during the years 1871–1873, was found in Constantinople, on what mission and service for the Holy See, I do not know.

The Bulgarian question and schism still preoccupied the Great Church, and the resulting upheaval had not yet concluded. Anthimos Koutalianos was Ecumenical Patriarch, and, as we heard, Nikodēmos of Kyzikos the so-called philosopher and Neophytos of Derkoi were favored members of the Holy Synod around him.

The archimandrite Phōtios, a native of Chios and a humble man of gentle character, succeeded Anchialos Basileios to the directorship of the School. Anchialos Basileios, known for his pious observance of the Fathers, had directed the School for two years after the announcement of the schism, and afterward became Metropolitan of Smyrna. Aside from Kleanthos Charalambidēs the Turkish professor (I do not remember the French professor; they changed and varied often), the lay teaching staff of the school was composed of Ēlias Tantalidēs, Basileios Grēgoriadēs, Christos Papadopoulos (who afterward became professor of philosophy at the University of Athens), Iōannēs Basmatzidēs, and Geōrgios Lianopoulos (the latter two from Hadrianopolis). The clergy were Iōannēs Anastasiadēs (my fellow Constantinopolitan, who became director of the Great School and Metropolitan of Caesarea); Grēgorios Zygabēnos; Kōnstantinos Bapheidēs; Ilariōn Kanakēs from Crete; and Basileios Geōrgiadēs, at that time the lay theologian of exegetics who also had taken on the chair of Hebrew and, at a very young age, was among the recent graduates of the Theological School and National University, [and] who now, as Basileios of Nicaea, gloriously occupies the patriarchate.

At that time, I was about twenty-two years of age, appropriate to the sixth class of the School, which numbered only six students, instead of the seventeen or eighteen that it had at the beginning of the third year. In addition to my own erudite self from Cappadocia ('Ινδζὲ σουλοῦ), there was Geōrgios Karakatsanēs from Kydonies, Apostolos Charalambidēs from Madytos, Hierodeacon Germanos Kaligas from Cephalonia (who later became Metropolitan of Athens and prematurely died to the Church), and two others named Panagiōtēs: the one I think was from Ganochora and the other from Sinop. This latter one had received the nickname of *Boukouvala*[3] (I do not know who gave him the nickname or how) and was known in the class and in the entire school under this name rather than under his own proper one. He was a *sui generis* type, quarrelsome and difficult, who took pleasure in being a champion among those who have a boisterous and disobedient character, until in his last year he was expelled from the School on account of insolence and obstinate insubordination, because he did not understand that he must conform to the prevailing order of the School—that candidates for graduation who were not clergy preach their sermons while neither ascending to the pulpit nor having a lectern before them, as he thought himself worthy. Kaligas was no less than a model of honor (φιλοτιμίας), a sincere zealot, pious and of good character, who, although he was one of the rather older students of the School, nevertheless managed to keep up with others, and was faithful in every service, and whenever he was seized by any anger, as we say, "τὸ κεφαλλωνίτικο,"[4] he immediately forgave everything, and was the same good-natured and eager fellow in every service. Our class was named after him as the "class of Kaligas," just as the one immediately above us was called the class of Olympios after its preeminent student in all things, Dēmētrios Iōannides Olympios, from Thessaly, who intended to serve the School with studies in Germany but was compelled to remain in Athens due to fragile health and distinguished himself as both a professor of the normal school there and by the profitable works he performed for earnest youth. Aside from Nikodēmos Alexandros, I think that no one is left from that class, as neither from our own class, except me, unless Karakatsanēs may still live somewhere. We were left with only "four" when the other

Panagiōtēs, from Ganochora, was expelled, but on account of an entirely different reason than that for which *Boukouvala* was expelled, a reason that was tied to one who was found at that time in Constantinople and who at the outset was named Vanuteli.

Visitation of our school and its library was always accessible and without special formalities for those who wished—not even the ones who came from the Latin clergy were excluded; neither the authorities nor the students of the School ever thought that Western priests and monks might also come for the purpose of proselytizing for the *Unia*. And nevertheless it appears that such a purpose was not foreign to them when visits of the colleagues of the aforementioned clergymen took place during the years 1871–1872; and they found such a courteous and sincere reception among the guileless students that he [Vanuteli] encouraged them to also cast baits for catching as many as they could. And their baits were certainly enticing ones, for example, that they send them to Italy and Rome for more advanced and comfortable studies and provide them a future much more bright than could be hoped for among us. It is no wonder that they found among the sixty to seventy students at least a few who paid close attention to the suggestions and promises, and indeed three also even proceeded with secret understandings: Panagiōtēs from Ganochora from our class was one, and the other two from the upper classes, one from Sinai (I forget his name, from among those of considerable age) and another whose origins are unknown to me. It appears that these understandings did not escape the attention of some students, and when they were confirmed inspired indignation and irritation among them, all the more as a decided day was also revealed for their flight from the School.

It was during the Nativity fast, if I am not mistaken. Dormitories and study rooms did not exist at that time. Two or three or even four lived together in one room. I occupied the second room directly at the top of the south staircase on the old southward side of the School. I had for a roommate the priest Grēgorios Nestoridēs, from Thessaly, who was in a lower class but was elderly, an excellent man who had been a parish priest in the Orthodox church of the expatriate (ὁμογενοῦς) parish in Budapest, and who knew a little German. Desiring a more advanced religious and theological education, he had given up his position there and had come to study at Halki. He was humble and honorable, among those qualities that one is also compelled to respect and love. In spite of age and difficulties that certainly during the first years put him to the test, he was able to graduate from the School with the customary diploma, so that after a few years he departed this life "in good repute," as the presiding priest of the Church of Saint John in Chios.

Neither my roommate nor I had an exact knowledge of the arrangements, especially because we were preoccupied on that day with the composition of "an encomium on the Apostle Paul," a homiletic exercise, later eliminated, but at that time required for the students of the sixth class. A competition developed over who could compose the better exercise, whose winner, after obtaining the approval of the proper professor, was also announced publicly in the more prevalent tradition of the School when the professors of theology and students of all the classes were certain to be present.

On a day of the Nativity fast, just returning from the customary walk and lighting my lamp—and at that time olive oil was used for lighting, and not petroleum—I had begun work again on the finishing touches to the encomium, and suddenly I heard unusual movement and much hubbub in the corridor. Those who were causing the commotion proceeded to search for and capture the three who were preparing to flee. Aside from the aforementioned *Boukouvala* and Kaligas, also Loukas Petridēs (a hierodeacon, from an upper class and, in any case, advanced in years, who afterward became bishop of Ainos and Philadephia) led the commotion. He discovered the ones being searched for and confined them to a room, which was next to mine, the first after the aforementioned staircase. Panagiōtēs roomed there. I am not able to express now and describe what I felt at that time when I saw the three under confinement and guarded. It was more a feeling of pity and sympathy for the suffering, even though they were guilty, than anger against the guilty. On the following morning, they were brought securely to the patriarchate with the appropriate letters from the director to the trustee board and never returned (nevertheless, they still went over to the *Unia*).

But a distress and indignation of another type took possession of us who were not up to this time participants in the commotion, an anger against those authors of the truly painful events—how those clergymen of the Western church, who came in sheep's clothing to the School and were considered worthy of every sincere courtesy and welcome, had so behaved and acted, and had been able to act like ravenous wolves for this very reason—and we decided without delay to send immediately a bitter letter to the author himself, as we thought, Vanuteli, with bitter complaints regarding such conduct. It was decided to write the letter in Latin, and its composition was assigned to the Cappadocian. He did not object. The letter sent certainly could not be Ciceronian, nor do I recollect now, after almost fifty-five years, either its language or content. Nevertheless, I still remember two points: first, that it contained those words of the Lord to the scribes and Pharisees, that "they traverse land and sea to make a single proselyte, and when he becomes one, they make him twice as much a child of hell"[5] as themselves; and second, that the name "Vanuteli" in the address was divided and written "*Vano telo*,"[6] as Homer would say, "ἐτώσιον βέλος."[7] The first points were fair, most fair. However, the second was not proper. What wrong did the name commit in the culprit's deed, so that it might be judged worthy of such dissection and distortion? But youth, when in a state of excitement, often goes beyond what is proper.

But we did not also behave badly on account of youth alone. "Introduction to the Holy Scriptures" and "Patrology" were assigned to one of the clergy professors (neither name nor place). A faulty memory (even in the very slightest details) is to the detriment of judgment—and judgment is indispensible to the aforementioned classes. His attempted argumentation against those holding opposing views concluded stereotypically; it is true, "even if opponents disagree." We proceeded to tradition (παράδοσιν) with sure expectations that we would find new disagreements and never be mistaken. Indeed, the question of the authenticity of the writings of Dionysius the Areopagite was an inexhaustible source of such disagreements. It swallowed most of the year, and we did not succeed in going through the Apostolic Fathers. I was one of those students who also studied some German privately in order to employ German writings in classes. German scholarship at that time was viewed as the *norma* and *regula* of wisdom. I had obtained the patrology of Alzog (a Catholic, and yet he also acknowledges their inaccuracies). I also shared the material with others. As if I had not done enough! A new pretext and material for *Boukouvala*—"The very thoughtless one himself, the very one suitable to night, the very plotter himself divisively wastes our time in disagreements so that we might learn by heart his drivel!" And where did you seek and find Panagiōtēs? In the director's office—"And again, holy headmaster, the question of patrology!" It goes without saying that nothing was corrected. But we imperceptibly became accustomed to the idea of breaches, and not of the walls of the treasuries (θησαυροφυλακίων),[8] but with persons who disagreed with us. Certainly Msgr. Vanuteli had a good guardian angel, and the tearing apart was confined only to his name.

If the person in question is the same, certainly His Eminence will remember (even if it be ever so indistinctly) these sad episodes of those times, and we will presume that he also condemns the vicious things done then and perhaps still done (even if it be to his name alone) in order that we do not now praise all the things that youth and the juvenile pen committed, in any case, as sins at that time.

NOTES

1. Basileios Antōniadēs (1851–1932) was born in the city of Ἰντζὲ-Σου (Indje-Su) in Cappadocia. He studied at the Great School of the Nation in Constantinople and later graduated from the Theological School of Halki (1874). From 1874 to 1879, he taught religious studies in Constantinople. In 1879 he traveled to Germany and was supported by the School for theological and philosophical studies at Heidelberg and Göttingen. From 1885 to 1888, he was professor of theology and philosophy at the Theological School of the Holy Cross in Jerusalem. When the school was closed in 1888, he studied and received a doctorate of philosophy at Leipzig (1890) for his thesis "Die Staatslehre des Thomas ab Aquino." He also worked in Paris, London, and finally in Moscow, where he was declared a doctor of theology. From 1890 to 1926, he taught theology, Christian ethics, and philosophy at Halki. He left Halki for reasons of health in 1926 but continued his academic work, including editing the journal of the Ecumenical Patriarchate, *Orthodoxy*, in which the present article was published on July 1, 1927 (*Ὀρθοδοξία* 2 [1927]: 125–29). He died on March 27, 1932, in Athens at the age of eighty-one. His publications were diverse and extensive. For additional information, see Νικολ. Μητσοποῦλος, "Ἀντωνιάδης, Βασίλειος," in *Θρησκευτικὴ καὶ Ἠθικὴ Ἐγκυκλοπαιδεία* (Athens: A. Martinos, 1962), 2:955–56.

2. This is most likely Vincenzo Cardinal Vannutelli (December 5, 1836–July 9, 1930), who became a priest in 1860; was consecrated as a bishop in 1880; and was created a cardinal in 1889, which was announced publicly in 1890. He would have been ninety years of age and the oldest living cardinal on December 5, 1926, as Antōniadēs observes. Vannutelli's career involved work in seminary faculties and the Roman curia. In 1872 he was working in the Vatican Secretariat of State and was given foreign postings. He served as apostolic vicar of Constantinople from January 23, 1880, until December 22, 1882. Among his accomplishments was his major contribution to the development of the 1917 Code of Roman Catholic Canon Law. For additional information, see "Em. Vannutelli (Vincent)," *Annuaire Pontifical Catholique* 33 (1930): 130–31; and Remgius Ritzer and

Pirmin Sefrin, *Hierarchia Catholica Medii et Recentioris Aevi* (Padova: Il Messagero di S. Antonio, 1978), 9:35.

3. A *Boukouvala* (Μπουκουβάλα) was an irregular soldier initially under Ottoman allegiance but who later rebelled and participated in the Greek Revolution of 1821. These soldiers were found in the areas of present-day Greece and Albania.

4. Cephalonians were reputed to be quick to anger. The noun "τὸ κεφαλλωνίτικο" refers to this supposed tendency.

5. A loose adaptation of Mt. 23:15.

6. "A vain missile" (cf. Titus Livius, *Aenid* 21.8).

7. "A vain missile" (cf. Homer, *Iliad* 14.407).

8. This appears to be an allusion to the patristic use of the word *treasury* (θησαυροφυλάκιον) as a metaphor for the soul as a "treasury for divine truths or virtues" (cf. John Chrysostom, *Homilies on John* 9.1).

Index

F

G

H

I

J

K

L

M

N

S

T

www.ingramcontent.com/pod-product-compliance
Ingram Content Group UK Ltd.
Pitfield, Milton Keynes, MK11 3LW, UK
UKHW040318101026
476515UK00004B/182

9 781501 791635